Planning the Fourth Migration:
The Neglected Vision of the
Regional Planning Association of America

**Planning the Fourth Migration:
The Neglected Vision of the
Regional Planning Association of America**

Edited by Carl Sussman

The MIT Press
Cambridge, Massachusetts, and London, England

Figure Sources

Survey Graphic (May 1925). 1: p. 155. 2: p. 157. 3: p. 192.

New York State Report of the Commission of Housing and Regional Planning
(May 7, 1926). 4: Plate II, p. 20. 5: Plate VIII, p. 23. 6: Plate IX, p. 24. 7: Plate
XIV, p. 32. 8: Plate XV, p. 32. 9: Plate XVII, p. 33. 10: Plate XVIII, p. 34, 11:
Plate XIX, p. 34. 12: Plate XXV, p. 44. 13: Plate XXI, p. 41. 14: Plate XXII,
p. 41. 15: Plate XXXII, p. 48. 16: Plate XXX (graph only), p. 47. 17: Plate LII,
p. 78. 18: Plate LIV, p. 80. 19: Plate LV, p. 80. 20: Plate LIII, p. 79. 21: Plate
LVI, p. 81. 22: Plate LVII, p. 82. 23: Plate XLVI, p. 62.

This book was set in IBM Composer Journal Roman
by Technical Composition,
printed on R & E Book
by The Colonial Press Inc.
and bound in Columbia Milbank
by The Colonial Press Inc.
in the United States of America.

Library of Congress Cataloging in Publication Data

Main entry under title:

Planning the fourth migration.

   Includes bibliographical references and index.
   1. Regional planning—United States—Addresses, essays, lectures. 2. Cities and
towns—Planning—United States—Addresses, essays, lectures. 3. Regional Planning
Association of America.
I. Sussman, Carl.
HT392.P55   309.2'5'0973   76-26075
ISBN 0-262-19148-2

To Lewis Mumford

Contents

Preface

People are more apt to know the names of those who belonged to the Regional Planning Association of America (RPAA) than to know the name of the organization itself. Clarence Stein and Henry Wright, for example, are prominent names in architectural and planning circles. "Housers" probably recognize the names of Edith Elmer Wood and Catherine Bauer Wurster. And Lewis Mumford, of course, has attained international prominence.

But if people are aware of the RPAA's collaborative work at all, their awareness is probably limited to the group's contributions to community planning. That actually represented just one topic in the RPAA's broad assessment of the quality of metropolitan life in America and alternatives to it. The group's primary objective was a new approach to regional planning, which Mumford captured in the image of the fourth migration. Surprisingly few people seem to be cognizant of this valuable aspect of the RPAA's work. While that alone would justify republication of these writings on regionalism, my interest was ignited by the accuracy of the group's predictions and the attractiveness of their alternative solution.

Thus this anthology is primarily a work of appreciation and advocacy. Admittedly the group's foresight begs for historical recognition, but its members deserve more than a posthumous salute. They offered a normative alternative to the then-emerging, and now well-established, metropolitan form. Their alternative had validity in the 1920s. Today, after we have endured the racial, urban, and environmental crises of the past decades, the fourth migration constitutes a compelling program of social reconstruction. Existing efforts to revitalize cities or control development should be at least compared to the RPAA's program. The resulting contrasts will testify to the narrow focus and ultimate futility of established strategies.

Fresh exposure to the normative quality of the fourth migration should reactivate a long-standing dispute among planners. Members of the RPAA rejected conditions that most other planners accepted as necessary, albeit unfortunate, constraints. RPAA members scoffed at all regional planning that accepted the continued spread of metropolitanism as inevitable or, worse still, desirable. As the final part of this book indicates, their intolerance was not a pious point of professional ethics; it personified an essentially political clash between opposing social visions.

This collection should also rectify what is rapidly becoming conventional wisdom: that antiurbanism and the garden city constitute the RPAA's philosophical legacy. Political antagonisms also breed these erroneous impressions. It is easier to falsely accuse the RPAA of antiurbanism or of having a nostalgic love for small towns than to deal with the complexities of the group's indictment of metropolitanism. The most perverse accusation directed at the RPAA is that the group provided the intellectual rationale for suburban sprawl with its brief for decentralism. To the contrary, the RPAA members actually responded to what they perceived as the disintegration of urban values caused by this sprawl. And though they advocated the construction of garden cities as part of the fourth migration, they never completely embraced that frequently misunderstood concept either. They certainly never sought to enshrine the garden city as the exclusive urban form of the fourth migration. Rhetorical simplicities about so-called antiurbanism cloud the complex and very real distinctions between competing philosophies. Those who hold opposing philosophies should be able to disagree with the RPAA without either misinterpreting the group's views or, worse, dismissing them altogether.

It is a testament to the power of the RPAA's work that republication of these writings readily captured the imaginations of many people. I am particularly grateful to Carol and W. H. Ferry for their early and crucial support. The Ford Foundation generously provided the funds needed to conduct research and write the introduction for this book.

By far the greatest substantive assistance came directly from members of the RPAA: Benton MacKaye, Lewis Mumford, and Stuart Chase. They yielded papers and notes, sat for lengthy interviews, corresponded, and endured last-minute telephone inquiries. And after all that, they carefully reviewed successive drafts of my manuscript. I want to thank Lewis Mumford in particular. He supplied reams of material, including a set of the RPAA minutes. He corresponded extensively with me and remained genial even after repeated interviews. Later he proved to be a rigorous critic as well. When our opinions occasionally differed, he charitably tolerated my view as generational counterpoint that also had its place. His tolerance only increased my great respect for him.

Clarence Stein died at the age of ninety-two, during the first few weeks of this project. He was a giant in the fields of architecture and planning, and he literally led the RPAA. My work on this book ends on another tragic note, Benton MacKaye's death this past month. While I never had the opportunity to meet and talk with Stein, MacKaye and I met repeatedly. At ninety-six, MacKaye had grown frail. He was blind and had difficulty hearing. But his conversation and memory belied his age. He recalled the dates, street addresses, and even the attendance at meetings held decades ago. I verified the accuracy of all this information with the RPAA's minutes. I am thankful for Benton MacKaye's patient assistance and regret that he did not live to see the final product.

In addition to the members of the RPAA, two of the group's contemporaries, Charles Ascher and Albert Mayer, agreed to interviews that proved very useful to me.

Although I never met him, I also owe an intellectual debt to Roy Lubove, who has previously explored some of the same territory. He left a well-marked trail for me and for others who will study this important period of planning history.

A number of people read drafts of my introduction and offered helpful comments. Allan Brandt and Steve Whitfield made particularly useful remarks. In addition, some close friends, Ken Geiser, Jon Pynoos, and Nancy Lyons supplied both substantive comments and occasional moral support. I also owe thanks to Ken Demsky, who typed several drafts for me.

It is common at the end of acknowledgments like these to find the thanks to a spouse. I realize now that the placement does not minimize the importance of the contributor; it suggests only that the thanks are most difficult to express. In this case Laura Lubetsky, my wife, gave me encouragement, understanding, and much more.

Carl Sussman
January 1976

Planning the Fourth Migration:
The Neglected Vision of the
Regional Planning Association of America

1 Introduction

Overview

The 1920s were a decade-long intermission in Richard Hofstadter's "Age of Reform": the Populists and Progressives on one side, the New Deal on the other. But while most reformers watched hard-won gains reversed in the twenties, one small and little-known group—the Regional Planning Association of America (RPAA)—voiced a wide-ranging and highly critical assessment of society. Although its members are known in some quarters for their advocacy of public housing and their important experiments in community and neighborhood design, the group's greatest collective contribution has been almost totally ignored: the members sought to replace the existing centralized and profit-oriented metropolitan society with a decentralized and more socialized one made up of environmentally balanced regions. Even today, the idea is radical. As one foreign observer explained, the group's "demonstrations of the region as the basic planning framework constitute one of the most important, and still unfinished, chapters in American planning history, now world-wide in their influence."[1]

1. Michael Hughes, ed., *The Letters of Lewis Mumford and Frederic J. Osborn: A Transatlantic Dialogue 1938-70* (New York: Praeger Publishers, 1972), p. viii.

This small but influential group (not to be confused with the Regional Plan Association of New York) included Lewis Mumford (b. 1895), the social critic; Benton MacKaye (1879-1975), the originator of the Appalachian Trail; Clarence S. Stein (1882-1975), the chief architect of Radburn, New Jersey, and Sunnyside Gardens, New York, and his coplanner Henry Wright (1878-1936); Catherine Bauer Wurster (1905-1964) and Edith Elmer Wood (1871-1945), two crusading housing experts; Stuart Chase (b. 1898), the economist; Charles Harris Whitaker (1872-1938), the editor of the *Journal of the American Institute of Architects*, and others.

The membership's writings and activities during their decade of cooperation read like chapter headings in a history of architecture and planning. They devised and developed Sunnyside Gardens and Radburn, experiments that pioneered in low-cost housing and community planning. Under the auspices of the New York State Commission of Housing and Regional Planning, RPAA members first introduced the idea of statewide regional planning. Wood, Wright, and Stein opened a new front for low-income housing. Pointing to figures showing the inability of the private market to adequately house a majority of the working population, they campaigned for a "constructive housing program" whereby the government or publicly supported cooperatives and limited dividend companies would build quality housing on a massive scale for low-income Americans. Housing experts today continue to cite statistics and urge policies that echo those first formulated by members of the RPAA.

MacKaye proposed the "Townless Highway"—a blueprint for automotive transportation that would have thwarted both "road towns" and the freeway invasion of the city before either inflicted their substantial wounds on the landscape. And Chase, who spent years studying social waste, promoted conservation of energy and resources and economic planning, ideas our crisis-weary academics are proposing at last today.

Members of this group and their ideas influenced the Tennessee Valley Authority, the Civilian Conservation Corps, the Rural Electrification Administration, and the greenbelt communities—constructive proposals begun but never brought to fruition in the New Deal or thereafter. The contributions of the RPAA members have never been intelligently appraised. Frequently, as with their concept of regionalism, they have been entirely overlooked.

Business imperatives and conventional wisdom posed a formidable barrier even to a group as experienced as the members of the RPAA. Their regional planning ideas threatened the perennial notion that metropolitan growth was good and speculative development necessary, regardless of the consequences. The substance of the RPAA's thought was plowed under almost as soon as it germinated. Though the group's practical influence was thus limited to a decade of experimentation between 1923 and 1933, the RPAA's work is still bursting with relevance for our time. Increasing numbers of people are demanding solutions to the urban, economic, and environmental contradictions that the RPAA exposed a half century ago. And perhaps the RPAA's long-ignored foundation—regionalism—may still serve this or succeeding generations, should they decide to solve these long-standing problems.

Unlike utopians who concoct celestial social visions off the top of their heads, members of the RPAA rooted their analysis in the deep soil of our nation's history. In one article, for example, Mumford described the urbanization process as a series of great internal migrations. The westward expansion comprised the first migration. It dispersed a farm population fairly uniformly across the continent. Then, with the beginnings of industrialization, the second migration occurred. This time the population moved back from the farms to the small towns that sprouted in the river valleys. There water produced both power and a convenient means of transportation. The railroads later reinforced this pattern. The population began collecting in the growing towns that the railroad trunk lines joined together in the river valleys. Technological advances continued to fuel the industrialization process after the Civil War, and a third migration began to the large cities. This produced the major congested metropolitan centers we know today. The automobile and skyscraper construction permitted the growth and spread of several cities of national importance. The urban concentration of the third migration also led to the depopulation of the countryside and of the industrial towns of the preceding epoch.

Mumford saw the prospect of a fourth migration as well. Unlike the previous ones, popular choice rather than economic caprice would prompt this population movement. For some members of the RPAA, the fourth migration became a metaphor to describe their regional ideal of a decentralized urban culture, which they hoped would replace the endlessly sprawling "metropolitan civilization" that at the time already seemed to be succeeding the third migration. Today, of course, the exodus to the suburbs and to megalopolis has turned into a rout, into a panicky attempt to flee from a constant threat of violence, high living costs, and shabby public services. Although the fourth migration materialized as unplanned suburbanization, the term *fourth migration* symbolizes the RPAA's alternative—planned regionalization.

Events transpired as members of the RPAA had predicted; this intensifies the magnetism of their vision. Not only has the growth of megalopolis occurred; it has also had disastrous effects on the quality of life. A pall of pollution hangs over every city. While mayors point with pride to new cultural and trade centers, alienation and poverty remain the birthright of the metropolis. Industry continues to abandon the big cities the way slumlords desert their once profitable holdings. And today many cities face the prospect of fiscal insolvency. All of these things and more were forecast by the RPAA decades ago.

These problems could have been avoided altogether if the nation had instead built economically and socially balanced regions along the lines described by people in the RPAA. Members of the RPAA imagined regions unlike the overbuilt monotony of metropolitan areas, where cities could maintain a stable and organic relationship to nearby wilderness and rural areas. And rather than concentrating the urban population in a single mass, the regionalists would have scattered it through many interconnected small cities and towns and through old cities rebuilt on a humane scale. Roads and transit would link them into a regional network. Regions would be drawn on the basis of climatic, cultural, and geographic unity, and they would be large and varied enough to provide the potential for a reasonable level of economic self-sufficiency.

The emerging technologies of the twentieth century provided the material basis for this regionally balanced urban and rural economy. Of course this included the RPAA's own contributions to community planning. But in addition, the people in the organization wanted to harness the automobile and long-distance power transmission—two relatively new advances—to stimulate the fourth migration. Associates of the RPAA felt that these two innovations in particular, when utilized in conjunction with a sound regional plan, could repopulate many declining towns and stagnant agricultural villages and salvage the special values derived from their very limitations. To insure an equitable and socially productive allocation of electricity, the RPAA strongly advocated public power. And finally, members saw the need for postcapitalist economic planning to guide the decentralizing process.

The members of the RPAA entered the planning field as open-eyed social critics. Although criticism of sprawl and suburbia became popular after the Second World War, the RPAA began to attack them back in the 1920s when the automobile first pushed suburban growth rates past those of the central cities. The members actively opposed the idea of megalopolis, the life style it nourished, and the quality of residential development it produced. Recent efforts to conserve land and resources and to stem urban growth have also unwittingly assumed some of the RPAA's positive proposals. Yet none of these subsequent crusades have so far captured the breadth of the RPAA's program. Wasted resources and suburbanization, for instance, were not isolated phenomena to the members of the RPAA; they were manifestations of society's blind commitment to profits and mechanical growth, evidence that society had lost sight of basic human and communal values. On this basis the RPAA avoided both the piecemeal approach and ameliorative role assumed by other professionals. Its members criticized the planning profession for limiting its activities, and still more its proposals, to what could be accomplished within the economic constraints that these regionalists saw as causing the problems. RPAA members asked themselves what was, what is, and what should be. And even if their proposals proved immediately impractical, they still had the prognostic virtue of indicating where society had to move to solve its acknowledged shortcomings. These were radical ideas in the 1920s, and one suspects that they remain so today.

In the final analysis, the group's long-range view accounts for the RPAA's enduring relevance. While the statistics may have changed dramatically in fifty years, the general trends have changed only slightly.

The following report, articles, and speeches by members of the RPAA demonstrate that the passage of time has heightened, not diminished, the importance of the RPAA's work. Thus this book is only incidentally a history; its fundamental purpose is to enliven the current debate on public policy with some long-ignored ideas. Although their own contemporaries failed to address the bold agenda for a fourth migration, we have the dubious advantage of an additional half century of pollution, congestion, and energy shortages to quicken our receptivity. We can learn from past mistakes and find guidance in the forgotten work of the RPAA.

Antecedents of the RPAA

Urbanization, by definition, demands the most fundamental type of social dislocation from an agrarian culture. For example, the emerging reign of the metropolis in this country during the late nineteenth and early twentieth centuries produced the heated conflicts of the Populist and Progressive periods—the struggles to resist, limit, or dominate the unfolding forces of urban industrialism. Farmers fought their loss of political power to the new urban masses and the captains of industry. Well-established urbanites championed municipal reform as a way to circumvent the growing influence of immigrant groups in their cities. Labor and management discovered their mutual antipathy. These conflicts reflected the entrance of a new social order that included the great metropolis. The clamor for reform waned in the years prior to the First World War, the great divide between the post-Civil War industrialization and highly centralized metropolitan civilization. But if the struggle seemed to die with the Progressive politician, the 1920 census proclaimed the symbolic victory of metropolitan and financial concentration: the majority of the population had by then moved to the cities.

The RPAA emerged in 1923 after the unrest accompanying urbanization had virtually disappeared. The members comprised the first group to critically assess the new urban order, a social system they called *metropolitanism* because, among other things, this form was too big and too congested to function as a city. Their condemnation of this urban form consolidated the fragmented protests of the preceding decades.

The First World War, in many respects, provided an immediate backdrop for the group's formation. Many of the first architects, social critics, and planners to join the RPAA took their apprenticeship with the government during the war. For the Department of Labor, Benton MacKaye prepared plans (that were never realized) for the postwar resettlement of returning soldiers. Robert D. Kohn (1870-1953), Henry Wright, and Frederick Lee Ackerman (1878-1950) worked for the Emergency Fleet Corporation, one of two entities that built the government's first public housing units. Stuart Chase was involved in the government's temporary economic planning apparatus. Under these extraordinary measures, the War Industries Board and other wartime departments successfully curbed the wasteful habits of private enterprise. The railroads were temporarily turned into a unified national system; as a result, industrial efficiency and productivity increased. All of these activities, in one way or another, suggested new roles for planners and expanded areas of governmental responsibility that eventually found their way into the work of the RPAA.

From 1913 until 1927, Charles Whitaker edited the *Journal of the American Institute of Architects (JAIA)*. This periodical reflected the traditional Beaux Arts approach to architecture and tended to host the aesthetic fallout of the "city beautiful" movement. The city beautiful movement emerged with the Chicago World's Fair of 1893; it promoted, among other things, the practice of city planning. But once city planning became established professionally as a recognized urban function, the city beautiful was little more than a bourgeois fascination with classic European architecture and civic design. Whitaker had been infected by more basic reform ideas than that. As the editor of the *JAIA* he led architectural thought away from the city beautiful by opening the journal's pages to a new strain of socially conscious writers, equipped with the new planning ideas that emerged during the First World War. Whitaker assumed the role of intellectual matchmaker too; he introduced most of the people who were to later join Stein in starting the RPAA.

One of the first socially conscious architects Whitaker drew under his publishing umbrella was Frederick Ackerman. Swayed by the work of Thorstein Veblen, as were many of his contemporaries in the RPAA,

Ackerman preached the need for fundamental social change. He wrote first about town planning and later focused on housing. In the fall of 1917 Whitaker sent Ackerman to England to study the large-scale housing projects being built there. Whitaker engineered the trip as part of a well-orchestrated campaign in the *JAIA*'s pages on behalf of a government program to build housing for war workers. Ackerman's reports appeared in a series called "What Is a House?" Although his objective was unstated, Whitaker was obviously trying to create professional support for wartime housing. But the articles reveal a broader objective than simply wartime housing; they point to the need for government to assume the responsibility for providing housing, regardless of military needs, when the private market fails to do so. Whitaker wrote the first two articles in the "What Is a House?" series as well as raising the same issues in his monthly column, "Shadows and Straws."

Edith Elmer Wood authored the sixth installment of "What Is a House?" When she had lived in Puerto Rico, she became interested in public health, which led her naturally to her concern with poor housing conditions. In her middle years she became a graduate student in housing economics. Her contribution to the *JAIA* outlined the work that distinguished her entire career and framed the housing debate from the RPAA's point of view.[2] She supported the program proposed by Whitaker and Ackerman, terming it *constructive housing legislation*. Unlike restrictive legislation where the public authorities "prevent the erection of bad houses through the establishment and enforcement of minimum standards," a constructive program requires an active public initiative in building adequate housing units. This might involve either direct government action or indirect support to nonspeculative builders. The point, as Robert Kohn explained in the same issue of *JAIA*, was that zoning and similar measures associated with the Progressive Era were inadequate. A complementary program of positive action was needed to supplement restrictive codes.

2. Roy Lubove, "Edith Elmer Wood," in *Notable American Women 1607-1950*, ed. Edward T. James, vol. 3 (Cambridge: Harvard University Press, Belknap Press, 1971), pp. 644-645.

The Progressive Era's housing movement had been an important agent of social reform since the late nineteenth century, with the passage of the New York Tenement House Law in 1901 and then New York's comprehensive zoning statute in 1916. But as the 1920s approached, the housing movement acquired the conservative posture of a well-established professional organization. Whitaker helped to start a new housing movement; he retapped the reform idealism abandoned by old-line housing reformers and turned it over to a new generation that espoused constructive housing legislation.

Government reports had already indicated the need for some sort of public housing to accomodate workers near the expanding centers of war production. Whitaker cleverly used the *JAIA* to support this initiative, and he also attempted to influence the quality of the housing through the reports appearing in the "What Is a House?" series. Ackerman's articles emphasized the theme that Britain was building permanent housing rather than temporary units that would become postwar slums. The British planning of Raymond Unwin and others also exemplified high standards of community design. This too Whitaker tried to incorporate into the government's war-housing aims. But his final goal was to rationalize the public's role in providing housing and in improving the overall standard of the well-planned house and community. Thus he used an article by Stein to fan public endorsement of constructive housing legislation; Stein's contribution indicated that productivity would increase if workers were comfortably housed. Edith Elmer Wood demonstrated that private enterprise would not adequately house the unskilled worker. All of the writers pointed to Europe as an example of public housing.

In the winter of 1918, under the added pressures of the housing shortage, Congress enacted the necessary legislation and, in the following summer, appropriated funds to the Emergency Fleet Corporation of the United States Shipping Board and to the United States Housing Corporation for the construction of permanent residential communities for war workers. Some of the most important people in the program turned out to be those associated with Whitaker's campaign. The Emergency Fleet Corporation hired Ackerman as its chief designer and Kohn to direct its Production Division. Henry Wright also worked on the corporation's design team.

The achievements of the government program and the future members of the RPAA were linked with one other important planning movement of the period: the garden city. The intermingling of the garden city and constructive housing ideas led to the study of community planning in this country; the members of RPAA initially anchored their work in this new discipline.

People interested in constructive housing legislation invariably knew of the English garden city movement. In 1898 Ebenezer Howard promulgated the scheme to build new towns rather than adding population to the large cities. Each garden city would be surrounded by a wide greenbelt to inhibit population growth beyond a predetermined point and to reunite town and country. Of particular interest to Whitaker and the *JAIA* were the principles of the single tax movement that Howard had ingeniously molded into his plan. With all the land in common ownership as prescribed by Howard, the whole community would benefit from the land value appreciation that accompanies urbanization and had previously enriched shrewd speculators. Letchworth, the first garden city, was already under construction in England. It represented a breakthrough in the theory of city building, equivalent to the impact Copernicus had in the field of astronomy. It released creative energy and opened new territory for exploration.

The garden city appealed to many reformers at the turn of the century who identified congestion as the root of urban disorder. People in the settlement house movement, for example, blamed many slum pathologies on the overcrowded conditions. This brought them into alliance both with housing reformers who advocated restrictive building codes and with park and playground advocates led by Jacob Riis who wanted to create more usable open spaces than existed in the city. Henry George's work influenced many of these reformers because they viewed congestion as an inevitable consequence of rising land values. Thus the German practice of zoning and the English garden city became the two popular solutions to congestion—popular with reformers, that is. Zoning won acceptance in New York only after large Fifth Avenue retail stores began to feel threatened by the garment district spreading into their exclusive domain. They joined forces with reformers in an effort to protect their property values. As a consequence, in 1916 New

York enacted the first comprehensive zoning statute. It regulated the use, bulk, and height of structures and was copied almost verbatim throughout the country.

The garden city scheme, based on municipal ownership of land and long-term rentals instead of on private ownership, was designed to control residential property values by limiting growth and by returning the increment from rising commercial and industrial property values back to the community. Its advocates hoped that the population would be attracted to the new cities by low rents and a less congested environment. But the reform movements of the period lacked the strength to mount the necessary assault on the financial basis of the metropolis.[3] And very often, as with Lawrence Veiller's active leadership in the housing movement, the reformers were actually committed to the capitalist values that the garden city obviously rejected. This in part explains why Veiller and his associates could never cross the bridge from the Progressive Era to join the new movement that attempted to supplement restrictive with constructive housing legislation.

Constructive housing legislation to allocate public resources for low-income housing met the determined opposition of realty speculators and investors. To them, public housing smelled of socialism. Mel Scott, for instance, observed that congressmen "suspected that war housing would be but the first step toward something almost as abhorrent as German Imperialism—socialism."[4] When Congress finally passed the measure for war housing, the legislation stated the intention to sell the housing units after the war. Congressional fear of public housing was so great that a month after the armistice—less than a year after it appropriated funds for them— Congress halted work on all projects that were less than 75 percent complete. Thus most of the proposed units were never built. Those that were, following the example of Britain's garden cities and other European housing experiments, established a new standard for community design and worker housing.

3. Lubove, *The Progressives and the Slums: Tenement House Reform in New York City* (Pittsburgh: University of Pittsburgh Press, 1963), pp. 337-344.

4. Mel Scott, *American City Planning since 1890* (Berkeley: University of California Press, 1971), p. 171.

The wartime housing, along with the neighborhood and community center movements, provided the new impetus for community planning. "Once we called it City Planning," Whitaker wrote in December 1918, "Tomorrow we shall call it Community Planning, for the narrow and inelastic idea which once fluttered its brief and worse than futile, existence under the title of 'city beautiful' has become humanized at last." As Whitaker explained it, "The forces with which Community Planning must deal, in order to achieve any measure of success, are not merely the physical forces which inhere in streets and squares, sewage and water-supply, transportation, and buildings." Those "physical forces" were the exclusive concerns of city planners under the influence of the city beautiful; community planners, on the other hand, would also address such things as economic forces in the "struggle for a more rational life."[5]

Recognizing this evolving product of a constructive housing program and the wartime communities, the American Institute of Architects (AIA) created a Committee on Community Planning (CCP) in 1919. An able Philadelphia architect, John Irwin Bright (1869-1940), became its first chairman. Bright repeated the pattern established by others who would later form the RPAA: he entered the circle through the pages of the *JAIA*. He had previously chaired the Special Committee on Housing and Transportation for the Philadelphia chapter of the AIA. Whitaker observed that the committee's reports broke new ground in their acknowledgement of the interdependence of environmental elements. Stein and later Wright succeeded Bright as chairman of the CCP. The CCP advanced community planning ideas that the RPAA later elaborated. When Bright's successor began publishing reports in 1924, the CCP's unofficial secretary, Lewis Mumford, was called upon to draft them. Mumford, who first met Whitaker after the *JAIA* published an article of his in 1919, became a frequent contributor to the periodical. Whitaker, in turn, drew him into his growing constellation of progressive urbanists. Mumford, who was still in his mid twenties, had already established contacts with European regionalists, partly through his correspondence with the Scottish biologist and town planner, Patrick Geddes. But as a writer, Mumford was able to reach a wider audience.

5. Charles Harris Whitaker, "Shadows and Straws," *Journal of the American Institute of Architects* 6 (December 1918): 549-550.

In an article for the *Nation* in 1919 Mumford critically reviewed three dominant housing reform movements. "The Single Tax by itself has only fulminated against the tenement," he argued. "Housing reform by itself has only standardized the tenement. City planning by itself has only extended the tenement." As a result housing remained inadequate, and slum rents kept rising, making it difficult for families to improve their health or other basic conditions of life. "It is fatuous to suppose that private interests will correct this condition, for it is for the benefit of private interests that it exists," he concluded. Then, sounding a note which in the late sixties became a refrain, Mumford suggested, "The housing problem, the industries problem, the transportation problem, and the land problem cannot be solved one at a time by isolated experts, thinking and acting in a civic vacuum. They are mutually interacting elements, and they can be effectively dealt with only by bearing constantly in mind the general situation from which they have been abstracted." This was exactly Whitaker's attraction to Bright's work in Philadelphia. Community planning, as it was represented in both the Emergency Fleet Housing Communities and the CCP, embodied this notion that planning had to be a coordinated many-sided activity. It would in the most sweeping sense become an element in the RPAA's approach to planning.

Whitaker drew Benton MacKaye and Stuart Chase into the RPAA by introducing them to Stein. During the war Whitaker and Chase took part in a small group of progressive Washingtonians that had congregated around MacKaye. MacKaye, a forester, later contributed an article to the *JAIA* that brought him into contact with Stein and the CCP. In the United States Forest Service, MacKaye worked under Gifford Pinchot, the active leader of the conservation movement. Then, during the war, MacKaye shifted briefly to the Department of Labor, where he worked this time for a single-taxer, Louis Post. While there, MacKaye began to formulate a new approach, using the particularly progressive threads of the conservationists' ideology. In lieu of their generalized rebellion against the private monopolists of natural resources and the complementary effort to substitute public management of the nation's resources to permit orderly industrial development, MacKaye proposed a communal and collectivized approach to stop resource exploitation.

In effect, MacKaye was beginning to forge a link between the conservation movement and the community planners.

In 1919 the government published *Employment and Natural Resources*, MacKaye's treatise on postwar employment for returning soldiers. He proposed that the government develop agricultural and timbering communities that could be operated on a cooperative basis. The timbering communities would utilize modern forestry practices whereby trees are "farmed" rather than "mined." On this self-renewing principle, logging can be done from a stable community rather than from temporary lumber camps. Similarly, new agricultural developments would replace the outmoded homestead approach, in which homesteaders were given unimproved land, and even if the settler could finance needed improvements, the land may have been inaccessible to markets. MacKaye thought the government should provide improved land that people could farm cooperatively with neighboring farmers and should locate these farming communities to ensure their access to city markets.

His ideas therefore necessitated the use of physical and industrial planning outside the city. This extension of the bounds of planning to include more than just the city or isolated elements in it represents one of the most viable contributions of MacKaye and other planners between the First World War and 1923. During this period they also adopted the community as the basic social unit upon which to base plans.

MacKay joined Whitaker's AIA coterie in 1921. During a visit to Whitaker's farm at Mt. Olive, New Jersey, MacKaye told Whitaker about his conception of an Applachian Trail from Maine to Georgia. Whitaker saw some exciting parallels in the trail proposal and in the work of the CCP. He introduced MacKaye to the CCP's chairman, Clarence Stein, who was in the area designing a building for the Hudson Guild Farm near Netcong. Stein enthusiastically embraced the idea and offered the CCP's support. With that Whitaker handed MacKaye a pencil and some paper. MacKaye spent his next few days in Whitaker's New Jersey home writing an article for the October 1921 issue of the *JAIA*.[6] Its title expressed a new thrust for community planners: "An Applachian Trail: A Project in Regional Planning."

6. Interview with Benton MacKaye, 10 June 1974.

The CCP circulated reprints of MacKaye's article. To it Stein append-
ed a brief introduction in which he wrote,

The Garden City would preserve something of the outdoors within
reach of the urban districts. But this is tame. We need the big sweep of
hills or sea as tonic for our jaded nerves—And so Mr. Benton MacKaye
offers us a new theme in regional planning. It is not a plan for more
efficient labor, but a plan of escape. He would as far as is practicable
conserve the whole stretch of the Appalachian Mountains for recreation.
Recreation in the biggest sense—the re-creation of the spirit that is being
crushed by the machinery of the modern industrial city—the spirit of
fellowship and cooperation.

MacKaye described it as "a project to develop the opportunities—for
recreation, recuperation, and employment—in the region of the Appalachian skyline." The chain of mountain ranges that parallels the eastern
seaboard was still primeval, although part of it was within a day's ride
of the majority of the urban population. The problem facing society,
as he saw it, was the growing imbalance of town and country. The nation was turning overwhelmingly urban. Decreasing numbers of people
had access to the country, and many lived amid oppressive urban congestion. Because of its size and accessibility, MacKaye felt that the
Appalachian skyline should be protected from private exploitation. As
a place for people to escape the city, MacKaye believed the wilderness
area would introduce people to some of the advantages of rural life. In
other words, people would begin to repopulate this area for nonurban
use after sampling its ambiance through recreation. Thus, he wrote,

This project is one for a series of recreational communities throughout
the Appalachian chain of mountains from New England to Georgia,
these to be connected by a walking trail. Its purpose is to establish a
base for a more extensive and systematic development of outdoor
community life. It is a project in housing and community architecture.

The best-known feature—the backbone—of the plan was a trail con-
structed and maintained by local voluntary groups under "general
federated control." This of course was initiated just fifty years ago under the Appalachian Trail Conference. In addition, MacKaye proposed
the construction of shelters for camping, spaced a day's hike from each
other. Some trail clubs in New England had already begun this task.
More substantial community camps for "outdoor non-industrial en-

deavor" would be located "on or near the trail." MacKaye added that the community camps "should not be allowed to become too populous and thereby defeat the very purpose for which they are created. Greater numbers should be accommodated by *more* communities, not *larger* ones." All of these various elements were to be planned carefully beforehand as the product of voluntary cooperative endeavor, always operating without profit or public funds.

Finally, MacKaye proposed a series of "food and farm camps": "Special communities in adjoining valleys." These communities resembled those he recommended in *Employment and Natural Resources*. Beginning as self-sufficient communities for vacationing urbanites, they could become permanent rural communities. "Coming as visitors they would be loath to return" to the city, MacKaye suggests. "They would become desirous of settling down in the country—to *work* in the open as well as *play*. The various camps would require food. Why not raise food, as well as consume it, on the cooperative plan? Food and farm camps should come about as a natural sequence. Timber also is required. Permanent small scale operations could be encouraged in the various Appalachian National Forests."

The Appalachian Trail has probably done nothing to redistribute the population. But it has undeniably contributed to the fuller utilization of this region and provided a welcome refuge for several generations of city dwellers. And MacKaye proved absolutely right about the kind of cooperative spirit that could be harnessed for a voluntary undertaking of this magnitude.

MacKaye's proposal became the first rallying point for the members of the RPAA. Here was a planning scheme that embraced more than a particular city or even the urban environment alone. It was a project, as MacKaye stated, in regional planning; it encompassed a vast geographical area, related urban and rural planning, encouraged conservation, and sprang from a genuine concern for the quality and goals of life. It was, in short, a compelling image for a planning philosophy. When the members of the RPAA came together for the first time on April 18, 1923, along with the garden city they reached for MacKaye's proposal as elements embodying their shared philosophy.

the time being on self-education rather than propagandizing. Friendship and a generally shared vision held this group together, not a set of
documents or a ten-point program. In fact, the RPAA never established
a formal organizational doctrine. While there was a general level of
agreement among the members on most matters, they consistently
avoided the temptation to define their beliefs too narrowly and thereby
alienate some of their comrades. Self-education seemed like a sufficiently ambitious task and one that did not require energetic attention to
overly restrictive definitions. Thus someone like Catherine Bauer could
participate comfortably in this group's deliberations even though she
was skeptical about the regional ideal. And even while the rest might
have believed in the philosophy of regional planning as it was typically
handled within the group, very few agreed on the size of a region. Mumford, who had most thoroughly explored the regional concept as a
geographic and cultural phenomenon, remembers that "All of us
thought of planning in terms of some larger corporate organization than
the community: MacKaye thought in continental terms, and even liked
—to my horror—to speak fondly of the Appalachian Empire . . . . Stein
thought originally in terms of the State or the Region, as the latter was
very vaguely defined in his own mind."[10] Only on the most abstract
level can we safely speak of the RPAA collectively typifying the concept of Mumford's, MacKaye's, Stein's or any other member's regionalism.

   To many of its members this informality and smallness were among
the virtues of the RPAA. An elementary bond held this fairly diverse
collection of people together. Chase would later admit that he "was
never disappointed that they never had more impact. I was glad to meet
with them and share information." He found the experience of interacting with other members rewarding enough. It was a "group with a
different point of view and a lot of information."[11] The surviving members frequently refer to the intimate friendship shared by all of them.
Mumford recently reminisced:

10. Mumford to Carl Sussman, 24 August 1975.

11. Interview with Stuart Chase, 17 June 1975.

It would be hard to exaggerate my debt to the people in this circle; but it was not the debt of a student to an older teacher: it was rather such a debt as married people owe to each other: the benefit of a constant sharing, so intimate that no one could tell, at any moment, who has given and who has received.

In our most intimate days, we could sign each other's memoranda without undue boggling or haggling, and at deliberations we almost never took formal votes. This made my own Miltonic role as secretary an easy one. We thus proved in our group two things that the Greeks knew well: that friends hold everything in common, and that there is no possibility of friendship except in a society of equals.

When in my teaching days at Penn. and M.I.T. my students would give vent to their discouragement and cynical reactions—well justified when one considers the lunatic world that the power complex has prepared for them—I would tell them the story of the Regional Planning Association of America. . . . I sought to show that personality is more important than organization, and that small groups can do directly what large groups are impotent to do: *their members can teach each other*. When friendship and daily intercourse bring people together for a common purpose, that association itself is sufficient reward to those who participate, no matter what the outward success of the enterprise. We enjoyed each other's company and shared a significant part of our life together.[12]

The RPAA also drew solidarity from a generally shared though diverse body of ideas. In his introduction to Stein's book on new towns, Mumford listed "the civic ideas of Geddes and Howard, the economic analyses of Thorstein Veblen, the sociology of Charles Horton Cooley, and the educational philosophy of John Dewey, to say nothing of the new ideas in conservation, ecology, and geotechnics" as forming the "intellectual foundation" of the organization's doctrines.[13]

The diversity of ideas mirrors the varied professional backgrounds of the people in the group. Architects accounted for less than half the membership. The rest were planners, a forester, a writer, an economist, an educator, a sociologist, and a businessman. According to Stuart Chase, their values and political views, although vague, helped unify the membership. "We were mildly socialist though not at all communist;

12. Mumford, unpublished manuscript, 5 August 1975.

13. Clarence S. Stein, *Toward New Towns for America* (Cambridge, Massachusetts: The MIT Press, 1966), p. 14.

liberal but willing to abandon large areas of the free market in favor of a planned economy. So we were not doctrinaire socialists. We were open-minded; kind of Fabian Socialists."[14] But even that misses the scope of the group's outlook and understates the intensity with which individual members rejected capitalism's urban wasteland.

Members of the RPAA communicated their ideas through books, articles, exhibitions, reports, and practical demonstrations. Sunnyside Gardens and Radburn, two experimental residential developments, made some of these ideas visible. They were, as Stuart Chase noted, "definite achievements: something you could kick with your feet." As a result, people commonly associate the RPAA with these two developments, overlooking the group's central concern with reorienting the whole social basis of urban development. These two projects merely symbolize the RPAA's effort to build an American garden city, an undertaking clearly identified by Mumford as "just a single thread in the new warp and woof" of their ambitious concept of regional planning.[15] The first project, Sunnyside, was a preliminary exercise in neighborhood planning and housing. Radburn was an ambitious though disappointing attempt to build a garden city. But even though most members of the RPAA viewed this garden city experimentation in the context of their program of regional reconstruction, Radburn and Sunnyside are recognized instead for their important housing and planning innovations.

The postwar housing shortage lent credence to earlier contentions by Kohn, Whitaker, Wood, Stein and others that a capitalist housing industry was unable to serve low-income households. The limited dividend form adopted by the CHC—the body established by Alexander Bing in 1924 with a view to ultimately building a garden city—departed from the practice of building for the richest third. It belonged to a modest tradition of philanthropic model housing—typically limited dividend— dating back to the nineteenth century. By imposing a low ceiling on profits, limited dividend companies provided better quarters at lower rents than slum landlords. As charitable undertakings, some limited

14. Interview with Chase, 17 June 1975.

15. Mumford, "The Fate of Garden Cities," *Journal of the American Institute of Architects* 15 (February 1927):39.

dividend housing projects also became experimental stations for new housing techniques. Their promoters wanted more than cheap housing; they wanted models that exemplified improved housing standards. Sunnyside was particularly significant in this respect.

Stein and Wright related housing to planning by providing a common green in the middle of each block or by clustering some Sunnyside residences around open courtyards. Grouping one, two, and three family houses in broken rows or clusters reduces construction costs and expands the usable open space, as Wright demonstrated.[16] A study recently compiled by the federal government, *The Costs of Sprawl*, generally confirms Wright's findings on this subject, testifying to the thoroughness of his analysis and to the slow rate at which ideas percolate through the dense filter of professional and business thought. In Sunnyside the residences were primarily row houses of varying sizes, along with a few apartment houses. Mixing these different kinds of units together around a large open green or an intimate court was a daring and successful social experiment. The variety added aesthetic appeal too, when compared to the monotony of subdivisions, even those using detached single-family houses. The courts were set aside for communal use with deed restrictions. In addition, the CHC donated and equipped a small playground with tennis courts to supplement the open greens. The Sunnyside Community Association still maintains the playground.

With the completion of Sunnyside Gardens in 1928, the CHC embarked on its garden city: Radburn, New Jersey. Even before the untimely bankruptcy of the CHC during the Great Depression, the garden city aim was abandoned. The depression relegated Radburn to the status of a suburb, albeit distinguished and unique. By most definitions garden cities incorporate a unified system of community land ownership, a greenbelt, and a balance of land uses that includes industry and housing for workers. In the end, Radburn had none of these. And when the depression prematurely ended the construction, Radburn's population was only a fraction of the planned 25,000. Still *The Radburn Idea*, as it has been called, occupies an important place in planning history.[17]

16. See Henry Wright, "The Road to Good Houses," in this collection.

17. See Stein, *Toward New Towns for America.*

At Sunnyside the city's rigid gridiron street pattern limited the CHC's opportunities for demonstrating just how economically the project could be built by eliminating unnecessary streets. Radburn presented none of these obstacles. Liberated from New York's inflexible platting, Stein and Wright devised a neighborhood unit comprised of superblocks —large irregularly shaped blocks penetrated by short dead-end lanes. The cul-de-sacs protected houses from through traffic and terminated in a spacious interior park with walkways weaving through the rest of the neighborhood, the school, the swimming pool, and stores. Following Olmsted and Vaux's fine example in Central Park, Radburn's planners almost completely separated vehicular and pedestrian traffic. Where a footpath crosses a road, a bridge or underpass separates them. The application of the Central Park plan to a residential community, the revival of the midnineteenth-century suburban technique of building on cul-de-sacs, and the creation of interior parks all represented planning innovations of some importance in the United States.

Roads received a revolutionizing treatment in Radburn, too. The prevailing practice at the time was to construct all streets to serve as through-traffic arteries, but Stein and Wright assigned specific functions to each street and consequently built them to different specifications. Thus cul-de-sacs had narrower paving than the collector roads that ringed each superblock. Yet these were more modest than the through streets. In itself, this appears trivial; when executed with the large blocks, however, the total savings in road construction and utility connections roughly equaled the cost of Radburn's interior parks. In other words, Radburn's residents paid the same price for their homes and parks, walkways, and quiet lanes as other people paid for comparable subdivision homes without Radburn's amenities. Radburn lived up to its promoters' appellation—"A Town for the Motor Age"—because it kept the automobile from interfering with its real purpose. Radburn was designed to be a town for living.

Radburn's final achievement was in the realm of social planning. It provided the first full demonstration of Clarence Perry's neighborhood unit. Perry helped frame the policy for Radburn at an RPAA conference held in the fall of 1927. Building by neighborhood units reflected the RPAA's concern with establishing the meaningful social life existing in some urban neighborhoods and small towns, which was threatened by growing urban congestion and suburban sprawl. In Radburn, each neighborhood revolved around its own elementary school and shopping center and comprised several interconnected superblocks.

Radburn and Sunnyside were examples of community planning. They demonstrated some of the techniques later employed by English new town planners. These were components of the regional outlook, but they do not represent the regionalism of the RPAA nor were they evidence of regional planning.

What is commonly—and (according to the RPAA) incorrectly—called regional planning made its first appearance in the United States before the close of the nineteenth century. In Boston, three metropolitan commissions had been established to supply water, sewage, and park facilities for the many small cities and towns that comprised the metropolitan area. Massachusetts served as an incubator for planning ideas that took years to hatch elsewhere. The Massachusetts Homestead Commission, for example, built the first public housing in the United States. The creation of these regional commissions was so premature when compared to the rest of the country that their survival is remarkable. Regional planning in the rest of the nation followed in the 1920s. Responding to the frenetic pace of urban growth and its spillover into suburban districts, private and public bodies began to copy the few cities that were trying to coordinate their own planning with that of neighboring jurisdictions.

This type of regional planning was sometimes conducted by a county and other times by a special district. Often it merely represented ad hoc cooperation between various local communities. And, as in New York City, regional planning was occasionally conducted by private groups. But regardless of its form, this kind of regional planning looked like city planning applied to the expanded domain of the motorized and subdivided metropolis. Like city planning, this new brand of planning sought to solve the problems of growth. Its practitioners were at best nonchalant about growth itself or the nature of urban life. They limited themselves to such mechanical dilemmas as road access and water supply, measures that assured continued urban growth and the life style it spawned. This particular variety of regional planning also found support among the powerful interests who wanted to protect urban property values. Regardless of whether such planning arose to protect property or to innocently minister to the consequences of growth, it guaranteed both continued growth and increased urban land values. One historian has concluded categorically that "No commission presented plans which aimed at diverting the growth of metropolitan cities because their sponsors never questioned the assumption that bigger was better. The regional commissions were supposed to facilitate growth."[18] The RPAA was perhaps the only voice systematically criticizing the reign of the metropolis.

Quite naturally, the RPAA rejected this so-called regional planning. First, it was not regional planning at all; it was metropolitan planning. More importantly, by facilitating growth and congestion, metropolitan planning compounded even the mechanical problems it supposedly solved. Finally, metropolitan planning lacked any "conception of a norm," unless of course, it was growth for its own sake.[19] Frederick Ackerman pessimistically concluded "that the nature and character of [modern city] growth is largely a function of pecuniary value," rather than human aspirations. Its "development and growth . . . is of a highly impersonal character. It does not express, in its details nor as a whole, the desires, aims or ideals of the individuals who consititute its population."[20] The difference between metropolitan planning and the RPAA position, Mumford insisted, was "not a difference over facts, but over fundamental beliefs, particularly as to the character and the destiny of our present form of civilization."[21] When their group organized a conference on the subject in 1931, Wright explained "that the reason . . . regionalism was chosen for the Round Table, rather than regional planning, was to . . . [divert attention from] . . . the more obvious and mechanical expres-

18. Joseph L. Arnold, *The New Deal in the Suburbs: A History of the Greenbelt Town Program* (Columbus: Ohio State University Press, 1971), p. 14.

19. Mumford, "The Culture-Cycle and City Planning," *Journal of the American Institute of Architects* 14 (July 1926):293.

20. Frederick L. Ackerman, "Cities of the Nth Degree," *Journal of the American Institute of Architects* 14 (July 1926):289-290.

21. Mumford, "The Culture-Cycle and City Planning," p. 291.

sions of planning, and get down to the fundamentals of a newer and better organization of life and its relation to its natural inheritance, in contrast to the life now developed in the most 'advanced' portions of the country."[22]

The RPAA looked to England, France, and Germany for examples of their brand of regionalism. In Europe regionalism took the form of a protest against centralization and standardization, two products of the industrial order that the RPAA dubbed "metropolitan civilization." The great cities were the capitals of this new industrial empire. The Europeans responded with movements to reclaim local culture and to build provincial institutions, attempts to counteract the homogenizing effects of metropolitanism. This was the general tenor of thought that the RPAA tried to bring to the United States. Sometimes when the group got together on weekend retreats, MacKaye would call folk dances. To its members, folk arts expressed and symbolized the indigenous regional culture threatened by the rise of a metropolitan civilization. Regionalism, particularly during the thirties, became an important movement in art and literature throughout the United States.

Some members of the RPAA found in Oswald Spengler's *The Decline of the West* a description of what they saw happening to the metropolitan centers. Spengler studied the life cycles of societies from their creative phase as a "culture" to their rigidified decline as a "civilization." Mumford called the first the "spiritual form" and the latter, the "material fact." Culture, as Benton MacKaye interpreted Spengler,

. . . is the tendency in society (and in ourselves) to develop and to *grow*, while the other [civilization] is the tendency to become mechanized and then merely to *expand*. One is an evolution of mind, the other—a multiplication of facts: Shakespeare is an outcome of the one, the bathroom is a product of the other. Both are useful and important: culture evolves the ends of life, civilization produces the means of life; one is living, the other is "getting ready to live."[23]

In the final stages of cultural decline a highly mechanized metropolitan, perhaps even megalopolitan, civilization completely supplants and subverts the rich urban culture from which it grew.

22. Wright to Mumford, 1931.

23. MacKaye, *The New Exploration: A Philosophy of Regional Planning* (Urbana: University of Illinois Press, 1962), p. 126.

The RPAA critique represented a radical challenge to the dominant social ideals of the period. Jumping to the defense of these metropolitan values, the RPAA's critics hastened to dismiss the group as being romantic about agrarian life or of harboring antiurban biases, indeed, seeking to destroy big cities. These charges are really the urbanists' hysterical equivalent to political red-baiting. They effectively place the RPAA's views outside the realm of consideration. In the introduction to their reader, *Regional Development and Planning*, John Friedmann and William Alonso typify this defense of the status quo. They dispose of the regionalism of the thirties "as an oddity . . . in the United States with its exceptionally fluid social patterns."[24] But Spengler and the RPAA viewed that fluidity as a manifestation of cultural disintegration.

In place of a world, there is a *city*, a *point*, in which the whole life of broad regions is collecting, while the rest dries up. In place of a true-type people, born and grown on the soil, *there is a new sort of nomad, cohering unstably in fluid masses*, the parasitical city dweller, tradition-less, utterly mater of fact, religionless, clever, unfruitful, deeply contemptuous of the countryman. . . . This is a very great stride towards the inorganic, towards the end.[25]

Culture, recreation, work, and every other phase of life becomes standardized, machine-made, and abstracted from life itself. Finally, "the creative forces diminish and a period of hardening and encystment sets in, marked by no fresh departures, but rather by *a technical elaboration of the existing elements*" [italics mine].[26] In effect, that is what the RPAA saw happening in the metropolitan centers; streets were widened, buildings were made higher, subways were extended, suburban areas were subdivided, all repetitiously expanding the metropolis and its monetary values. Therefore "it is inevitable" that metropolitan planners, as unwitting supporters of cultural decline, "should devote their efforts chiefly to matters of external technique; matters which will

24. John Friedmann and William Alonso, eds., *Regional Development and Planning: A Reader* (Cambridge, Massachusetts: The MIT Press, 1964), p. 12.

25. Mumford, "The Culture-Cycle and City Planning," p. 292.

26. Ibid.

keep supreme and dominant the present financial and political institutions, and the classes which direct them and profit from them."[27]

If, as some of the group argued, settlement patterns reflect a society's goals, political structure, and economic conditions, their own normative ideal, captured in Mumford's image of the fourth migration, challenged the very essence of the social system. The alternative, as expressed by one of its members, was "a more or less conscious choice of continuing an old and hardened civilization or of beginning to foster the fresh growth of a new culture."[28] The RPAA chose a new culture. As they imagined it, the new culture would begin with a migration from the metropolis into stable and balanced communities. This population movement had none of the trappings of a retreat toward a primitive life style; it would depend instead on the wise use of new and emergent technologies. For example, the rapid growth of the automobile from 2.5 million vehicles in 1915 to 9.2 million in 1920, and then to 20 million in 1925 presented a massive problem in the congested urban centers. But automobiles could potentially supply access to communities that were long abandoned in the migration to the industrial towns and urban centers served by railroads and river transportation. Similarly, long-distance power transmission meant that industries could locate far from traditional power sources. Power could be inexpensively distributed throughout large regions. In short, the technical and industrial justification for metropolitan growth had evaporated. Technological advances supported a new migration, which could either reinforce the metropolitan pattern with sprawl or replace the increasingly dehumanized metropolitan environment with a life-sustaining one.

Only the city prospers under the metropolitan regime. The rest is a hinterland colony drained of its resources and vitality. Compare that to the indigenous environment. As MacKaye envisioned it, the indigenous environment comprised three elements: wilderness, rural, and urban habitats balanced with each other in an organic relationship. The group's best representation of that balanced relationship can be found in this volume—*The Report of the New York State Commission of*

27. Ibid.
28. Ibid., p. 293.

Housing and Regional Planning. Like Mumford's preceding piece, "The Fourth Migration" (which also appears in this anthology), the report establishes its roots in the rich loam of premetropolitan life.

Thus Henry Wright, the major author of the report, describes the shift from New York's partly self-sufficient agrarian economy to a centralized industrial one. The report uses maps extensively to illustrate the distribution and size of towns, their economic activities, and a great deal of other statistical information. The maps reveal two distinct periods in the state's development. "First there was scattered, small-scale industry serving local markets. It was the period of the water-wheel, hand-driven tools, the wagon road and canal and the town."[29] At the height of this first epoch, roughly 1840, "the typical citizen lived in a small and almost self-sufficient rural community, about 500 of which were scattered all over the State. He might be on a farm, raising crops and tending animals, taking his wheat to the grist mills, his hides to the near-by tannery, his wool to the small carding, spinning and weaving plants which came to supplant clothmaking at the home. . . . The life had hardships and uncertainties of its own; it was rigorously simple and knew few luxuries."[30] With the second epoch "came the age of steam, the machine, rail transportation, and the city. The small plant gave way to the modern factory, sales forces canvassed the national market, the town declined, the city rose. In New York State the topography which determined the location of rail transportation forced almost all of the growth into one narrow [Mohawk] valley that extends from Buffalo east to Albany and thence [via the Hudson] south to New York."[31] Half the state's population lived in this L-shaped valley system in 1875. By 1920, four times as many people lived in the valley than in the rest of the state, and most of these lived in cities.[32]

At the end of the second epoch the typical citizen dwelt in the industrial center; he worked in a factory or an office with ever growing

29. State of New York, *Report of the Commission of Housing and Regional Planning to Governor Alfred E. Smith* (Albany: J. B. Lyon Co., 7 May 1926), p. 49.

30. Ibid., p. 37.

31. Ibid., p. 49.

32. Ibid., p. 36.

hordes of fellow employees and with automatic machinery always increasing in complexity. He lived often in congested tenements. His food and water supply came from greater and greater distances. Meanwhile many of the farmers found themselves hanging on to land no longer profitable. Their local markets had dried up. Only those who could ship to the cities continued to support themselves.

Such was the situation in New York State when, in 1921, electricity passed steam in importance as a motive power and the automobile had supplanted the railroad for many important classes of traffic.[33]

These were the conditions the New York State Commission addressed in suggesting a plan. Following the line of argument advanced in "Dinosaur Cities," an article (in this volume) by Clarence Stein, the commission predicted that among the sweeping consequences of electricity and the automobile, places of business would move from the congested urban centers, and people would travel to work from suburban areas. Rural electrification and the flexibility of motor transportation also suggested an increase in farm productivity in some areas abandoned during the second epoch. In these indications of a vast redistribution of population, the commission perceived an opportunity to remedy the social ills and economic waste associated with urban congestion. Change, as the report concluded, was "in the air."

Past experience with uncoordinated development implied the need for a plan to insure that impending social changes would "improve the conditions of life rather than to promote opportunities for profit."[34] At the very least, this meant that the state should act in the provision of roads and the like in a coordinated manner, based on a plan. The resulting outline provides a pure example of what MacKaye called the *new conservation*. The commission superimposed maps of the state's topography, soil, natural resources, and climate. The resulting map indicated the areas that naturally lent themselves to intensive use. Another composite showing rainfall, catchments, land utilization, and farmland values produced a general picture of areas unsuited for either agricultural or industrial use and therefore ripe for reforestation. The commission's analysis disclosed that large areas abandoned with the spread of

33. Ibid., pp. 37-38.
34. Ibid., p. 64.

the steam engine should remain unpopulated and be returned to a natural wooded state where they could provide lumber, permit recreation, and control soil erosion.

Thus the studies supported the continued development of the valley system of epoch two with one important exception: the valleys natural-ly conducive to intensive development were in fact far broader than the concentrated pattern permitted by the technology of the preceding epoch.

Within the state the commission saw the outlines of regions that "form a complete social organism." The northern part of the state bor-dering Lake Ontario and the St. Lawrence River was one such region. It had the variety of resources and environments to fill the RPAA's definition of a region: it combined an overall cultural and geographic unity with the variety of resources to insure a measure of self-suffici-ency. "The regionalist attempts to plan such an area so that all its sites and resources, from forest to city, from highland to water level, may be soundly developed, and so that the population will be distributed so as to utilize, rather than to nullify or destroy its natural advantages. It sees people, industry and the land as a single unit."[35] This particular region provided ample land along the lake shore and to the east where climate and soil conditions made agriculture promising; the region's industrial resources were also ample. Railroads served the area and the hydro-electric potential of Niagara Falls, the St. Lawrence River, and the Adirondack Mountains was impressive.

The commission noted:

The actual development [of this locale] does not take full advantage of the great resources of the region. The district is not integrated. Cities like Rochester, Buffalo and Syracuse have grown to such a point as to introduce problems of planning, traffic and housing that might be avoided if smaller industrial centers were developed. The vast industrial and agricultural activity of which this entire region is capable must be related to the hinterland.

For example, they suggested the following:

The lower hills, rising 1200 to 1600 feet above sea level are favorable for dairying and grazing. The highlands should serve for forest reserve

35. Mumford, "Regions—To Live In," *Survey Graphic* 7 (May 1925):151.

and water supply. Access to these and to the beautiful Finger Lakes
section in the center of the State would provide recreational escape
from the cities. With foresight and planning, such a region might take
full advantage of all its resources and might provide a setting for a multitude of prosperous and healthy communities.[36]

The development of such a region would inevitably rely on many of
the specific techniques that intrigued the RPAA's membership, including ecological planning and the garden city. Although they accepted
the basic principles underlying Ebenezer Howard's garden city, members of the RPAA did not share Howard's panacean faith in the concept. They wanted more variety in city size and layout for example.
Nonetheless building new cities was a logical way to go about repopulating regions. Even without orthodox adherence to Howard's overall
conception, numerous planning principles elaborated by him found
their way into the RPAA's plans for regional reconstruction. Thus new
and replanned communities would be limited by greenbelts from repli-
cating metropolitan growth patterns. Common ownership would likewise eliminate the speculative pressures endured elsewhere and reduce
the cost of housing and community facilities. Howard's garden city concept also conveyed the idea of industrial and residential balance, self-
government, and an intimate relationship between town and country.
Members of the RPAA valued these notions.

The original garden city concept was also a regional idea. Howard proposed that ten garden cities be grouped contiguously to form what he
called *social cities*. These resemble what members of the RPAA began
to call *regional cities*. Although separated from each other by greenbelts, rapid transit would connect them. So as Howard pictured it,
"each inhabitant of the whole group, though in one sense living in a
town of small size, would be in reality living, and would enjoy all the
advantages of, a great and most beautiful city; and yet all the fresh de-
lights of the country . . . would be within a very few minutes' walk or
ride."[37] The RPAA's interest in garden cities, as exemplified in the

36. State of New York, *Report of the Commission,* p. 71.

37. Ebenezer Howard, *Garden Cities of To-morrow,* ed. F. J. Osborn (Cambridge,
Massachusetts: The MIT Press, 1965), p. 142.

CHC's attempts to build one, was instrumental to the goal of regional reconstruction, and not an end in itself.

The RPAA wanted to introduce other new techniques besides the garden city to aid in the regionalizing process. The automobile, for example, which the RPAA perhaps too optimistically welcomed, required special treatment in order to fulfill its potential role in the fourth migration. Otherwise, as events were already proving to this small band of critical observers, the automobile would reinforce the hegemony of the metropolis and further undermine the quality of urban life. Benton MacKaye found the clue to road planning at Radburn, where the automobile and the community were segregated to the advantage of both. Radburn was safer and more tranquil, and motoring was more efficient than in other communities.

In March, 1930, MacKaye wrote an article for the *New Republic* proposing that the principle be extended to interurban highways—*townless highways*, he called them. The railroad supplied MacKaye with an analogy. Trains had their own right-of-way with only an occasional grade crossing where they could possibly impede other activities and vice versa. Why not build roads without access or grade crossings except at long intervals? MacKaye compared points of access to railroad stations, but unlike the railroad terminal, these stations would be located well outside of town. They would have all the services motorists might need, like gas stations and restaurants, but nothing more. Thus only those travelers destined for a particular city had to enter it, and they would use local roads. Access to the townless highway at any other point would be prevented by public ownership of all abutting property. This effectively eliminates the parasitic "road slum" that affixed itself like a leech to other automotive arteries. Its commercial blight and turning traffic could be abolished. In some respects, the townless highway set the standard for modern high-speed roads—limited access, median dividers, public ownership of abutting land, even the elimination of billboards. But the successors to the townless highway deviated significantly from MacKaye's design. Too often they penetrated the fragile urban fabric to deliver cars to the urban core on a stream of through traffic.

The most glaring perversion of MacKaye's idea can be found in his own state. In 1930, he advanced the concept of a multipurpose bypass around Boston.[38] The semicircular road would divert through traffic. MacKaye wanted to broaden the insulating layer of greenery along the road to two miles. In this way the "Bay Circuit" would also serve as a massive park; a greenbelt barrier to continuous urban sprawl. Built eventually without this greenbelt, Route 128 destroyed MacKaye's farsighted idea. Despite limited access to it, the road became a magnet for commercial and industrial growth and a model for state bureaucrats throughout the country who, like children throwing rocks into a mud puddle, appreciate the concentric pattern of sprawl emanating from the old urban centers.

Like all techniques, the townless highway could serve many ends. Instead of facilitating regionalization, the automobile rode on another kind of highway; one that spread the metropolis until it ultimately formed the megalopolis.

Economic planning represented another potential instrument of regional reconstruction. Stuart Chase was first alerted to the benefits of economic planning during the First World War and he later wrote an influential book about it, *The Tragedy of Waste*. In it he observed that "the war had its by-products of technical achievement." Chief among these "was the elimination of industrial waste made possible through the co-ordinated control of the economic structure."[39] With a quarter of the work force diverted to the war effort, Chase reported that "the standard of living held its own and probably increased somewhat."[40] Without luxury production, the position of the lower classes improved relative to the higher income groups. All of this was possible because the War Industries Board, the Food, Fuel, and Railroad Administrations, the United States Housing Corporation, and numerous other federal bodies allocated materials and distributed goods in order to eliminate waste. "War control lifted the economic system of the country, stupefied by decades of profit seeking, and hammered it and pounded it into an intelligent mechanism for delivering goods and services."[41]

38. MacKaye, "Super By-Pass for Boston," *Boston Globe* (31 October 1930).

39. Chase, *The Tragedy of Waste* (New York: Macmillan Company, 1925), p. 4.

40. Ibid., p. 7.

41. Ibid., p. 10.

The system of industrial control expired with the armistice. Normalcy returned amid an economic slump. President Harding unceremoniously fired Chase and some of his companions for "criticizing business profits."[42] But the implications of wartime controls impressed the RPAA. As conservationists, the results supported their contention that resources were being wasted. The Soviet Union's Gosplan supplied further evidence that economic planning made sense. Chase studied the Soviet's five-year plan as part of the first American trade union delegation to visit Russia. He returned impressed with "their economic methods but not their political methods." The experience fortified his belief that planning regions as economic units would reduce resource consumption. Without the then-emerging capitalist practice of national marketing and its resulting cross-hauls, Chase believed prices would decrease. This in turn would improve the standard of living for everyone. Economic planning was also a vehicle for building viable and balanced regions. In lieu of the old laissez-faire system of industrial location, factories could be directed to locations where they were needed. So, for that matter, could housing, as the United States Shipping Board had shown.

Rural electrification represented yet another structural member in the RPAA's blueprint for regional reconstruction. Electricity, like almost every other commodity, flowed primarily to the urban centers. This of course intensified the industrial dominance of the great cities. But just as automotive technology might have helped to overcome the rural population's growing isolation, long-distance power transmission was seen by the RPAA as a way to restore balance between the city and the country. Rural electrification became a realistic possibility with these lines. Hooked into an electrical system, small towns could support industry. Similarly, electricity could transform the drudgery and isolation of farm life.

The garden city, the townless highway, rural electrification, economic planning—each was a block of granite from the same intellectual quarry. Except for the RPAA's theoretical exercises, these blocks were never fabricated into the regional configurations for which they were excavated.

42. Interview with Chase, 17 June 1975.

But neither were they entirely overlooked. The RPAA influenced the New Deal; no administration before or since has been so committed to national planning. And certainly regionalism had a special appeal to Franklin Roosevelt and some of his advisors, particularly Rexford Tugwell. The New Deal introduced the first national constructive housing program since the short-lived attempt that accompanied the First World War. But the government sampled the RPAA's ideas selectively and never stayed for the main course. The Greenbelt Town Program, for example, was too small and too suburban to do justice to the RPAA's regionalism; the three towns that did finally negotiate the political obstacle course and were built—Greenbelt, Marlyand; Greenhills, Ohio; and Greendale, Wisconsin—exemplified the rising standards in community planning. Henry Wright, Clarence Stein, Frederick Bigger, Robert Kohn, and Catherine Bauer all made at least some direct contribution to the program's limited success. If the greenbelt communities had been the next stop after Radburn on the route to a comprehensive garden cities program, instead of the terminus, features like its now-lapsed public ownership would seem more impressive today.[43] But after forty years, the greenbelt program is a historical anomaly. If the country was ever committed to the Greenbelt Town Program's latent idealism, it has long ago retreated from it.

In his history of the Greenbelt Town Program, Joseph L. Arnold acknowledges the New Deal's great intellectual debt to the RPAA.[44] Without the RPAA's decade-long advocacy of a program of publicly developed garden cities within a new regional framework, the Greenbelt Town Program would probably never have been conceived at all. The RPAA even had direct contact with President Roosevelt, although, paradoxically, this may have been less influential than the cumulative impact of their writings. Eleanor Roosevelt, a greenbelt supporter, had served on the CHC board. The president himself had attended and addressed the RPAA's Round Table on Regionalism in 1931. Two years

43. Members of the RPAA and Stein in particular lobbied to prevent federal disposal of the communities. Stein to Wurster, 3 January 1949, Catherine Bauer Wurster Papers, Bancroft Library, University of California, Berkeley, California.

44. Arnold, *The New Deal in the Suburbs,* pp. 14-15.

later the RPAA wrote to Roosevelt encouraging him to locate "and design new communities in connection with industrial decentralization with the object of building a usable environment." But as finally adopted, the program focused on relocation of displaced country dwellers, a policy that reflected Roosevelt's limited conception. Even the members actually employed in the New Deal administration were not in positions to influence the ultimate direction of programs, although their earlier work had in part inspired them. Thus the Greenbelt Town Program lacked the decentralizing quality so critical to the RPAA's design for regional reconstruction.

By contrast, the Tennessee Valley Authority (TVA) looked like the embodiment of the RPAA's greatest hopes. "Your Tennessee program," Stein wrote to Roosevelt on behalf of the RPAA, "offers the opportunity of broadly developing this environment in terms of the house itself, the neighborhood unit, the balanced industrial and agricultural unit, the community and the region. It should serve as an example for the development of much of the country."[45] Benton MacKaye joined the TVA staff, and Tracy Augur, one of the RPAA's last members, served as chief town planner. Stuart Chase declared himself a self-appointed publicist for the program. "Here, struggling in embryo," Chase wrote in one book, "is perhaps the promise of what all America will some day be."[46] TVA was a multipurpose agency responsible for the development of an entire region; it was dedicated to the idea of democratic planning.

A new regional concept—the river basin as an integral unit—was created which had a special responsibility neither national nor state-wide in scope. . . . Further, and in one sense more important, a broad vision of regional resource development—in a word, planning—informed the conception, if not the actual powers, of the new organization.[47]

The river system and the publicly financed improvements to it defined the TVA's mission, but its influence extended inland, with a less

45. Stein to Franklin Roosevelt, 1 March 1933.

46. Chase, *Rich Land, Poor Land* (New York: Whittlesey House, 1936), p. 287.

47. Philip Selznick, *TVA and the Grass Roots: A Study in the Sociology of Formal Organization* (New York: Harper Torchbooks, Harper and Row, 1966), p. 5.

specific mandate to consider and respond to the social repercussions of the TVA's primary activities. Thus, rural electrification supplemented the power-generating program. The TVA built three modest new towns —Norris, Pickwick Landing, and Wheeler. It supervised reforestation projects and helped create numerous parks. As Philip Selznick discovered, however, weaknesses in the TVA's design limited its authority as a regional planning agency.

... It must be said that although the agency and its program have symbolized concentrated effort and planning, in fact the TVA has had little direct authority to engage in large-scale regional planning. The powers delegated to it were for the most part specific in nature, related to the primary problems of flood control, navigation, fertilizer, and power. In addition, authority to conduct studies and demonstrations of a limited nature, but directed toward general welfare objectives, was delegated to the President and by him to the Authority. This became the basis for some general surveys and demonstration work in forestry, local industrial development, community planning, and for work with cooperatives.[48]

As a result, "TVA never fulfilled itself as an experiment in regional planning; it remained chiefly a corporation to produce and sell power and fertilizer."[49] Thus even in the most promising of the New Deal programs, the RPAA's goals were unrealized.

In the decade prior to the New Deal, few were receptive to the RPAA's message. The group's warnings went unheeded and regionalism was scoffed at. The New Deal seemed to change all that. The Roosevelt administration looked like fertile territory for the proposals of the RPAA. One by one its members boarded trains out of New York. Robert Kohn became the first director of the Public Works Administration's Housing Division; MacKaye joined the TVA; Frederick Bigger assumed the position of chief of planning for the greenbelt program; other members followed. Although the RPAA had a general ideological impact on the administration, these officeholders did not occupy positions that allowed them to determine specific policy. The essential thrust of a decade of RPAA activity was blunted in Washington. Meanwhile, the RPAA, al-

48. Ibid., p. 6.

49. William E. Leuchtenburg, *Franklin D. Roosevelt and the New Deal* (New York: Harper and Row, 1963), p. 165.

ready weakened by the dissolution of Stein and Wright's long collaboration, was abandoned in New York as its members pursued the opportunities for active planning and the illusion of significant change offered by the New Deal.[50]

Merely by creating these opportunities for individual members of the group and by appearing to share the RPAA's ideas, the New Deal contributed to the group's gradual disintegration and unintentionally muted the RPAA's persistent voice for a new mode of regional planning.

Nevertheless, most of the RPAA's members managed to escape the worst threat posed by the New Deal's beguiling appeal. Although they served the administration as technicians, they did not later defend the New Deal for successfully implementing their program, as Progressive reformers had done when city councils and state legislatures recast their comprehensive goals into narrow laws. The farsighted publicists of the Progressive Era became the nearsighted bureaucrats of the next.

In the early years professional planning was affiliated with the . . . housing and other municipal reform movements which espoused normative goals and broadened the planner's perception of his function. Increasingly, however, the professional planner evolved into a technician who minimized normative goals—structural or institutional innovation—and became the prophet of the "City Scientific" or "City Efficient." Technical matters relating to zoning, law, finance, capital expenditure, and transportation became his province. He did not seek fundamental changes in urban form and structure, but projected existing demographic and institutional trends into the future as a basis for planning.[51]

The New Deal's offer of political legitimacy similarly tempted members of the RPAA, but they escaped the fate of Lawrence Veiller and other Progressive reformers. The regionalists who served Roosevelt's administration as either supporters or technicians eventually realized that in the process of instituting the first significant wave of reform

50. Stein and Wright had begun to move in different directions after Radburn, Stein tenaciously spreading the gospel of "The Radburn Idea" and Wright seeking out still newer forms. Wright joined with Mumford and Albert Mayer to form the Housing Study Guild to train young architects in the techniques pioneered by the RPAA.

51. Lubove, ed., *The Urban Community: Housing and Planning in the Progressive Era* (Englewood Cliffs, New Jersey: Prentice-Hall, 1967), p. 14.

since the Progressive period, the New Deal had only extracted disjoint-
ed fragments of the RPAA's carefully evolved regionalism. The Rural
Electrification Administration, for example, ostensibly undertook the
RPAA's drive to bring public power to the countryside. Without the
complementary efforts to industrially stabilize the rural population as
outlined by the RPAA, however, rural electrification would inevitably
increase agricultural productivity and fuel a still increased migration to
cities already lacking in opportunities and amenities for previous mi-
grants. The Roosevelt administration also instituted a constructive housing program. It too was pursued independently of the regional framework that the RPAA proposed as essential to a constructive housing
policy. The New Deal adopted public housing primarily as a means to
re-employ construction workers and to stimulate allied industries; only
secondarily was public housing to supply new housing to people who
could not otherwise afford it.

Regionalism as defined by the RPAA and set forth in this volume is a
policy framework. Housing, power development, highway building, and
the like reinforce and give substance to that policy. But the New Deal
administered these programs as dosages of economic adrenalin. They
were rarely even ends in themselves. Regionalism, on the other hand, is
a complex objective. It demands the kind of commitment and social coordination we associate with the most fundamental sort of change. Apparently, some of the RPAA's members temporarily lost sight of that
fact in the intoxicating rush of New Deal rhetoric and power. Instead of
maintaining their integrated program, many of them promoted specific
reforms independent of the regional vision.

Catherine Bauer and Edith Elmer Wood, who were most interested in
housing anyway, became advocates for a public housing program and
later worked for the United States Housing Authority.

Despite the fact that Catherine Bauer was close to the higher-ups in the
national Housing Administration, Stein and Wright's fresh contributions
to community planning played hardly any part in their work; and the
farther they went, the farther they departed from Wright's demonstrations. By the time they built Fort Greene houses they had committed
themselves to the High Rise Slums, as [Catherine Bauer] later regretted.[52]

52. Mumford to Carl Sussman, 30 July 1974.

Thus even after Bauer had distanced herself from the integrating principles of regionalism, she compounded her folly by failing to apply even the proven community planning practices that had emerged from experiments in Sunnyside and Radburn—despite the fact that she had worked closely with Stein on Radburn.

As Mumford subsequently observed, "both the economic and the political situation favored opportunism rather than long-range thinking; and Roosevelt was the prince of opportunists, taking a bold stand one day and contradicting it the next."[53] Members of the RPAA were not immune to these temptations, particularly after years of intellectual isolation. The naturally interdisciplinary quality of their program yielded to parochial interests during the New Deal. Like nineteenth-century English and European socialist town planners and American Progressives, the members of the RPAA who worked in the New Deal devoted themselves to piecemeal reforms that restored political and economic legitimacy and stability to the metropolitan order they had set out to change.[54] As competent technicians they helped effect forward-looking reforms that marginally improved the lot of many Americans within the context of the existing order. By unintentionally allowing these reforms to reinforce the old patterns of metropolitan congestion, many members of the RPAA undermined the implicit aim of their regionalism: to create a new social and economic order.

Belatedly, they acknowledged their mistake and began to regret the organization's untimely disintegration. "The fact is," Mumford recalls, "we dispersed and none of us were as good after as we were together."[55] In 1948 Clarence Stein spearheaded the revival of the group as the Regional Development Council of America, but the unique conditions that made the group thrive in the twenties could not be reproduced. Within a few years it too dissolved.

Looking at the general situation today from the perspective articulated by members of the RPAA, nothing has really changed in the fifty years

53. Mumford to Sussman, 14 December 1974.

54. Leonardo Benevolo, *The Origins of Modern Town Planning*, trans. Judith Landry (Cambridge, Massachusetts: The MIT Press, 1967), p. 110.

55. Interview with Mumford, 26 April 1974.

since they first began their campaign against metropolitanism. "But if," as Mumford maintains, "a full realization of our ideas required a complete reformation of our dominant personal incentives and social objectives, a change from a Money Economy to a Life Economy, it would have been childish to anticipate an early consummation."[56] And they did call for a massive restructuring.

Almost predictably the conditions the RPAA deplored in the twenties have worsened. By 1920 just half of the nation's population lived in cities. By the same statistical standard, the figure now approaches three-quarters of the population. More importantly, a large proportion of these people live in the overextended metropolitan areas; most, live in suburbs. Even now the migration continues. Financiers still control urban development, although they now depend on federal complicity. Slums abound. National markets are the rule. The move away from the human scale takes increasingly bizarre forms. The country weathered an urban crisis without any real change in national attitudes toward the city. Environmental conditions have seriously deteriorated. Yet the nation remains committed to the same discredited metropolitan ideal it pursued decades ago. The years since the New Deal bear out the RPAA's predictions of crime and congestion, urban fiscal crises, and wasteful suburban sprawl. These are the still crumbling ruins of our metropolitan civilization, and they vindicate the RPAA's critique.

The great task outlined by the RPAA still confronts us. The members of the RPAA make a convincing argument, buttressed by the excesses and destruction of an intervening half century, that every effort to resolve the contradictions of metropolitanism, while still maintaining its economic and political foundation, will only deepen the original crisis. The situation, in short, cannot be ameliorated without embarking on a bold new course. The RPAA offered such a course. If suburbanization has preempted Mumford's label for their regional alternative—the fourth migration—then perhaps the RPAA's vision can someday be realized as the fifth migration. But despite all of the political obstacles to change and the ideological momentum to keep things more or less as they are,

56. Interview with Mumford, 5 August 1975.

the members of the RPAA demand a fundamental commitment. Instead of working in the name of pragmatism on meaningless civic improvement projects, they argue for a dedication to a new social order where people have decent homes, a stable community life, a healthy and varied environment, and a genuinely urban culture. That is the real message and the ultimate challenge to be found in the following selections.

I Metropolitan Civilization: Its Rise and Fall

"We may be fully aware that the accelerating congestion of urban centers cannot continue indefinitely. But we have based our wealth upon the prospect of continuous and accelerating growth, expansion and congestion."

—Frederick Ackerman

Introductory Note

Although the members of the RPAA coalesced around a shared vision, their combined viewpoint remained largely private and poorly articulated until 1925. Months before the International Town, City, and Regional Planning Conference convened in New York, Robert Bruère, the education editor of the *Survey Graphic,* sat in his office talking with Benton MacKaye. They discussed the RPAA's role as the conference's host. Bruère suggested a special regional planning issue of the *Survey.* They quickly formulated a tentative outline, which MacKaye delivered to Mumford, with their request that he edit the issue. Mumford accepted. As a result, in May 1925, the *Survey Graphic* published its "Regional Planning Number."

Although a couple of the articles have been reprinted elsewhere, the importance of the issue as a whole has been overlooked. Both as individual statements on a seemingly wide variety of subjects and as a comprehensive statement by the RPAA, the "Regional Planning Number" possesses that rare quality found in literary classics—it can be read today, fifty years later, for an understanding of our own time. In 1968, for instance, Lewis Mumford republished one of these essays as a preface to *The Urban Prospect.* "I'll warrant that most readers won't realize till they reach the end," he confided to a friend, "that it was all written more than forty years ago. My little joke."[1] Clarence Stein endowed his article, "Dinosaur Cities," with the same enduring quality. He exposed the fallacy in the popular idea that new urban growth and more intense use of urban land improve a city's financial health. Yet the mayors of most American cities still cling to their growth strategies even as they struggle to forestall bankruptcy. One has to look no further than Frederick Ackerman's article for an explanation for their obstinacy. His interpretation foreshadows a recent wave of radical urban analysis. Henry Wright detailed the case for cluster housing and for planned unit development in his article. These two concepts gained professional recognition in the 1960s; in the future they are likely to become the standard for most new housing. In his contribution, Stuart Chase indicted the national transportation system for generating enormous social waste. The same facts alarmed the nation during the 1974 energy shortage.

Some of the articles stand out as seminal works. Lewis Mumford's "The Fourth Migration" was such an essay. In it he depicted three stages in America's urbanization. Historians, such as Sam Bass Warner, continue to use this periodization of America's urban development.[2]

The *Survey Graphic* articles reveal the individuality of approach, style, and emphasis that differentiates the RPAA members. MacKaye's piece exemplifies his preoccupation with naturalism and his faith in ecological planning. Alexander Bing's business acumen and his commitment to actually building an American garden city reveal themselves in his article.

In the clipped and measured cadence of magazine articles, the *Survey Graphic*'s "Regional Planning Number" presents a harmonious composition about the condition of urban life and a program for change. Its critique of metropolitan civilization and description of an alternative regional system based on new technologies and social institutions con-

1. Michael Hughes, ed., *The Letters of Lewis Mumford and Frederic J. Osborn: A Transatlantic Dialogue 1938-70* (New York: Praeger Publishers, 1972), p. 432.

2. Sam Bass Warner, Jr., *The Urban Wilderness: A History of the American City* (New York: Harper and Row, 1972), p. 60.

vey the essential thought of the RPAA. The basic propositions can be reread today, among other things, for their fresh insights into the sad state of metropolitan life and our inability to use technology humanely.

1 The Regional Community

This is the Regional Plan number of *Survey Graphic*. It owes its under-lying idea to a long-bearded Scot whose curiosity would not let him rest until from his Outlook Tower in Edinburgh he had seen clear through the pother of civilization to the land which sustained it and, in spite of human fumbling, controlled it.

This number has been written by a group of insurgents who, as archi-tects and planners, builders and rebuilders, have tried to remold cities in conventional ways and, finding the task a labor of Sisyphus, have pinned their faith boldly to the new concept of the Region. One of them lives in a Brooklyn flat and writes wistfully of Connecticut villages; one spends his best hours felling trees and clearing mountain trails; one is a prophet crying in the wilderness of the city, his heart in the crumbling country towns. Among those who have shaped it and put it together is a man who clings to a tiny communal patch of green set in the midst of tenements; a woman who takes her sweltering way twice daily beneath the length of Manhattan; a man who gives three hours a day to journey-ing between his desk and a crabapple tree. The Regional Plan number, in a word, has been made by people who are loath to live fractional lives

Reprinted from *Survey Graphic* 7 (May 1925): 129. This introduction to the fol-lowing articles appeared without credit to an author.

in either city or country—and refuse to admit that civilization requires of them perpetually the sacrifices they must make today to reconcile the means to live with a way of living. It will be read by thousands who share their discomfort and their hope.

For it is not enough to decry the manifest disabilities of the great city as a place to live in, or to ease them momentarily by the patching and straightening that engrosses so much of the effort of the city planner. Nor is it enough to plaster the billboards of the city with fervent appeals to Own Your Own Home. Back-to-the-land campaigns reckon neither with the creeping paralysis which threatens our agricultural communities nor with the anomalous situation of the suburb—which is often a mere castle in the sand, swallowed up sooner or later by the swelling tide of city congestion. Lewis Mumford gives the clue to genuine progress in *Sticks and Stones*:

To see the interdependence of city and country, to realize that the growth and concentration of one is associated with the depletion and impoverishment of the other, to appreciate that there is a just and harmonious balance between the two—this capacity we have lacked. Before we can build well on any scale we shall, it seems to me, have to develop an art of regional planning, an art which will relate city and countryside in a new pattern from that which was the blind creation of the industrial and territorial pioneer.

Here *The Survey* opens its pages to the Regional Planning Association of America. These pioneer planners have watched the drift of population and gauged the promise of its shifting currents. (So the number, which like a region has a plan, opens with a rapid sketch of these lines of flow.) They have probed beneath the surface of the great city which we accept so carelessly as the capstone of civilization, and have found the foundations crumbling. (So the number next gives space to a group of articles which appraise the performance of the city, its psychology, and its attendant hurly-burly of transportation.) Then they have studied with technical precision the possibility of a new pattern of power, of industrial distribution, of housing and play, of the interlock between natural resource and human uses. Generalizing from their data, they have devoted the greater part of this issue to presenting, facet by facet, a new kind of human environment—the regional community. They define it;

they show it as an end toward which New York with its Regional Plan Commission and Pennsylvania with its Giant Power Survey Board are already moving; they portray it as a place of more satisfying homes, as a place where children today and their children tomorrow may find a fuller life.

This then is the first rounded statement in magazine form of a new plan of relating masses of population to the land. This plan harks back to the robust "geotechnics" of Patrick Geddes—and through the summer we shall publish a series of brilliant articles from the pen of this seer of cities. The plan is closely linked in spirit and practice with the garden cities of England, whose founder, Ebenezer Howard, is a delegate to the New York Conference on Town, City and Regional Planning; it has frequently been dealt with, since the war, in the *Journal of the American Institute of Architects*: it binds up the common hopes of scattered planners in many cities. Here it is newly set down in broad outline for what it is worth—tentative as it must be, prophetic rather than descriptive, yet full of exhilarating promise.

2   The Fourth Migration

Lewis Mumford

In a period of flow, men have the opportunity to remold themselves
and their institutions. The great migrations that swept over Europe in
the past; the migrations that surged past the water-boundaries of Europe
and crawled through the formidable American wilderness—these great
tides of population, which unloosed all the old bonds, have presented
such an opportunity. To some of us it seems that in America we are in
the midst of another such tidal movement of population—and for convenience, we have called it the fourth migration.

Historically, there are two Americas: the America of the settlement
and the America of the migrations. The first America consists of the
communities that were planted on the seaboard and up the river valleys
during the seventeenth and eighteenth centuries. By 1850 these communities had achieved their maximum development; they had worked
out a well-rounded industrial and agricultural life, based upon the fullest
use of their regional resources through the water-wheel, mill and farm
and they had created that fine provincial culture, humbly represented
in the schools, universities, lyceums and churches, which came to a full
efflorescence in the scholarship of Motley, Prescott, Parkman and Marsh,

Reprinted from *Survey Graphic* 7 (May 1925): 130-133.

and in the literature of Emerson, Thoreau, Melville, Whitman and Poe.

The second America is the America of the migrations; the first migration that cleared the land west of the Alleghenies and opened the continent, the work of the land pioneer; the second migration, that worked over this fabric a new pattern of factories, railroads, and dingy industrial towns, the bequest of the industrial pioneer; and finally—and this brings us down to the present period—there is the America of the third migration, the flow of men and materials into our financial centers, the cities where buildings and profits leap upward in riotous pyramids. These three migrations have covered the continent and knitted together its present framework; and our efforts to promote social welfare, to "make crooked cities straight," and to conduct industries efficiently are based for the most part on the notion that this framework is complete and satisfactory—and final.

But the mold of America has not been set: we are again in another period of flow, caused like the flows of the past by new industrial methods, new wants and necessities, and new ideals of life, and we have before us the great adventure of working out a new pattern so that the fourth migration will give to the whole continent that stable, well-balanced, settled, cultivated life which grew out of its provincial settlement. We can hinder this tidal change and rob ourselves of its potential benefits by adjusting our plans to the forces that were dominant in the recent past; or we can remold our plans and guide our actions in terms of a more desirable future. This alternative goes down to the very roots of social philosophy. John Dewey has implicitly warned us of the fallacy of the first attitude; for in dealing with social facts that lie in the future, our hypothesis and our working plan are among the elements that determine the outcome. The sheaf of articles presented in this issue uncovers a new set of facts and presents a fresh set of alternatives, which seek not to create the fourth migration—that is already under way—but to guide it into positive and fruitful channels.

In order to put the fourth migration in perspective, let us consider briefly the three great movements of population which every civilization in Europe has experienced at some time in its history. In America this experience was crowded into the short space of a little more than a century; and these three movements had certain peculiar characteristics which left their mark on our landscape and our life.

The first migration was the clearing of the continent; and its symbol was the covered wagon. Before the Revolutionary War America was in reality a fringe of Europe: here was a Biblical "city of refuge," there a penal colony, and in another place an experimental society. From the close of the war the colonists found themselves bound by an unprecedented urge to take possession of the continent; and the history of the pioneers is the history of restless men who burned the forests of the Mohawk valley in order to plant farms, who shifted into the soft glacial deposits of Ohio in order to cleave their plows through its rich soil; men who grabbed wheat land and skinned it, who grabbed urban sites and "turned them over"; who staked out railway lines, sometimes strategically, like the Lehigh, and sometimes stupidly, like the Erie, in a mad scramble to cover the continent.

During the period from 1790 to 1890, when almost the last good free lands were disposed of, the farmers and woodmen and miners of the country lived symbolically, if not actually, in the covered wagon. The little communities that clustered about the mine or the railway station were towns and villages only by courtesy of the census taker: they lacked the traditional resources of a common life—their games, their religious revivals, their intellectual stimuli, were all of the crudest. Pleasure never interfered with the "business" of the early pioneer; because business *was* his pleasure. The gospel of work needed no Carlyle for preacher in pioneer America.

It is conceivable that the first migration might have been made soberly; that there might have been a consistent prospecting for good sites, an attempt to sort out the newcomers by directing them to the type of land and community they needed, and an effort to secure stable farming and a sound exploitation of resources. The "necessity" for opening the continent was largely mythical: it was, in all probability, a rationalization of the land-hungry European. All these better methods were, perhaps, conceivable; but as things stood, they didn't come to pass; and ever since 1890 we have been feeling the effects of the disorderly first migration: the butchered forests; farms gone to ruin or into a ruinous system of tenantry; villages so sterile that they drive all their ambitious or sensitive young people to the big towns. The conservation movement is a belated attempt to repair the evils of the first migration, and to use the land and its resources with some respect to their permanent productive capacity. Its chief weakness is that, in protest against our misuse of the remaining resources it tends to be negative, and is only beginning to develop a consistent regional program for their proper social use and development. As conservation passes out of this negative state, it tends to find common cause with the rural side of regional planning. But this is to anticipate.

The second great flow of population in America was from the countryside and from foreign countries into the factory town; the covered wagon gives way to the iron horse. Up to 1820 the chief concentration of people had been in the trading centers of the seaboard and the river junctures. With the introduction of steam power, factories were erected in places where power, as in the mill towns of Pennsylvania, or factory hands, as in the seaports, seemed most available. Cleveland in 1820, Columbus in 1830 and Chicago in 1840, with the rapid growth of all the industrial towns in the industrial expansion of the Civil War, tell a graphic tale of the westward march of men and manufactures.

The conditions that determined this flow of population were narrowly industrial: a city was considered solely as a place of work and business opportunity. That children need a chance to play and grow, that families need decent shelter and privacy and a few amenities, that learning and culture are worth encouraging for their own sake—these things were too often forgotten and ignored by the men who fostered the new industrialism. The result is familiar, and there is scarcely a town with more than 10,000 people and a working population which will not serve for example. Homes blocked and crowded by factories; rivers polluted; factories and railway yards seizing sites that should have been preserved for recreation; inadequate homes, thrown together anyhow, for sale anyhow, inhabited anyhow. The result was called prosperity in the census reports, but that was because no one tried to strike a balance between the private gains and the social losses.

To offset the depletions and dilapidations of the second migration, a special kind of "conservation" was instituted. The housing movement began in New York when a group of public-spirited citizens discovered that vice, crime and disease were largely by-products of an impoverished and congested environment. City planning came later. Meanwhile in every industrial center remedial agencies from soup kitchens to building and loan associations, from social settlements to employment bureaus, have been endeavoring to supply, partly from private means, the necessary facilities for living and enjoyment that were left out in the growth and expansion of the industrial town.

On certain sides the deficit has been terrific; scarcely any large town founded before 1880 has attempted to house the whole community with a respectable minimum of light, air, garden space and playgrounds, to say nothing of parks and access to open country; and although a great part of mechanical industry is burdened with overproductivity—which it recovers from by periodic shutdowns at the expense of the workers—it waited the suggestion of Peter Kropotkin, and the technical innovations of Henry Ford, actually to hold out the prospect of an environment in which industrial idleness might be bridged over by a certain sustaining minimum of agricultural labor. In short, if the first migration denuded the country of its natural resources, the second migration ruthlessly cut down and ignored its human resources. This, too, is the history of a wasted opportunity. With every chance to begin afresh, the industrial revolution in America reproduced—if we ignore a few isolated villages—all the bad characteristics of industrialism in Europe. Dickens' Coketown duplicated itself in Pittsburgh, Chicago, St. Louis, Newark, Bridgeport, or where you please.

The magnet of the third migration was the financial center. As the industrial system developed in America productive effort came to take second place to financial direction, and in the great consolidations of industry that began in the eighties, in the growth of banking and insurance facilities in the nineties, and in the development of advertising for the purpose of securing a national market, that got under way in the present century, the sales and promotion departments have absorbed, directly or indirectly, a large part of the population.

The greatest concentration in all these departments took place, of course, in New York, whose overseas connections put it into a peculiarly strategic position; but within the past generation a similar development has taken place in the regional sub-metropolises, that is to say, in the twelve cities which now have a nominal population of over 500,000 and in most cases an actual population, when suburban areas are considered, of over a million. With the exception of New York, which controls very largely the journalism, banking, insurance and advertising of the whole country, and of Chicago, which operates similarly in the middle west, these sub-metropolises—as a glance at their position will show—are really regional centers whose natural growth has received an additional stimulus from these peculiar financial opportunities.

The third migration has resulted in a steady drain of goods, people and pecuniary resources from the industrial towns and villages of the earlier migrations, and along with it the new sub-metropolises have acquired cultural resources which the rest of the country has lacked, or has achieved only tardily. The art museums, libraries, universities, research institutions, and theaters were at first monopolized by the older cities of the seaboard; and it has been only with great effort that the sub-metropolises, with their original industrial base, have begun to equalize the financial advantages of New York. As it is, no one can do first rate scholarly research in many lines without going to New York or Boston, Philadelphia or Chicago; and by the same token, it is New York that monopolizes the theaters and sends out road-companies to the rest of the country, as Dives might scatter the crumbs from his table.

When we speak of the disadvantages of the third migration, it is important that we should distinguish between the economic basis of that migration and its cultural by-product. So far from looking for the growth of regional centers of culture to cease, we should perhaps count upon its increasing as soon as the social and economic disadvantages of excessive concentration are done away with.

There are two things that should be noticed about the first three migrations. The first is that the movement of population is not from farm-village, to industrial town, to financial metropolis: the migrations rather come as successive waves, and while one wave recedes as the next comes foaming in, the first nevertheless persists and mingles with the second as an undertow. The present migration to the fruit farming and dry farming areas, or the new migration to the reclaimed swamps, marks the continuance of the first migration. Each migration represents a particular type of economic and social effort: the life that Daniel Boone sought is a different life from that a Wall Street broker or advertising man thinks desirable. The first migration sought land; the second industrial production; the third, financial direction and culture; but as a matter of fact, each of these types of effort and occupation is needed for a stable, all-round community. Only here and there have we even fitfully attempted to utilize the land intelligently, relate industry to power, resources and market, and provide an adequate "human plant" for the community at large. To effect this union is the task of the fourth migration.

What, then, is the basis of the fourth migration? Its basis is the technological revolution that has taken place during the last thirty years—a revolution which has made the existing layout of cities and the existing distribution of population out of square with our new opportunities. The first change is that which has taken place in transportation: the railroad line is no longer the sole means of rapid transportation. The automobile has brought goods and markets together, not linearly, as the railroads tend to do, but areally; so that a great deal of ground untouched by the railroad has been made accessible to the automobile. Chain stores have been quick to grasp the advantages of covering territory in this fashion, and the truck that makes its rounds through the small villages and towns receives the current surplus of eggs and butter, for distribution beyond the local market area.

Similarly, the automobile has increased the radius of the school and the library service, and it has likewise provided a basis for a system of direct marketing which now exists, unfortunately, only for summer-communities, but which could, were summer-communities made permanent, be made the basis for a year round supply of milk, eggs, butter, poultry and garden produce. In many parts of the United States the summer-community has assured the farmer of a stable income which his remoter metropolitan markets did not assure him. The railroad, moreover, tends to concentrate population near its lines; and there are city planners who, thinking in terms of the railway era, look forward to a complete consolidation of population in the seaboard and lake areas, along these lines. The railroads themselves have done what they could to promote this concentration by subsidizing a large commuting population, in order to increase the amount of noncommuting traffic.

Mark the contrasting type of development brought in by the automobile. The motor road does not depend upon concentration of population for its upkeep; indeed, instead of concentrating on main highways or trunklines, the motor highway system is best kept up, without heavy wear and tear on one hand or practical disuse on the other, by spreading the load of traffic and taxes. The tendency of the automobile, in other words, is within limits to disperse population rather than to concentrate it; and any projects which may be put forward for concentrating people in Greater-City areas blindly run against the opportunities the automobile opens out. Whether the airplane will work centrifugally or centripetally it is hard at the moment to tell: at present, with the volume of traffic slight, aviation has tended to develop air-lanes; but if the volume increases an aerial network, less bound to linear movements than even the automobile, seems at least a likelihood.

The second factor which bears upon the new layout of population is our new means of communication. The set towards urban concentration in industry and social life dates before the days of the telephone, when all personal contacts had to be made on the spot. Today the spot can be any point in a large area—in theory the whole United States, in practice the ten cent call zone—and still the contact can be effective and personal. In certain lines, where the bargaining between buyer and seller is still intimate, face-to-face meeting is a necessity; but this concerns the business end of production more than the factory end, and a great many factories, which are now on the periphery of Chicago, St. Louis, or Philadelphia, might with equal success be conducted at any point in a much wider region, even if the eventual market for the product were concentrated. The telegraph symbolically follows the railroad; the telephone, with kindred symbolism, follows the motor highway. So much for the business end of communication.

Socially, the popularization of the radio has made concentration even more obsolete, for today the songs, the news, the gossip and the speeches, which were once available only by taking a journey and sitting in a hall, are now increasingly the property of anyone who possesses a radio outfit; and the remote countryman is just as near the events and amusements which many people regard as the indispensable benefits of the big city, as the flat-dwellers of the Bronx or the rabbit-hutch dwellers of Philadelphia. In other words, the radio is potentially a distributive and decentralizing agency. Finally, the parcels post has placed the rural dweller who has the postman collect the mail from his door even nearer to his market or his neighbor than the city dweller, who must walk to the post-office to mail a package. Our modern methods of transportation, in fact, have reduced many of our boasted metropolitan advantages to nil.

Finally, electric transmission, in its recent phase, can send energy over a wide area without undue loss, and here again, instead of being tethered to the railroad and its coal shipments, industry can move out of the railroad zone without moving out of the power zone. Where water-power is available, the location of the factory need have no relation at all to the older technology. Moreover, for the economic distribution of power, engineers have found it advisable to have a balanced load, that is to say, a day-consumption (industrial) and a night-consumption (home) within the same local area; for when these two types are separated, the equipment that serves the daytime city lies largely idle at night.

All this, it goes without saying, means that our modern power facilities are favored by, and favor, a wide distribution of population. The three-hundred mile transmission belt, plus the motor highway, has made the coal railway center an antiquated industrial site. Industry under modern technology has a much wider choice of site than ever before. It if does not exercise this choice it tends to lose in efficiency of operation and personnel. As yet, it has scarcely begun to exercise it, partly because the inertia of custom and business enterprise has bound it to the old centers, and partly because its attention has not been directed to the advantages that would accrue to it; and finally because it can make no move which does not involve the housing of its workers and the provision of municipal services. An occasional factory or steel plant has made the attempt; but industry as a whole has not. It remains for regional planning to develop all these factors at once, as part of the technique of the fourth migration.

Now the third migration has not produced a good environment: it has sacrificed home, health, and happiness to the pursuit of business enterprise designed to produce maximum profits. Those centers which have concentrated most feverishly upon business efficiency are farthest away from having adequate homes and all the accessory institutions that round out a well-developed community. The forces that are concerned soley with business enterprise lose no opportunity for stressing the necessity of continuing the third migration; and city planners who fall in line with it plan for the agglomeration of ever-greater urban regions. This method and this attitude take altogether too much for granted, and if they have the great advantage of following the line of least resistance they too easily ignore the significance of new methods and new procedures which shift the direction of that line.

It is evident that each great movement of population, in sum, presents a new opportunity and a new task, and wisdom consists in taking advantage of the movement while it is still fluid. Fortunately for us, the fourth migration is only beginning: we may either permit it to crystallize in a formation quite as bad as those of our earlier migrations, or we may turn it to better account by leading it into new channels. To suggest what these new channels are, to show how necessary it is for us to trench them open, and to indicate how much the future may hold for us if we are ready to seize our destiny and shape it freshly—that is the purpose of the present articles. Even if there were no fourth migration on the horizon it would be necessary to invent one. It is at least a more fruitful hypothesis than any of those we are now blindly following!

3 Dinosaur Cities

Clarence S. Stein

Most of us see the great city as in a dream. It is the sum of all our possible aspirations. A picturesque skyline, massive towers, romantic beauty! Crowds swaying through the lighted streets in pursuit of pleasure; flashing lights, dancing feet, and delightful foods with the flavor of Rome, Paris, Vienna, Peking or London. A far cry from the Ladies' Social of Gopher Prairie! Libraries of rare books, vast museums and universities, the grand opera and the concert hall—the city of culture!

Our dream does not stop here; it has also a practical side. We see successful lawyers, engineers, advertising men, seated behind wide mahogany desks, protected and padded by secretaries, or speeding out to the golf-links and the country estate—the city of great opportunities! Chicago and New York, or at least Philadelphia, Boston, St. Louis and Los Angeles, lie at the end of that long, long trail which winds into the land of our dreams. Even if we remain in the home town, our aim is to make it grow fast enough to put us in the same class as these cities.

It is cruel to put the hard realities of daylight alongside these dream cities. But sooner or later most of us in the great cities awake to find that we have been grasping after a bubble, and that many of the real

Reprinted, without illustrations, from *Survey Graphic* 7 (May 1925): 134-138.

opportunities of living have slipped through our hands. For the city of our dreams is lost in another city which could occur to a sane mind only in a nightmare. It is in this second city that the great mass of people who swell the census statistics live and work and marry and die.

Look at the great city in its entirety: the turbid mass of traffic blocking the streets and avenues, the slow-moving crowd of people clambering into street-cars, elevateds, subways, their arms pinioned to their sides, pushed and packed like cattle in ill-smelling cars, with a mingling of bodies which would be indecent were it not for the suffocation and discomfort that acts, as it were, as a counter irritant. Look at the dingy slums of the East Side, Long Island City, the stockyard neighborhoods, the Hump, or where you will: there is little enough to choose between the dark unsanitary tenements of lower Manhattan (some of them among the worst in the world) and the grey minimum of decency that West Philadelphia provides. What part does art, literature, culture, or financial opportunity play in the lives of the millions of men and women who go through the daily routine of life in our great urban districts? The city of dreams is as far away from them as it is from the denizen of Winesburg, Ohio.

To the few the great city gives all: to the millions it gives annually less and less. In spite of sanitary codes, tenement house laws, and various other urban reforms, the prospects for decent human living have become distinctly worse in New York during the last generation. And New York, unfortunately, represents the goal towards which all our bigger centers are striving with might and main. For this reason I propose to examine New York's plight in greater detail, and to ask: Why the great city? What are we putting into the great city, and what are we getting out of it? How long can we stand the strains and difficulties that are peculiar to our large congested centers? What particular promise is there in planning for an increasing population in other large centers, if all these efforts are doomed eventually to result in the same difficulties? Is the great city still the goal of our legitimate desires, or is it a monstrosity, a bloated spider that lures us into its web only to devour us?

One can get a better notion of the present plight of the great city general if we follow the greatest city, New York, through a series of breakdowns that have attended its growth.

Historically, the first great breakdown of the metropolis came in housing. The crowding of the population into the growing port of New York had, as early as 1835, created a housing shortage and a slum area. Here conditions were so wretched that they drew down the attention of the Health Commissioner; and the Report of Housing Conditions in 1842 was the first of a long list that dealt with the housing problem. It is safe to say that New York has never caught up with its original shortage. To-day half the population of Manhattan are living in quarters which are below the standard fixed as safe and sanitary by the tenement house law of 1901: these tenements are within reach of the unskilled worker because they do not possess running water, the heating apparatus and the sanitary facilities which represent the minimum standard for safe living quarters today. But what of the new law houses? The new tenements meet a minimum standard of sanitation and ventilation; but they do this at a price beyond the reach of two-thirds of the population; while their bleak courts, their white-washed walls, their dull streets, their occasional glimpse of the sun are still a long way from being the kind of environment in which mothers and children can flourish. Jane Addams showed us a long time ago what happened to "the spirit of youth in the city streets" when it was denied normal outlets for its energy and zest of life: but what have these bleak and overcrowded homes to offer the adolescent boy and girl?

Congestion is such a normal process in the great city, and decent living quarters require such a restriction on the profits of the speculative builder, that even on the edge of the city, where the price of land remains comparatively low, four and five story tenements are erected. Superficial observers talk of this housing breakdown as if it were a product of the war. On the contrary, there is a chronic deficiency that has been piling up in every great city—in London, Paris, and Berlin, as well as in American cities—for the last hundred years. In the great city there are not enough decent quarters to go round; and even the decent quarters are not good enough. That is the sum and substance of the housing breakdown. In the acutest stages of the housing crisis the smaller centers in New York State did not feel the shortage as keenly as the great city. One can almost put the case in a mathematical form: the bigger the city the remoter are its chances of solving the housing problem. This does not, of course, ignore the fact that other causes than congestion have created housing difficulties quite frequently in small cities, and even villages.

The second breakdown of the big city occurred in its water-system and its sewers. In 1842 New York was compelled to push back into the Croton watershed for a sufficient supply of clear water, and by the beginning of the present century the shortage threatened so acutely that a new system was planned, with reservoirs in the Catskills and the Adirondacks. If the thirst of the big city is not unquenchable, its tendency to grow has not at any rate been diminished: as a result, the necessity for still further aqueducts has already been recognized. This process must come to an end either when the existing areas have been drained dry, or when the cost per capita for water mains reaches a point at which water will become a luxury—supplied at an *uneconomic rate* for the same reason that bread and shows and baths were provided in ancient Rome, namely, to keep the population contented. Through this continual reaching back for new water supplies New York City is draining away, quite literally, an essential resource from other communities, dependent upon their immediate supply.

A different sort of loss and disaster results from sewage-congestion. The difficulties that Chicago has experienced in getting rid of its sewage are notorious. The spread of sewage in the Hudson, the East River, and the Harbor has not merely destroyed the opportunities for bathing and caused the practical disappearance of North River shad; it has also, according to the latest report of the Joint Legislative Committee at Albany, cut the city off from 80 percent of its shellfish, increased the dangers of typhoid (as nearly a thousand cases in the past winter testify) and now threatens the bathing beaches of Coney Island and Brighton.

In this case, the great city can avoid a complete breakdown only by building an elaborate plant and equipment which enables it temporarily to meet the problem. But it does this with blind disregard for expense. The growth of the city might be illimitable if its purse were illimitable; since the ingenuities of engineering can solve many of our difficulties if we can disregard the expense. The point is that the expense is becoming unbearable. The "overhead" of the city is increasing to a point at which it will outmeasure any of its tangible or intangible benefits. Then something must happen: something which will not be more growth and more expense.

We come now to the breakdown of the street system, and the inability of our overground and underground ways to carry the load of traffic. Our older cities were planned for four-story buildings at most. With the rise of the six-story building in the middle of the last century, traffic difficulties were felt in the shopping district of lower Broadway. An experimental safety bridge was even built. Today, not only in the lower part of Manhattan, but in vast sections between the Pennsylvania and the Grand Central Railroad stations, up Park Avenue and Broadway, and even over in Brooklyn—*today from two to six cities* have been piled up one above the other. This would be bad enough if only foot traffic and public vehicles were considered: the automobile has added the proverbial last straw, for each car, with its two or three occupants, occupies at least twice, and sometimes three or four times the space of pedestrians walking. Since our zoning in the built-up parts of the city has all been done in subservience to rising land values, none of our zoning provisions touch this problem; on the contrary, even in parts of the city where the four-story town has lingered, the twenty-story town is permitted—in fact, is being built. If our avenues were wide enough to carry comfortably the present and potential load of traffic, there would not, in a great many parts of the city, be room for the buildings themselves.

Our city officials and engineers are now hinting that the "solution" lies in building overhead streets. But even if it were conceivable that a complete system of aerial streets could be built for the population, this could be done *only at a cost which would fall back upon the land in the shape of taxes—and in turn this would make it necessary to build higher buildings and more streets!* To call this circle vicious scarcely does it justice. In point of fact no large city, however unbalanced its budget, attempts to keep up with its need for free channels of circulation. Every day the congestion increases—in spite of traffic policeman, curb setbacks, one-way streets, electric traffic signals. Even in Los Angeles, whose growth was coincident with the auto, the cars have multiplied faster than the streets have been widened. The end here is already in sight. There must come a time when every street in New York will be regulated as the streets in the financial district now are: individual vehi cles will not be permitted to circulated through the business and industrial sections during the day. This is what happened in prosperous commercial Rome when its congestion reached something like New York's present pitch; and it is inevitable here. It is equally inevitable in Pittsburgh's triangle, where it is now actively discussed, and in Chicago's Loop. And all the while the costs are piling up. The hard, practical men who think they can avoid this conclusion while they continue to congest the population and raise the land values are living in dreamland: they simply have not the courage to face the results of their own handiwork.

The breakdown of the mechanical means of transportation follows hard upon the collapse of the street system; the same causes are at work. As the city increases in height it increases also in area; for the railroad and subway must be introduced to carry the main load of passengers from the central district of skyscraper offices and lofts to the outlying areas. When the vacant land on the outskirts is filled up, the net result is congestion at both ends. This causes a demand for additional means of transportation. Beyond a point which big cities reach at a very early point in their career, more transportation routes mean more congestion. The only way this could be avoided is by duplicating the existing transportation lines; but this method would reduce the earnings of the existing lines by distributing the load, and it is never even considered except when an equal degree of congestion can be assured to the new line. The cost of all these facilities increases steadily as the lines are lengthened into more remote areas so that in one way or another a subsidy must be introduced to support them at a price per ride the ordinary commuter can afford. At the present time New York, with its five cent fare, is losing more than $12,000,000 annually on the money it paid for constructing subways, and it will lose even more on the new lines, which the transit engineers estimate will be three times as costly.

This is one of the concealed costs of living in a great city: it parallels the hidden cost of other services, including sewers, elaborate street paving and complicated utilities but all the while this cost is pressing down on the economic well-being of the average citizen. In addition to the half billion or so that New York is preparing to spend in future on its subways, increased suburban facilities are now needed. D. L. Turner, the engineer of the New York Transit Commission, has suggested an expenditure of some three quarters of a billion dollars, of which he proposes that one-half be paid in taxes, partly by the city and partly by the suburbs: this will, in his opinion, take care only of the increase of traffic in ten years (to April, 1934) when the octopus-city must again face another colossal expenditure, if its bloated growth is to continue. It is possible that the annual saving in man-power, equipment and coal through such a regional redistribution of population as would enable the majority to walk to work, would pay the larger part of the necessary plant and equipment for new communities.

As things go now, on the other hand, there is no way in any of the large centers of avoiding a continuous breakdown in its transit facilities. They are, and they must remain, perpetually inadequate so long as people and industries, instead of being redistributed into planned communities, are sucked blindly into the metropolitan areas.

But perhaps all this congestion is justified by the fact that industry is conducted more efficiently in the big city? Perhaps this more than equals the other losses? Not at all; just the contrary in fact. In most industries it actually costs more to carry on manufacturing on the congested island of Manhattan than it does in smaller industrial centers. The reasons are plain. The transportation of goods through the streets and on railways is the very life-blood of industry; and in all our big centers these arteries are clogged. Lacking streets to keep pace with the multiple-city, the trucks in New York City spend less time in active hauling than in unproductive work—locked in congested streets, or waiting at the crowded loading stations and stores. The few hours a day that the trucks actually move at snail's pace has already made the automobile uneconomical; and so the greater part of trucking is still done by horsepower in order to lower the overhead charges. The periodic congestion of freight terminals and docks—with the spoiling and rotting of perishable foods—present another facet of the same difficulty. At the pier, in the railway yard, at the factory, congestion obstructs the normal processes of industry.

Finally, the crowded conditions of the city have increased the overhead within the factory. The garment industry, for example, stands fourth among New York's manufactures; and many of its shops have moved into great skyscrapers in the central district. Here the high rent, the high taxes, and the high cost of fireproof structures have so raised the overhead costs that New York manufacturers, on their own confession, already find it difficult to compete with those in smaller cities, where these costs are lower. The higher cost of housing in the metropolitan area is likewise reflected in proportionately higher wages for the same type of work—or else it is borne by the worker in impoverished living conditions.

Certain industries are inevitably associated with great seaport and traffic junctions, like Philadelphia, New York and Chicago; but as the city increases in population the disadvantages for other kinds of manufacturing tend to counterbalance the advantages of the local market. When the local overhead cannot be shifted, and when smaller centers are, in spite of their poorer financial and business facilities, able to make their industrial advantages felt, the great city's industries will have to migrate or declare bankruptcy. We are still in the day of postponement; but the day of reckoning will come; and it behooves us to anticipate it. The question then will be whether industries are to migrate into the free area that lies immediately around the great city, or whether it will not pay, once moving must be faced, to locate at some point in a much larger area, where land values are not so high and where a finer environment may be provided more easily, without the risk of being gobbled up eventually—as Pullman was gobbled up by Chicago, and as Yonkers and Mt. Vernon are now being gobbled up by New York in its steady growth.

Inadequate housing facilities, inadequate water supplies, inadequate sewage, inadequate streets and inadequate transportation—these are but the larger and more obvious ills that derive from the congestion of population. They are enough, however, to show that the great city, as a place to live and work in, breaks down miserably; that it is perpetually breaking down; and that it will continue to do so as long as the pressure of population within a limited area remains. I have used New York merely for the sake of concrete example. New York's problem of housing in 1850 was Chicago's problem in 1890; New York's transit solution of 1900 is now Chicago's solution of 1925—and promises no better; and so on with the other details in the breakdown. Other cities can avoid New York's breakdown only by making an effort to avoid New York's "greatness."

Now all these breakdowns are costly in themselves; unfortunately the effort to put them off becomes even more costly. The result is that money and effort which should go into making the city more liveable—the money that should be spent on the education of children, on the maintenance of health, upon art, education, and culture—all this money and effort is devoted to expenditures which do no more than make the physical side of congestion barely tolerable. It is not merely that the effort to supply sufficient transportation routes, to widen streets sufficiently, is inevitably doomed to failure: what is worse is that even if it were successful it would be foolish and extravagant.

If we saw a family with ragged and neglected children, in a tumble-down shack, half of which was unfit for habitation, spending all its income and savings in providing a tiled bathroom and an automobile, we should conclude that this expenditure was unbalanced: the house should be put in order, the children clothed, the rooms sunned, aired and dusted, and the toilet arrangements adjusted to a decent sanitary minimum. Yet the expenditures of the great city are quite as wild and unbalanced as this. In order to reduce the horrors that result from the breakdown of housing and transportation, the city spends all its funds on futile palliatives. It lives in the midst of a sort of perpetual cataclysm. The great city—if I may sum up the case in a different metaphor—is like a man afflicted with hardening of the arteries, a man so conscious of his condition and so preoccupied with carrying out the incidental medical treatment (hopeless though it be) that he has no time to work, to think, to play, to create, or to perform any of those acts which separate a state of invalidism from a state of health.

All the breakdowns we have been studying are the result of a congestion of population; and the greater the magnitude of that congestion the more chronic the breakdown becomes, and the more completely does it embrace all the activities of the city. The big city is bankrupt. The little city that has adopted a program of mere expansion—and where is the little city that does not boast its first skyscraper—is headed in the same direction.

Once we actually face the situation, we shall, I am confident, be roused to the drastic public efforts to deal with it. The day of the palliatives and the patent medicines is passing—in city-growth as in the fight on disease. We must do all that is necessary to combat the forces of congestion at their source. For in that direction lie the fundamental things that men and women care most deeply for—a beautiful environment, a home for children, an opportunity to enjoy the day's leisure and the ability to ride on the Juggernaut of industry, instead of being prostrated under its wheels.

4 Our Stake in Congestion

Frederick L. Ackerman

The modern city man believes that good things will come to him in abundance as the by-product of the inflation of values. So firm is his faith in the Good to flow indirectly from accelerated growth that he is not at all disturbed by plans for the future of his city which must by the nature of things work out to make each day of his urban life a day of added complexity—as New York, for example, is groping for ways and means of financing more subways, bus lines, tunnels and bridges, two and three story streets, and more houses with apartments of fewer and smaller rooms, so that ultimately thirty or forty millions may live and do their work, with a constantly greater waste of time and energy, within the city's taxable area. If, in the face of mounting costs and difficulties he entertains the thought that some limit had better be placed on growth and concentration, he is instantly confronted with a host of his own pre-conceptions which frantically shout at him that this would be suicidal.

To account for this attitude on the ground that it is due to instinctive action—the herd instinct—is to overlook the historical background of the peoples whose descendants inhabit the city. For the most part, that background was a life conditioned by a rural environment and contact of

Reprinted, without illustrations, from *Survey Graphic* 7 (May 1925):141-142.

individuals within small groups. Nowhere in the life history of these peoples do we find anything which even remotely resembles the organization of the modern urban center. Not so long ago it was true that the size and rate of growth of a community were of little moment to those who lived in it and who gained their living, for the most part, in materially productive work. That is not to say that the people of our early American communities, for example, gave no thought to such matters; but it is rather that within a short period of time a revolutionary change has taken place in the way city growth and size are regarded.

A community with a stable population is now referred to as a "dead one." It is not viewed as a promising field for investment nor does it invite the merchant. For the return upon an investment, the appreciation of values, the volume of business and the rate of "turn over" in the process of buying and selling are matters of primary concern, and the prospect is rated good or bad according to what the future seems to hold in store on these counts. If the community is growing, if concentration, congestion and traffic are increasing, the prospect is good. If not, it is poor. This point of view constitutes the core of the problem of the great city.

Responsibility for the shift to this point of view, like responsibility for the change in the character of our communities, may safely be lodged with two factors—machine industry and credit economy. It was, we may say, by historical accident that these two factors arrived upon the scene at about the same time. One operated to augment the effect of the other, so that the total effect constitutes a revolutionary change in the nature and character of the material environment and in the point of view under which men live and do their work.

The immediate effect of the introduction of the machine, the rise of the mill town and its further effect in the development of great industrial centers are so fully appreciated that we may pass the point without further reference. But how credit economy played a part in accelerating the drift into urban centers is evidently not so well understood, for we speak lightly of "distribution" or of "decentralization" of population —of the "garden city"—as if these could be achieved while men are animated by their present point of view; as if little more was involved than the moving of one's personal effects from one place to another. It may be that those who are growing restless and neurotic under the increments of discomfort which stalk the increments of value created by growth and concentration, look wistfully toward decentralization. But to count upon this as of sufficient driving force to bring about a change is to overlook, or at least to underestimate, the strength of absentee ownership and the appetite for congestion.

For when we look into the case of the city man—how he lives and upon what he depends for his living—it is readily seen that he has woven himself into a complicated web of inflated values and capitalizations *which involve the necessity of growth and concentration.* He may be the owner of land and buildings; probably he holds a minimum equity, bought with the hope of "return" and appreciation. The magnitude of that appreciation hangs upon the rate of growth and concentration. As a general proposition the purpose for which credit is used in the case of purchase of urban lands and the erection and purchase of buildings is to capture the appreciation of value which is a function of growth, concentration and even congestion. No speculator in urban lands and buildings will interest himself in an enterprise unless the prospects surrounding it show the promise afforded by growth and concentration. What holds true with respect to investor and speculator holds true also in the case of those who lend upon enterprises of this sort. Stability is not sufficient for the enterprising buyer or lender; there must be the promise of something more.

Going a step further away from the primary transaction, suppose that our city man holds stock in a local enterprise. In most cases the capitalization of such enterprises is based not upon cost or upon the materially productive effort involved, but upon the prospect of return. It is not ordinarily viewed as businesslike to embark in an enterprise where in establishing the capitalization something cannot be added to inital cost. And that depends upon the prospect of growth and concentration.

But the net is wider still. The city man may depend for a living upon a salary or professional fees, or on wages that fall short, but this condition does not modify his point of view as to what would be likely to add to his income. For he assumes with those others who benefit directly through ownership that any increment of value which might arise out of expansion, concentration and congestion would ultimately work out to benefit him also.

So it would require many words to list those whose welfare seemingly hangs upon inflation of values in the urban center: that is hardly necessary. The upshot of it all is that the urbanite has an interest at stake—the income from property, land and buildings, profits, dividends, salaries, fees, wages, annuities, insurance, pensions, income of one sort and another—which seems to hang directly or indirectly upon the question whether the rate of growth, expansion and congestion keeps pace with the rate of capitalizing these prospects.

Whether the urbanite in his several interests stands really to gain or to lose when these promises are fulfilled is quite beside the point.

Having placed his eggs in the basket of "progress"—which means a bigger city—it is hardly to be wondered at that he pauses in alarm before any proposal that seems to threaten them. So the mere mention of stability in population is quite sufficient to send values tumbling and so scare off those who would seek a way out of the dilemma by any act that would put a check on growth.

But the problem has other roots. In every community outside the cities a younger generation is being educated. Running through that process of education and serving as its excuse and aim is the distinction drawn, as to status, between those who engage, as "workmen," in materially productive labor and those who do not. Periodicals of vast circulation carry the tales of the "successful" who forsook their home town with its simple employments and its "limitations," went to the city and ultimately became presidents of great corporations. Except for a few variations, as (possibly) in the case of agricultural education, the educational process in the rural areas is largely that of saying "move on." So throughout the rural areas and the small communities the forces of our culture are directing a host to our urban centers to sustain the capitalized values which are based upon the certainty that this host will come.

With the stage set for such a constant migration into urban centers from the rural areas, it is not difficult for the urban centers to draw from these same rural areas the funds available to serve as the reserve against credit advances to urban enterprises. Nor is it difficult to bring the rural investor into line. Stocks and bonds in city enterprises which rest for their security on the prospect of increasing growth and congestion may readily be disposed of among those whose aim in life is in harmony with the selfsame prospect. The recent rapid development of the use of mortgages upon urban properties as a basis for small investment, and the wider distribution of stock ownership in city enterprise of every character make us aware how widespread has become the vested interest which looks toward city concentration to produce income.

Hitherto, the gains to be had from the growth and intensive use of city land have been imaginary rather than real to the majority of those who live and do their work within them. But the wider distribution of stock to employes in banks and stores, in manufacturing plants, in co-operative or joint ownership enterprises, is rapidly giving a quality of reality to what was imaginary. The resulting frame of mind may be illustrated by reference to a sign displayed in a "cooperative restaurant." The sign was an invitation to invest in the enterprise; to insure its appeal the proposition was put this way: "The more you eat the greater your profit."

We may be fully aware that the accelerating congestion of urban centers cannot continue indefinitely. But we have based our wealth upon the prospect of continuous and accelerating growth, expansion and congestion. Paper securities carry face values that represent nothing more tangible than this prospect. So, with income from investment, the very aim of modern life, dependent upon an ever accelerating migration, can it be wondered at that the proposal to bring this to a close would arouse opposition?

The ground of current common sense is not likely to shift short of the time when the pressure of necessity will force a change of attitude. The prospect of pecuniary gain is not likely to be dispelled by theoretical prophecy. So congestion runs its course. We are not likely to avoid the collapse that will follow the deflation of values when our cities reach the saturation point and stability succeeds the fever of expansion.

5 Coals to Newcastle

Stuart Chase

From the standpoint of communities planned and designed to furnish a maximum of economic goods with a minimum of human effort, how much of the current movement of men and goods in the United States can be written off as loss, leakage and waste? On the basis of profitable investment, the philosophy of "what the traffic will bear," and present technical operation, there is waste enough in transportation, as Mr. Hoover himself will tell you. The minute, however, planned values are substituted for going values, the figures of the efficiency engineers take to cover before a margin of leakage which gaps like the jaws of a crocodile. From the latter standpoint we venture the assertion—calculated to outrage all the admittedly hard-working traffic managers of all the two hundred and fifty thousand miles of railroads in these states—a good part of transportation is not economically necessary.

An aeroplane observer with a quite celestial eyesight, cruising over the continent of North America, would see certain physical things—natural resources, the plant for their conversion and distribution, and the people concerned with producing and consuming them. These people, on the whole, except for wandering streams of the unemployed and

Reprinted, without illustrations, from *Survey Graphic* 7 (May 1925): 143-146.

a sprinkling of those psychological twins, the gentleman of the club window and the gentleman of the road—are extremely busy with their resources and their plant. They are blasting coal and iron out of mountains, and pumping oil out of the ground, and felling the virgin stands of the forest at a rate unprecedented in human affairs. Lumber is being cut four and one half times faster than it is grown, and more oil has been won since 1913 than in all the previous years of history. Such of this raw matter as they do not waste in the mine and the well and the forest and the farm—about half the total loosened from the crust of the planet—they proceed to move with great speed and dispatch, here, there and everywhere, and sometimes back again, to be hammered and shaped and pounded in the mills and factories; moved, amidst the tears and the exhortations of purchasing agents, from process to process—cattle into green hides, hides into leather, leather into boots—rerouted, reshipped, consigned and returned, loaded, unloaded and reloaded; moving in a gathering cloud of advertisers, drummers and go-getters—beseeching and praying like drivers around a stampeded elephant. So it goes on through jobbers and wholesalers and commission men, in and out of warehouses, up and down elevators, over the rails to the retailers—where the advertisers again crack their larynxes—into trucks and out of them, onto shelves and down from them; and at last—so much as hasn't been joggled off and crushed and spoiled in transit—into the hands and the stomach of the consumer.

An incomparable display of energy and rush, an altogether praiseworthy disregard of life and limb as fabricated fragments of terra firma are hurled from Maine to California and from California to Maine. Gilbert and Pogue have estimated that the mechanical energy alone released in this process (150 million horsepower) is the equivalent of the labor of three billions of slaves—or thirty helots for every man, woman and child in the country! How many slaves are making as against how many are moving, they do not specify, but it is safe to assume that transportation accounts for a considerable fraction of the total.

Thirty servants! Greece in her prime only averaged five helots per family. As good Americans, this news increases our chest measure; but as consumers we find a certain difficulty in getting our helots to do the specific things that we want done. We could use them—if we could find them. But they are too busy building industrial plants—when the unused capacity of the existing industrial plants runs better than 40 per cent; or moving lumber from Oregon to New England, or apples from Washington to New York, or shunting train loads of soft coal in and out of Chicago, or pumping people, very unhappy people, back and forth in subways, or driving ten oil wells to the acre when the technology of oil recovery calls for not more than one, or telling the world in letters of flame and fire (there is a single electric sign on the Cleveland Credit Company's building which burns more current that the city of Illyria) that what the country needs is more chewing gum.

The aeroplane pilot observes the consumer, who is also the producer, who is also *homo sapiens* and whose wants presumably are the reason for all this grinding of wheels, deploying of products, and rushing about of mechanical slaves. He is bunched into cities where only an hydraulic press could pack him any closer, or scattered in lonely farm houses over rich and unutilized spaces. If literate, he may read the statistics of the total tonnage of coal mined, the board feet of lumber cut, the square feet of sign board area, the total freight train miles, the gross output of automobiles—which, if placed end to end . . . the four quadrillion words turned out annually by the indefatigable printing presses of his Republic, the twelve acres of forest which go into the Sunday Times-Examiner —his head reels and his bosom swells, but the landlord keeps right on raising the rent, and it costs no less to eat.

Now what, specifically is the matter? Where does energy, particularly transport energy, go to waste, and how would planned communities reduce this waste so that the wayfaring man instead of falling behind, or making unheard of efforts to keep where he is, can begin to gain ground against the cost of living? As we said in the opening paragraph there are two basic aspects involved: first, the waste which flows from current transportation methods assuming no change in population grouping or industrial plant location; second, the waste which arises because communities are not regionally planned. The former is illustrated by the historic charge of Brandeis that the railroads were wasting a million dollars a day, the latter by the unbearable congestion of New York City, or by the failure to locate eastern industries nearer western raw materials. We try to answer the question primarily from the second point of view, but many of the following facts and figures come from investigations dealing with the going mechanism.

The Massachusetts Commissioner of Agriculture recently reported for the Boston market "the arrival of eggs from China, peaches from Africa, various fruits and vegetables from Argentine, and iceberg lettuce shipped 3,000 miles across the continent from the Imperial Valley in California." And he pointed out that nearly all those products are grown or could be grown in New England.

The Geological Survey made, in 1921, a study of cross-hauling in coal. It found Kentucky lump coal moving into Indiana, Illinois and Ohio past mines in these states producing coal of an identical quality. It found West Virginia coal supported by a special rate differential moving to the Great Lakes to compete with Ohio coal which only needed to travel half the distance. The result had been a serious overdevelopment of West Virginia mines to take—or try to take— a traffic for which it was economically unfitted. Equal grades of coal are solemnly moved from Illinois mines to be sold in Ohio, and from Ohio mines to be sold in Illinois. Coal cars, at the dictation of spot market speculation, "move into Chicago and out, and back to Chicago again, like dice in a gambling game." During the war, the Fuel Administration saved 160 million car miles by "zoning" coal; that is by adopting the regional principle and making deliveries to consumers from the nearest mine. With the return of normalcy, these savings collapsed.

Pulp wood is imported from Norway and shipped 1,000 miles inland. The center of production of lumber—according to the accredited laws of "skimming the cream"—has shifted progressively from New England to the Pacific coast. The shipments of Western timber to the East, where the mills are concentrated, is increasing all the time. The usual route is via the Panama Canal to New York and thence by rail inland. Thus we have mills without forests in the East and forests without mills in the West. Meanwhile 60 million acres of potential forest lands accessible to the Eastern and Lake States are lying unproductive—their only crop an occasional devastating fire.

Fifty per cent of all manufacturing in the country is done in the northeast sea board region, 35 per cent is done in the Middle West, 9 percent in the South, 6 per cent on the Pacific coast. If we plot on a map the location of factories, and superimpose above it a map of sources of raw material—coal, cotton, wool, iron, ores, leather, lumber, grains— we will find that the lack of correlation is amazing. To supply the mills of the eastern seaboard, bulky raw materials must be moved by long haul from their points of origin in the West and South—cotton from Texas to New Bedford, hides from Kansas City to Massachusetts— there made up into finished products and flung back again in large part for ultimate consumption near the place where they started. Perhaps the supreme example—though it is not a local one—is the movement of kangaroo hides from Australia to Lynn, there to be made up into shoes and carried *in toto* 10,000 miles back again—for only Australians will wear kangaroo boots!

Loose cotton, according to the Bureau of Foreign and Domestic Commerce, is now hauled long distances to be compressed and then hauled back over the same route duly baled. Two cars of baled can carry the equivalent of four cars of loose cotton. E. G. Booz, writing in the Annals of the American Academy of Political and Social Science, finds that the average retailer only sells 10 per cent of the coffee used in his own logical territory. The other 90 per cent is subject to cross-hauls from illogical territory. The Joint Commission of Agricultural Inquiry reports the condition of the Chicago wholesale provision market which, though a local reorganization is now in process, may fairly represent city marketing problems. It is located on a narrow street in the congested Loop district. To it through the hurly-burly of the streets are hauled fruits and vegetables from terminals anywhere from two blocks to two miles away. Arriving, the foodstuffs are unloaded, sold, reloaded and solemnly hauled back again, often to the identical terminal from which they started their metropolitan tour.

Gilbert and Pogue point out, in America's Power Resources, the astonishing kindliness of nature in furnishing those regions in America which are short of coal deposits with abundant water power. Nature has balanced the power load. Do we take advantage of it? We do not. We haul coal into water power states, and develop water powers in coal states. The late Charles P. Steinmetz once worked out a power plan for New York. There is no coal in New York, but there is 4,200,000 of undeveloped horsepower to be readily derived from falling water, of which only 1,300,000 is now utilized. If all were utilized, Steinmetz concluded that it would take the place of some 40 million tons of coal now shipped into New York, would serve to electrify all the railroads, save the labor of 500 locomotives, 15,000 coal cars, save 400 millions in railroad equipment and give us smokeless cities. In short, the saving in transportation costs to be made from giant power regional plans is almost limitless: *today one-third of all railroad freight is coal.* Giant power by providing energy on a balanced load basis from water fall and central power stations at the mine mouth, could eliminate a large fraction of this traffic, and eliminate the untold cost of smoke damage along with it (See the Giant Power issue of *Survey Graphic*, March, 1924).[1]

To make a bad matter worse, Ford finds that freight cars are absurdly heavy. The weight, he says, ought to be in the load not in the car. Stronger steel cars at one-third the present weight would give vastly greater efficiency, for heavy cars "bang out the roadbed and bang out themselves." Furthermore, says Ford, we only get 6 per cent of the potential power of coal out of that burned in a steam locomotive. "If the primary purpose of the railroads is to buy coal this is all right, but if the purpose is to move goods as economically as possible we cannot continue to waste this power." Electrification will enormously decrease the transportation cost per unit moved.

Two-thirds of all railroad expenses are terminal expenses, and two-thirds of this is wasted in the unplanned, competitive chaos of terminal facilities, according to E. J. Clapp. He estimates that the prevailing competitive policy employs two to three times the manpower, equipment and material that a unified terminal plan would necessitate. Terminal markets are in continuous stages of choke and suffocation. In the testimony taken by the Federal Trade Commission in re the port of New York, a wholesale fruit dealer stated that enough fruit is lost in New York through inadequate facilities for handling to supply the population of a city the size of Pittsburgh. This waste can be largely reduced by railroad consolidation, irrespective of the element of decentraliza-

1. Giant power was the term adopted at the time for the publicly planned, large-scale distribution of electrical energy made possible for the first time through the development of long-distance power transmission lines. See Gifford Pinchot's definition on p. 116.

tion—as proved by the performance of the Railroad Administration during the war.

Through lack of regional planning Maine and New York farmers compete for the potato market. Great overproduction necessarily results. In some years 40 per cent of the Maine potato crop will be left to rot in the fields. And this clumsy process leaves room for the further folly of speculative marketing. Said the New York World on June 15, 1924, "Thousands of packages of cucumbers and other fresh vegetables were dumped on the New York offal dock today." In the fall of 1920 the author steered his canoe with difficulty through carloads of good watermelons which had been dumped into the Potomac from the Washington docks in order to keep the market from going below twenty-five cents. The New York Commissioner of Markets recently pointed out how two hundred carloads of Thanksgiving turkeys were held on sidetracks to enable dealers to face a holiday price of twenty-five cents a pound. The same gentleman quotes the case of ten carloads of Texas onions consigned to New York, worth $10,000 at prevailing prices, yet dumped on the Jersey meadows to prevent breaking the market. All the farmer received was a bill for freight charges!

But even more important than the elimination of such wastes are the savings to be made through decentralization of population. Henry Ford has discovered that highly standardized, highly subdivided industry need no longer become concentrated in large plants with all the inconveniences of transportation and housing that hamper such community arrangements. A thousand or five hundred men ought to be enough in a single factory; then there would be no problem of transporting them to work or away from work, and there would be no slums or any of the other unnatural ways of living incident to the overcrowding that must take place if the workmen are to live within reasonable distance of a very large plant . . . . "The belief that an industrial country has to concentrate its industries is not well founded."

Ford, not as a philosopher, but as a business man of unusual foresight, has not only eliminated much waste in the stream of production from ore mine to finished flivver but has been driven by the logic of operating costs to decentralize, and is now building valve plants and other small units out in the country where his workers may walk comfortably to their benches, and farm on the side if it pleases them. (See *Survey Graphic* for March and April, 1924.)

Consider what the jam and congestion of great cities cost us in added transportation load. Subways and tubes built and operated at enormous outlays, yet from the point of view of a planned region—and from Ford's new industrial point of view—quite unnecessary. The total investment in New York's rapid transit system is $541,000,000 to date, with over 100 millions more in new construction contracted for. The annual operating costs are $73,000,000 to pay for a total of 2.3 billion passenger rides. There are over 1,100 miles of subway, elevated and surface tracks. And state and city authorities are now at loggerheads over the expenditure of $275,000,000 more.

Finally the Congressional Joint Commission of Agricultural Inquiry, investigating wastes in distribution, has announced a conclusion which I can only regard as treasonable to all the immemorial canons of sturdy self-help upon which the Republic is founded. As a result of its researches it finds that the hope and glory of America—the national advertiser—in attempting to break down "sales resistance" and sell its wares from coast to coast is *costing the consumer more in uneconomic distribution than can be saved by large scale unit production*. National markets tend towards making goods cost less at the factory door, but the saving is more than eaten up by cross-hauling and the burden of high pressure salesmanship. "Manufacturer after manufacturer," says the Joint Commission, "has repeated this process of sales forcing until the public and the retailer are confronted by a confusing urge to buy more products in constantly increasing variety. Buying habits are upset and consumers cease to give their patronage to individual merchants, and not only scatter their buying within the community, but make purchases outside of it." Retailers, the commission finds, are thus ceasing to be an economic factor serving their local community with what the community wants.

What can we do about it?

We are already beginning to measure ourselves and our population-distribution in the higgledy-piggledy of "business as usual" against ourselves regrouped and relocated in communities planned for getting the most out of life. With the same population that we now have, consider what a difference there would be in the transportation load if people were grouped into communities and regions specifically planned for the maximum of local subsistence and the minimum of cross-hauling—interregional as well as local—communities based on natural economic and geographical considerations. An Appalachian region, a Pacific coastal region, and so on.

The regional planning of communities would wipe out uneconomic national marketing, wipe out city congestion and terminal wastes, balance the power load, take the bulk of coal off the railroads, eliminate the duplication of milk and other local deliveries, short circuit such uneconomic practices as hauling Pacific apples to New York consumers by encouraging local orchards, develop local forest areas and check the haulage of western timber to eastern mills, locate cotton mills near cotton fields, shoe factories near hide producing areas, steel mills within striking distance of ore beds, food manufacturing plants in small giant power units, near farming belts. Gone the necessity for the skyscraper, the subway and the lonely country-side!

Granting the psychological possibility of planning and operating communities with such unheard-of common sense—and no mean grant it is—we report again and finally: a good part of transportation is unnecessary.

6 Regions—To Live In

Lewis Mumford

The hope of the city lies outside itself. Focus your attention on the cities—in which more than half of us live—and the future is dismal. But lay aside the magnifying glass which reveals, for example, the hopelessness of Broadway and Forty-second Street, take up a reducing glass and look at the entire region in which New York lies. The city falls into focus. Forests in the hill-counties, water-power in the mid-state valleys, farmland in Connecticut, cranberry bogs in New Jersey, enter the picture. To think of all these acres as merely tributary to New York, to trace and strengthen the lines of the web in which the spider-city sits unchallenged, is again to miss the clue. But to think of the region as a whole and the city merely as one of its parts—that may hold promise.

Not merely a wistful hope of a better environment, but sheer necessity, leads us thus to change our approach to the problem. For cities, as the foregoing articles show are becoming too big; as they grow they fall behind in the barest decencies of housing; they become more expensive to operate, more difficult to police, more burdensome to work in, and more impossible to escape from even in the hours of leisure that we achieve. The forces that have created the great cities make permanent

Reprinted from *Survey Graphic* 7 (May 1925):151-152.

improvement within them hopeless; our efforts to plan them lag pitifully behind the need when indeed they do not foster the very growth that
is becoming insupportable. We are providing, in Professor Geddes' sardonic phrase, more and more of worse and worse.

Not so with regional planning. Regional planning asks not how wide
an area can be brought under the aegis of the metropolis, but how the
population and civic facilities can be distributed so as to promote and
stimulate a vivid, creative life throughout a whole region—a region being
any geographic area that possesses a certain unity of climate, soil, vegetation, industry and culture. The regionalist attempts to plan such an
area so that all its sites and resources, from forest to city, from highland
to water level, may be soundly developed, and so that the population
will be distributed so as to utilize, rather than to nullify or destroy, its
natural advantages. It sees people, industry and the land as a single unit.
Instead of trying, by one desparate dodge or another, to make life a
little more tolerable in the congested centers, it attempts to determine
what sort of equipment will be needed for the new centers. It does not
aim at urbanizing automatically the whole available countryside; it aims
equally at ruralizing the stony wastes of our cities. In a sense that will
become clear to the reader as he follows the later articles in this number,
the civic objective of the regional planning movement is summed up
with peculiar accuracy in the concept of the garden-city.

There are a hundred approaches to regional planning; it brings to a
head, in fact, a number of movements and methods which have been
gathering momentum during the last twenty or thirty years. But each
approach has this in common with the others; it attempts to promote
a fuller kind of life, at every point in the region. No form of industry
and no type of city are tolerable that take the joy out of life. Communities in which courtship is furtive, in which babies are an unwelcome handicap, in which education, lacking the touch of nature and of
real occupations, hardens into a blank routine, in which people achieve
adventure only on wheels and happiness only by having their minds
"taken off" their daily lives—communities like these do not sufficiently
justify our modern advances in science and invention.

Now the impulse that makes the prosperous minority build country
estates, that causes the well-to-do professional man to move out into

the suburbs, the impulse that is driving the family of small means out upon the open road, there to build primitive bungalows regardless of discomfort and dangers to health, seems to us to be a pretty common one. These people are in the vanguard of a general effort to get a little joy back into life. At present this exodus is undertaken blindly and, as Mr. Wright shows, all its promises are illusory, since a helter-skelter development such as is now going on in the countryside around our big cities promises only to spoil the landscape without permanently satisfying the hungry urbanites. The community planning movement in America, and the garden-cities movement in England are definite attempts to build up a more exhilarating kind of environment—not as a temporary haven of refuge but as a permanent seat of life and culture, urban in its advantages, permanently rural in its situation. This movement toward garden cities is a movement towards a higher type of civilization than that which has created our present congested centers. It involves a change in aim as well as a change of place. Our present congested districts are the results of the crude applications of the mechanical and mathematical sciences to social development; our garden cities represent fuller development of the more humane arts and sciences—biology and medicine and psychiatry and education and architecture. As modern engineering has made Chicago or New York physically superior to Athens, whilst the labyrinth of subways and high buildings is more deficient for complete living than a Stone Age cave, so we may expect that the cities of tomorrow will not merely embody all that is good in our modern mechanical developments, but also all that was left out in this one-sided existence, all the things that fifth century Athens or thirteenth century Florence, for all their physical crudity, possessed.

On its economic side, this movement towards a fuller human environment goes hand in hand with what has been aptly called the industrial counter revolution. For a hundred years in America business has been concentrating financial resources, concentrating factories and urban districts, attempting to create material prosperity by producing goods which could be quickly "turned over." The paper values have increased enormously even in the brief period from 1900 to 1920; but most statisticians seem agreed that the real wages of the majority of workers have remained nearly stationary. The new industrial revolution is an attempt to spread the real income of industry by decentralizing industry, by removing some of the burden of the business overhead and sale-promotion, ground rents in congested districts, and so forth. Far-sighted industrialists like Dennison and Ford are already planning this move, and business men like Edward Filene feel that business is at an impasse unless decentralization is followed as "The Way Out." Regional planning is an attempt to turn industrial decentralization—the effort to make the industrial mechanism work better—to permanent social uses. It is an attempt to realize the gains of modern industry in permanent houses, gardens, parks, playgrounds and community institutions.

Finally, regional planning is the New Conservation—the conservation of human values hand in hand with natural resources. Regional planning sees that the depopulated countryside and the congested city are intimately related; it sees that we waste vast quantities of time and energy by ignoring the potential resources of a region, that is, by forgetting all that lies between the terminal points and junctions of our great railroads. Permanent agriculture instead of land-skinning, permanent forestry instead of timber mining, permanent human communities, dedicated to life, liberty and the pursuit of happiness, instead of camps and squatter-settlements, and to stable building, instead of the scantling and falsework of our "go-ahead" communities—all this is embodied in regional planning.

It follows pretty plainly from this summary that, unlike city planning, regional planning is not merely the concern of a profession: it is a mode of thinking and a method of procedure, and the regional plan itself is only a minor technical instrument in carrying out its aims. The planners of the Ontario power project are genuine regional planners; Mr. Ford in his schemes for industrial decentralization is a regional planner; the Pennsylvania State Power Commission, as Mr. Bruére makes clear, is handling an essential element in regional planning. The Chicago Regional Planning Commission with its emphasis on transportation, power and industrial development over wide areas, the Sage Foundation Study in New York with parts of three states included in its "environs" mark the break with our old method of treating the city as a unit by itself. The New York State Housing and Regional Planning Commission has made a series of important preliminary studies which radically cut loose from the older tradition and employ the whole commonwealth rather than the large city as their base.

Moreover the aim of regional planning is not confined to those who are interested in the development of industries and resources. The cultural forces that have begun to challenge the dominance of the big city are plainly working in the same direction. So the little theater movement, by building local centers of culture instead of waiting patiently for the crumbs dropped from our metropolitan table, is essential to regionalism; and in the same way our new experimental schools, which have showed the rich educational opportunities that come from exploring and utilizing the whole living environment rather than sticking to the pallid routine of books, find themselves handicapped in the existing centers and demand a new environment patterned on the human scale, in which the school may work intimately in touch with the home and with industry and with the surrounding world of nature.

In sum, regional planning does not mean the planning of big cities beyond their present areas; it means the reinvigoration and rehabilitation of whole regions so that the products of culture and civilization, instead of being confined to a prosperous minority in the congested centers, shall be available to everyone at every point in a region where the physical basis for a cultivated life can be laid down. The technical means of achieving this new distribution of power and culture are at hand. The question before us is whether the automatic operation of physical and financial forces is to burke our rising demand for a more vital and happy kind of existence, or whether, by coordinating our efforts and imaginatively grasping our opportunity, we can remold our institutions so as to promote a regional development—development that will eliminate our enormous economic wastes, give a new life to stable agriculture, set down fresh communities planned on a human scale, and above all, restore a little happiness and freedom in places where these things have been pretty well wrung out. This is a question that cuts diametrically across a large part of our current political and social problems; some of these it places in a new light, and some of them it makes meaningless. Regionalism or super-congestion? Will man in America learn the art of mastering and ordering his environment, to promote his own fuller purposes, or will he be mastered by his environment, and presently, as in Samuel Butler's picture in Erewhon, or in Zamiatin's We, find himself without any purposes other than those of the Machine?

7   The New Exploration:
Charting the Industrial Wilderness

Benton MacKaye

"The last great earth story has been told." So spoke Peary upon his return from the discovery of the north pole. Amundsen and Scott soon
thereafter checked on the location of the south pole. These expeditions,
taken together, to the uttermost ends of the globe formed indeed the
last great earth story; they closed the drama of our planets' unfolding
which began with Marco Polo and Christopher Columbus. Man has con-
quered the wilderness and carried forth his civilization. But in dispelling
one wilderness he has created another. For the intricate equipment of
civilization is in itself a wilderness. He has unravelled the labyrinth of
river and coast line but has spun the labyrinth of industry. And the un-
tangling of this iron web is the problem of our time.

    The story of this interchange of wilderness is the story of men's wan-
derings over the surface of the globe and we shall do well to begin our
study of the new exploration at the four corners of the earth, though
we shall find it coming to focus, too, in a little Berkshire valley. J. F.
Horrabin, in his excellent little book on Economic Geography cites four
main chapters in men's wanderings.

Reprinted, with some illustrations, from *Survey Graphic* 7 (May 1925):153-157,
192, 194.

1. The river valley chapter, in which civilization (in the sense of a "settled life in a particular area") made its beginnings: Egypt, "gift of the Nile"; Mesopotamia "between the rivers"; the valleys of the Indus and the Hwang-ho.
2. The Mediterranean chapter, thirty-five centuries long. Men ventured on the water. But only gingerly. They sailed the inland sea but not the open ocean.
3. The unfolding of the world's coast lines, begun by da Gama, Columbus and Magellan. This took about three centuries, when European civilization (outside of Europe herself) was limited to a series of seaboard settlements connected by ocean routes.
4. The unravelling of the rivers and valleys within the continents—in Siberia, Africa, Argentine and in our own Far West: the chapter of the covered wagon and the "iron horse."

The "march of empire," then, has taken place in more directions than toward the setting sun: it has fronted every point upon the compass. But it has followed a definite purpose. The effort of the empire builder consciously or unconsciously is to develop a self-sustaining unit of civilization—and of industry. With the modern statesman this is a deliberate aim: as far as possible to be independent of the other Powers. Empire as here used is physical and not political; it refers to physical and geographic movements and implies no brief for imperialism. It is through the upbuilding (and downfalls) of physical empires that nature's wilderness has dwindled and the wilderness of industry has spread. If we would unravel the incognito of industry, as our forefathers unravelled the incognito of coast and continent, we must look into this matter of empire building—and empire charting.

There is a "physiology" of industrial empire. For empire is something more than territory. It is a working thing; it is a rough hewn organism—a system. Its "physiology," in certain ways, resembles that of a river system. It is a flow from source to mouth.

Take Britain: it's "sources" lie in India, in Africa, in Sumatra, in Australia—the lands around the Indian Ocean (and elsewhere). These lands contain *raw materials*—wheat, beef, cotton, wool, lumber. These, in large part, "flow" to England. They flow first across the Indian Ocean in various converging tributary routes to the Gulf of Aden; thence they flow in one main stream, through Suez and Gibralter, to the "mouth" (which is Great Britain).

But this is only half the picture. England consumes, but she also produces. She is source as well as mouth. She has iron and coal. With these
she converts raw material into *finished products*. And these flow back
again (through Gibraltar and Suez and Aden) to the lands of the Indian
Ocean. So these lands are "mouths" as well as sources.

Here is empire in a nutshell: (1) the *sources* of raw material; (2) the
"mouths" or *markets* for finished products; (3) the *routes* to the home
country whereby the latter controls the "flow."

Empire is industry: it is a flow from many sources to many mouths
through a controlling port. Not all the flow, of course, is through such a
port. Perhaps only a small part of it. But it is controlled therefrom. The
home port is the head; it is the integrator.

Empire is integration. It is a groping, unconscious effort to get world
order out of world chaos. But it brings its own chaos. For there is more
than one empire. And their lines of flow get crossed. That is what happened in 1904 at Port Arthur; and ten years later at Constantinople and
Bagdad. Empires are integrators. But they must be further integrated.
Industrial flow must be integrated. And first it must be charted and that
on a world-wide scale.

But let us take one continent at a time. Let us focus on America.

The biggest year in America's history is 1776. It marked the birthday
of her independence, and also of her expansion. For it was in '76 that
Daniel Boone crossed the Appalachian Mountains. Till then America
had been a remote seaside adjunct (politically and industrially) of a
growing, world-wide, maritime Power. After that year she became a
separate continental Power—in time to become the first big "railway
empire." Siberia, Africa and Argentine came later.

But she did not wait for the railway. For horses and oxen started Westward Ho a generation ahead of the locomotive. The trails of the covered
wagons followed those lines of least reisistance destined to become our
present lines of industrial flow. The Santa Fé Trail became the Santa Fé
Railway. The Oregon Trail became the Union Pacific. The wagons, followed by the engines, dispelled the wilderness of nature and set up the
wilderness of industry.

The territory of the United States forms a world industrial unit which
is almost self-sufficient. It contains the sources of food, clothing, fuel,

buildings and furnishings. Wheat, cattle and cotton come from the interior prairies, iron from the Mesaba Range and coal from the Allegheny Plateau, softwood comes from the Gulf region and the Pacific Coast and hardwood from the Appalachians. Semitropical produce comes from Florida and from southern California.

These *raw materials,* in a general way, "flow" eastward through Chicago and St. Louis and the Soo Locks, to the "mouths" of Pittsburgh and New York. Here and in other big power centers they are turned into *finished products.* Then (as in Liverpool and Manchester) the "mouths" turn "sources." The flow begins anew. The finished products (foods, textiles, furnishings) flow part of them to Europe and elsewhere abroad; the rest flow back westward to the sources now turned "mouths."

This "flow" takes place by rail, not water. Roughly speaking, it is east and west, not north and south. In time this may be modified. For the Mississippi Valley has two natural outlets by water to the open sea. One is through the Lakes and the St. Lawrence. This (like Russia's outlet through the Baltic) is a somewhat ice-bound way. The other is down the Mississippi River to the Gulf. This is a Pacific route as well as an Atlantic one. For New Orleans via Panama is about as near to Valparaiso and Vancouver as she is to Liverpool. It was this interior waterway empire, even now awaiting development, which was the dream of La Salle for France.

So much for a general picture of the world and of America. So much for the lines of flow across one continent and between some others. Are these lines as direct as they might be? Do they converge at the best located ports? Should there be more ports to handle the flow? Are there cross flows and duplicated routes? Are the sources themselves—of foods, textiles, and furnishings—developed within each region in sufficient variety? Could the manufacturing centers be better placed? These are a few questions which need answering about our modern web of industry.

Beneath this surface web, as it stands now, there lies another framework: this a potential one. This is the *most efficient framework* that geographic factors will allow. It is the framework that would enable the smoothest possible "flow" from the sources to the mouths; the framework which would achieve this flow with the minimum ton-mileage (and with minimum labor effort). The problem of finding and locating this "most efficient framework" is an extension of the problem of the civil engineer: the problem of relocating a railroad line between points A and B. Between these points there is a *most efficient route*—as to distance, grades, curves and general serviceability. The engineer's job is to find that route. Perhaps he never does it. But probably he finds the nearest to it that any man can find.

The job is *not to make* the most efficient route. It is already made—by nature. It lies there, a hidden potentiality. The job is to *discover* it. To do this the engineer must search for it: he must explore. His first job, then, is not construction but exploration.

And this is the job we have with regard to the *most efficient framework* for achieving industrial flow. Our job is *not to make* the framework. It is already made—by nature; and lies before us, a hidden potentiality. Our job is to *discover* it. This is something we, very likely, can never do. But by knowing what it is that we are after we can find the thing that comes the nearest. To do this we must explore. And this—the discovery of the most efficient framework for guiding industrial flow—is the job of the new exploration.

What clues have we for making our discovery? Where shall we commence in our process of unravelling the present tangled web of steel? Let us look at a sample of it. Let us take a cross-section of New England from mountain crest to ocean port: from the Berkshires to Boston harbor, along the Hoosac Tunnel Route of the Boston and Maine Railroad (Figure 1).

Three types of topography occur in this cross-section:

The Appalachian Barrier, illustrated by the Berkshire-Green Mountain Range of western Massachusetts and Vermont. The Hoosac Tunnel penetrates this range near North Adams, Mass.

The Threshold Plain, illustrated by the New England Plateau which covers three quarters of the total area. (This plateau is crossed by the alluvial plain of the Connecticut River).

The Seaboard, illustrated by the Boston Basin, a flat low area bordering the harbor and occupied by the cities which form Greater Boston.

Each of these three types of topography is occupied by a somewhat distinct type of industrial web. The Appalachian barrier is mainly a "source region," chiefly of water power and of forest growth. Crop soils

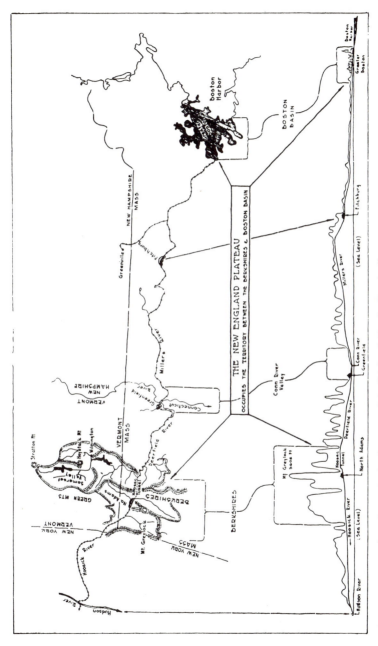

Figure 1. Cross-section of New England: a part of the "Atlantic Border Empire."

are limited to the narrow valley bottoms but many of the slopes afford pasture for cattle. This region, in New England, is the major source of water power and of hardwood lumber: and an incidental source of milk supply. The industrial web here occurs in its simplest form, consisting chiefly of power equipment, of logging equipment and of small plants.

The seaboard, on the other hand, is by and large a "mouth region." The industrial web here occurs in its most complex form. It consists practically of every type of manufacturing plant, of elevators and storage plants, of stores, office buildings, wharfs, railway yards, and the thousand and one combinations of industrial structures. To these are added transit lines and motor vehicles for the diurnal movement of office workers to and from the suburbs.

The seaboard is only one instance of the metropolitan regional type. This type is, of course, scattered throughout the country, occurring in all sizes from cities like Greater New York and Chicago, occupying whole counties, to the little "one-horse" factory town, occupying a few blocks. We have referred to such territory as the "mouth region." This it is for raw material; for finished products it becomes a "source region." The cities and towns shown on the map along the B. & M. Railroad (Fitchburg, Greenfield, North Adams) may be classed, therefore, as "Lesser Bostons." The city, whether large or small, presents the industrial web in its most complex form: it is the knottiest, thickest part of the industrial jungle.

Between these extreme types—of city and mountain range—lies the plain and plateau region which forms the bulk of the country's area (represented in our map by the New England Plateau). This is a farming region—the source in New England of milk and apples and fuelwood. It is a country of fields and woodlots. The industrial web is more simple than in the Seaboard, but more complex than in the Appalachians: it consists chiefly of barns and farming equipment, of creameries and various factories, and the roads to connect them with the nearby cities.

In which of these "geo-economic" types can we best begin our exploration—the search for that hidden potential framework which is our goal? Shall we begin in Boston or the Berkshires?

Where did our forefathers begin—the pioneers of the *old* exploration? They began in Boston. And for good reason. The wilderness in Boston was less intricate than that in the hills that came to be called Berkshire. Our forefathers, following the lines of evolution, moved from the simple to the complex. They moved from Boston toward the Berkshires.

Where should we begin—we of the *new* exploration—in Boston or in Berkshire? If we too would follow evolution we shall emulate our fore-fathers: move from simple to complex. But these have reversed their positions on the map. "The simple" has moved to Berkshire, and "the complex" to Boston. For in Berkshire the industrial web lies thinnest; here at the "source" industry greets nature; here industry begins; here it fastens in Mother Earth those initial strands along which the "flow" gets started. But in Boston the web lies thickest; there at the "mouth" industry greets man; there industry rests; there it links with the ultimate consumer those myriad final strands through which the "flow" ends. And so we shall begin in Berkshire, not in Boston.

Indeed Berkshire represents one sphere and Boston quite another. Berkshire represents what may be called the "sphere of origin"; Boston, the "sphere of distribution." A vital difference! The lines of industrial flow within the sphere of origin can be definitely segregated; but within the sphere of distribution they must be integrated. The source region is a "one industry" region (or a "few industries" region), while the mouth region is a region of many (or all) industries. Converting a tree into boards in the Berkshire forest can be planned all by itself; but delivering a wooden chair in Boston concerns the whole lumber industry: even more—it concerns iron and steel, and the whole cosmos of manufacture and distribution.

Some day, of course, we shall have to enter Boston. But on the same day we shall have to enter New York and Chicago and San Francisco (and perhaps even Liverpool and Hong Kong). For these are all in the sphere of distribution. They are nerve centers of a continuous flow which is continental (inter-continental) in its vastness.

"But," you say, "if the source region forms one end of the industrial thread and the mouth region forms the other, why not begin both in Boston and Berkshire and work both ends against the middle?"

A good idea. Let us by all means have our city planning. But let us not forget its roots in its vast hinterland. Let us understand that traffic congestion on State Street and subway congestion at "Park Street Under" are resultants of activities taking place in Dakota and Texas, in New York and Charleston, as well as in Somerville. It is a fairly simple matter to widen streets and build new subways; and this sort of emergency ditchwork may seem very necessary when the flood has come upon us. But it is not going to the roots.

When Pittsburgh began at last to tackle man-fashion the floods of the Allegheny and Monongahela Rivers, what was done? An urgent part of the city plan was for the disposal of these surplus waters. And the Pittsburgh Flood Commission went about it. They went *away* from Pittsburgh. They traced the waters to their sources. And this part of the Pittsburgh "city plan" included river drainage basins stretching over goodly portions of four states. At least seventeen reservoirs, scattered for hundreds of miles around, were found necessary to control the floods at Pittsburgh. The city itself was but one tiny spot on the map of this "city plan."

And as with the flow of waters so with the "flow" of other things. So with the flow of population, depending as it does upon the flow of industrial products. The *industrial flow* out of the Mississippi Basin through the North Atlantic ports is more terrific than the *water flow* which passes through the Mississippi Delta. The most terrific "gorge" is New York harbor: for here about one fifth of America's foreign tonnage squeezes through. New York is the biggest "Niagara." But Boston and Philadelphia and Baltimore are only lesser ones. Can this flow from our continent's interior be "shedded" with greater engineering skill?

And how about our "pools" of manufacture? Why should these congest in the metropolis? Are not the main line cities (Fitchburg or North Adams) as good for much of this as Boston? And (for some things) are not the branch line towns (Greenville, N.H. or Wilmington, Vt.) as good as Fitchburg or North Adams? And why not pool our factories even further back than this—back nearer to the sources? Coal and iron can get together anywhere east of the Mississippi. There is the Mesaba Range in the north and Birmingham, Alabama in the south. Electric power, direct by wire, from coal field or waterfall, can reach almost any portion of this territory. The hardwoods of the Carolina Highland and the (future) softwoods of the Lake States and the Gulf, are (or will be) near at hand. And all around grow the cotton and the corn, and the sheep and cattle, to clothe and feed us.

When Boston (and the others) make their real city plans as part of an industrial watershed, they will look beyond their ditchwork (their street widenings and subways) and do as Pittsburgh did with her flood waters. They will study the streams and springs that cause the flood. They will seek to control from the *source outward,* not from the *mouth backward.*

And now let us start our exploration: not in Boston but in Berkshire. We shall explore a sample region in the "sphere of origin." We shall take the basin of the Upper Deerfield River, the territory drained by this river and its tributaries above the big bend at Hoosac Tunnel, Massachusetts. Part of this territory is in Berkshire county, Massachusetts, and part within the state of Vermont. It consists of a series of mountain valleys along the main crestline of the Berkshire-Green Mountain Range. On one of these we shall focus our chief attention, namely Somerset Valley, at the extreme headwaters north of Wilmington, Vermont.

Somerset Valley is a miniature empire. It is 17 miles long, from four to eight miles wide, and covers 49,000 acres. It is a typical crestline valley, an almost perfect illustration of the "sphere of origin." It is shut off from the outer world by three of the largest mountains in this part of the range—Glastonbury on the west, Stratton on the north and Haystack on the east. Its outlet is at the southeast corner just above the town of Wilmington.

This little region has its own history; and it shows a definite rise and fall of "settled life." Daniel Rice, the first settler, entered the valley the same year (1776) that Daniel Boone crossed the Southern Appalachians. He and his followers, emulating the Egyptians, made their settlement in a fertile river bottom (now occupied by the Somerset Reservoir). Here, in 1780, Rice built the first sawmill and gristmill. The next community building was a church—built five years later out of logs. Settled life at Big Meadows as they called the community lasted about one hundred years, beginning with Daniel Rice in 1776 and ending with one last reported family in 1882.

The history of this century in Somerset Valley is the history of the rise and fall of a certain phase of the lumber industry, the phase of the ox team and the log drive. The one main export of the Somerset empire was lumber. Little sawmills (run by water power) were set up (and abandoned) from time to time along the main stream. In addition, one wood-working plant at least was built—a clothes-pin factory in 1846. Big Mea-dows and vicinity was apparently the center of the valley's life till the middle of the century, the population rising from 111 in 1790 to 321 in 1850. Thereafter the center seems to have shifted downstream to the settlement at Searsburg. But at this time life in the valley as a whole be-gan its decline: history reports the abandonment of sawmills rather than the building of them; and the combined population of both settle-ments dropped from 340 in 1860 to 169 in 1910.

In 1907 the "old empire" was supplanted by a new one: the coming of the logging railroad. A new phase of lumbering entered the valley— the railroad phase. But its very power made it short lived. The valley was planted with temporary logging camps and the logs hauled by rail to the big mills at Wilmington and further down the river. Before 1920 the remaining larger timber growth thus was taken out and the tracks pulled up after the last trainload had gone its way. And so the "second empire" ran its course and settled life in Somerset Valley now awaits its restoration.

This story is the story of the average wooded crestline valley in the eastern states. It is the history of one particular initial strand of indus-try, namely, lumbering. This industry, as in Somerset Valley, has spread its web and picked it up again. Our own problem, therefore, is rendered all the simpler. The "framework" we are looking for is not so deeply buried. We can build on a fairly clean slate. Indeed the very "ruins" of the web make firm foundations for our framework. The old railroad grades in Somerset would make excellent roads for reaching the various portions of the valley's future forest. Some of the old logging camps could be turned into logging communities. It happens in Somerset Val-ley that no great devastation has been made. Hence a regulated forest growth could readily get started.

As a sample, therefore, of our new exploration—of the charting of one particular strand of the hidden framework which we seek—a rough hewn plan has been drawn for guiding the potential outflow, year by year, of one of the raw materials which Somerset Valley can supply; namely, lumber. The gist of this plan is presented graphically—in the ac-companying map (Figure 2).

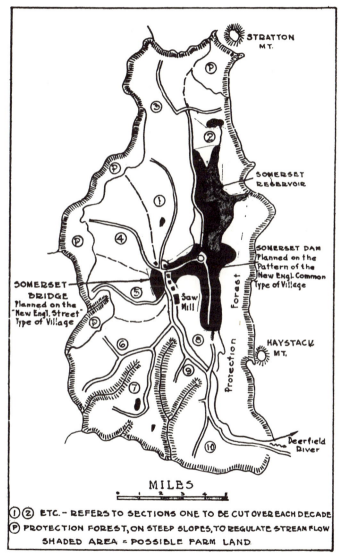

Figure 2. A forest plan for Somerset valley, upper Deerfield River.

The forest plan here presented is for that portion of the Upper Deer-field basin just described—Somerset Valley. It requires the adoption of what is known as "forestry." Forestry would develop the maximum potential wood growth of an area, just as the water power industry would develop the maximum potential horsepower from an area. The yearly cut is then limited to the yearly growth. Forestry, that is, cuts each year the annual forest "interest" in lieu of shoveling out, all at once, the forest capital. It is *forest culture* as against *forest mining*.

Forestry is all that will keep settled life in Somerset Valley in a truly settled state. For any community to be permanent must rest on a per-manent industry. So long as the forest industry is run on a "mining" basis it can support only a "camp" population; it must become a forest culture if it is going to support a settled life.

It takes from 50 to 150 years for a timber tree to grow to financial maturity. This fact necessitates waiting for more than a human lifetime to realize on the money investment. This in turn requires some form of long-time ownership and a consistent long-time policy. Hence some pub-lic institution is the logical (and the practical) owner—such as state, federal or municipal government. The present plan presupposes such form of ownership.

Our goal in this plan is to discover and chart the "most efficient framework" for regulating the outflow of lumber from Somerset Valley.

This framework (as nearly as we see it) is here mapped. It consists of a system of roads and of periodic cuttings converging on a central sawmill plant and wood-working community. (The community, as planned, is divided into two parts, one near the mill and the other near Somerset Reservoir.)

The plan as presented is merely a sketch plan. It is for purposes of illus-tration only, and so to keep it clear the sketch has purposely been made very crude and rigid. For actual working it would have to be modified.

Another important "raw material" to be supplied from the sphere of origin is water power. And as one more illustration of a potential frame-work for guiding the outflow of a resource from a region a power plan is here presented (Figure 3). We are saved the trouble of making this plan ourselves. For it has already been made (and in large part carried out) by the engineers of the New England Power Company.

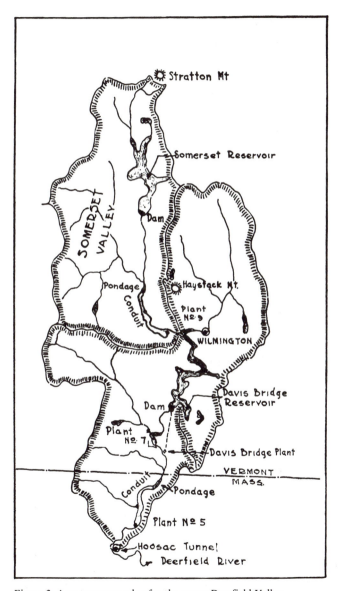

Figure 3. A water power plan for the upper Deerfield Valley.

These engineers are, in all reality, explorers in the new exploration. They realized, when they went about their job, that there was already laid by nature within the basin of the Upper Deerfield some one *most efficient framework* of power development (some combination of reservoirs, power sites and grades for guiding the stream's flow which would yield more power per annum, and more steadily, than any other combination). Their job was to *find* that framework. Whether or not literally they did find it, neither they nor we perhaps shall ever positively know. Perhaps even now they can see some better layout. But they have found a *framework* for securing and controlling the stream's power which certainly looks like that "most efficient framework" we are seeking.

We shall not go into the details of this framework. Its main lines, as with the forest plan, can better be presented graphically than by verbal description. The plan provides for developing the Upper Deerfield's power throughout its whole valley above Hoosac Tunnel. The plan is limited to the "sphere of origin." It is a framework for making available for use (in the form of electric power) the potential mechanical power of the stream's flow. *What use* (when available) this power should be put to is quite another story. That is a problem of another sphere, namely the "sphere of distribution." And this we shall not enter in this article. The problem of distributing power flow is part of the problem of distributing industrial flow generally; and power flow is part of that one great stream of industry which ultimately must be handled as one great unity.

Illustrations, within the sphere of origin, might be presented of other industrial strands: thus the "most efficient framework" for guiding the flow of coal power from the West Virginia mountains; the flow of milk and butter from the grazing lands of the New Jersey crestline valleys; the flow of wool from various grazing regions along the Appalachian ranges. The two examples given (of lumber and water power) are but hints in our industrial charting.

Indeed industry forms but half the story of a region's "settled life." The other half—its social development as a community unit— is a whole subject in itself. The problem there is to chart the framework for a community which shall make of it an environment fit for human living. Thus a forest community in the Deerfield Valley need not be primitive nor crude. On the contrary it is readily open, on its own modest scale, to all that a civilization can provide—not only in material needs but in social life and in culture generally. To chart the framework for real *living,* and not *existence* merely, is another fundamental of the new exploration.

"The last great earth story has been told." The *old* exploration has done its work. "Settled life," from its early homes on the flood plains of Egypt and Mesopotamia, has pushed nature's wilds aside and spread its web throughout the world: first on the shores of the Mediterranean, next on the coasts of trans-Atlantic lands, and finally in the hearts of the continents. In America the trails of the covered wagons, solidifying into ways of steel, have set, in the main, the mold of our industrial civilization.

But the end is not yet. "Settled life" is still not wholly settled. We have cleared one wilderness but made another. We have made an iron web of industry that threatens to strangle us. Beneath this web there lies a latent framework, namely that "most efficient framework" through which life substances must flow before we can be freed from useless toil and strife.

Our job is to find that framework. And the first places wherein to seek it seem to be those where it makes its start, and where too its strands are fewest and most simple. These places form the "sphere of origin"—the regions of the sources where each strand (each industry) can be segregated and charted as a separate entity. The framework for guiding the flow of lumber from Somerset Valley illustrates one such segregated strand; the framework for guiding the flow of water power from the Upper Deerfield River illustrates another. It is the mountain crestline, with the side valleys that adjoin it, that is the backbone of the sphere of origin.

But down in the city (on the seaboard or the railway) down in the "sphere of distribution"—the problem grows complex. Here the strands are woven on a continental scale. So when we seek our framework here we must deal, at once, with the flow from continents, not valleys.

And so we of today have our big search as our forefathers had theirs. They sought to chart the wilderness of nature; we seek to chart the wilderness of man. In purpose their trail and ours lie in the same direction—from the simple to the complex. But on the map they lie in different ways. Their trail—that of the covered wagon (of the old exploration), followed the valley way; our trail (of the new exploration) follows the crestline way. Their base of operations was the bottom of the valley (the river line) whence they worked up the side streams to their sources in the hills. Our base of operations is the top of the valley (the mountain crestline) whence we work downstream toward the mouths.

From source to mouth (of river and industry); from crestline to seaport; from sphere of "origin" to that of "distribution"; from the simple to the complex; such is the evolution of the new exploration. Our trail follows the crestline (of the Sierras, of the Rockies, of the Appalachians) and the new exploration may be symbolized in terms of the Appalachian Trail which is already threading its way down the backbone of our eastern states. For the crestline is the new frontier.

8 Giant Power—Region-Builder

Robert W. Bruère

Regional planning has come into being under pressure from our swollen, congested and unmanageable commercial cities. But it is only secondarily a metropolitan problem. Primarily it is a problem of staying the decline and re-invigorating the life of rural and small-town communities. It assumes that the alternative commonly expressed by the question, *Do you prefer to live in the city or the country?* is a false alternative; that healthy, vigorous, life-loving men, women and children want an environment in which they can enjoy the good things of both.

In spite of the rapid shifting of population from the farms to the cities, the United States is still an agricultural nation, and must continue to be if we are to maintain our domestic prosperity and our economic preeminence in the world. Fortunately what we confront is not an ethical imperative only; traditionally we are a land-loving people. The magnet which drew our adventurous millions from their European homes was land and the opportunities and freedoms implicit in it. We tend to forget the intensity of that land hunger as decades intervene between us and the era of free soil, and as census by decennial census, we watch the balance of population shift from the farms to the towns. But we con-

Reprinted, with minor changes, from *Survey Graphic* 7 (May 1925): 161-164, 188.

found symptom with cause. When only a little more than twenty-five years ago Oklahoma was thrown open to settlement, thousands and tens of thousands joined in the greediest "sooner" rush in our history. And that was before oil had been discovered there. Many went simply to get something for nothing; but many to strike root in the earth. If another Indian territory were available that spectacle would be repeated at the crack of the land agent's pistol. Our people would not by the millions be abandoning farms if they could overcome the hard isolation of American farm life and if tillage could be made economically profitable. In the last analysis, regional planning and the decentralization of population depend upon the stabilization and increasing prosperity of agriculture; and that depends in turn not only upon more abundant and cheaper fertilizers, but also upon the extension of modern mechanical equipment and energies to small-town and rural homes. Giant electrical power, if wisely controlled, can be made to yield both.

A year ago, in the Giant Power number of *The Survey* (March, 1924), I said that through the development of the electrical industry mechanical engineers were beginning to rebuild the technical and social framework of American life. Some readers were disposed at that time to see more romance than fact in the statement, but the intervening months have brought public confirmation of the data upon which it was based. One after another of the electric utility corporations has announced mergers preliminary to the construction of giant power lines from the coal mines in Pennsylvania and West Virginia to the Lakes and the Atlantic seaboard. The debates over Muscle Shoals in Congress have made every wide-awake layman aware of the prospective gathering of the energy resources of the country into a few pools of power upon which the future of industry, transportation and community life will increasingly depend. There is no longer any doubt as to the reality of the technical revolution which the mechanical engineers are unobtrusively setting in motion.

At the same time I deplored the fact that the human engineers—social workers and educators, health, civic and labor leaders—seemed hardly aware that a new industrial revolution was on; that they were facing the progress of electrical invention almost as naively as the philanthropists of the eighteenth century faced the revolutionary progress of steam.

The possibility remains that unless men and women of vision bestir themselves to forestall such a tragedy, the social history of the dawning electrical age may repeat that of the Industrial Revolution.

The report issued this spring by the Pennsylvania Giant Power Commission, and this regional planning number itself, may be regarded as two of the first concerted attempts by groups of social engineers to apply forethought and planning to this fundamental technological change, in ways which may help to avert its preventable evils and guide its tremendous forces into socially beneficent channels.

It is inevitable that such trail blazing work should have the tentative quality of all pioneering. But in view of the untoward symptoms that have already attended large scale electrical development, it has a most timely importance. Home-work, that stepmother of the sweat shop, is again on the increase in our great cities. The socially unimaginative exploitation of water power in parts of the South is building up new cotton mill towns on the motor-geared labor of women and children. The extension of cheap electricity from central stations to the coal mines of West Virginia and southwestern Pennsylvania is intensifying the struggle between the workers and operators by bringing a powerful ally to the operators in the non-union fields. While the general leveling up of standards of health and decency is having its protective effect, the new technical revolution tends in its social aspects to follow the familiar lines of the old. That this should be so is largely the fault of social workers and human engineers, public officers and civic leaders in failing to keep abreast of the mechanical engineers and to exercise their prerogatives as the outposts, educators and social guides of the rank and file of the community.

There are two places in the North American continent, Ontario and California, where, by grace of nature's arrangements, giant power has been diverted from the traditional channels and has built the frame work of regional areas. The southern arable portion of Ontario possesses the essential elements of a region as that term is used in this number. And giant electrical power has done for this Canadian state what the regional planners . . . hope it will do for New York. When hydroelectric plants were first built at Niagara Falls their promoters had in view the development of a concentrated industrial district between Niagara and Toronto.

They dreamt of an electrified Pittsburgh. Ontario had escaped the usual type of industrialization because it had no coal, and coal imported from Pennsylvania, Ohio or Great Britain was too dear to support an industrialized state. As a result it had retained much of its colonial character, remained a community of farms and small towns, with something of the charm of colonial New England. The very backwardness of the province, industrially speaking, proved a portentous social fact; it has helped it to leap over the stage of development which holds most of urban America in a vise.

When the engineers began harnessing the Falls, the merchants, manufacturers and craftsmen in the small Ontario towns, together with their socially interdependent agricultural neighbors, rebelled at the notion of a huge suction pump at Niagara which would draw the life out of their communities and leave them gossip-rattling, Main Street shells or mere suburban satellites. Accordingly they fought for the organization of the Ontario Hydro-Electric Power Commission, with a view to decentralizing the energy generated at Niagara and having it evenly distributed throughout the province in order that their small towns and rural communities might flourish after their kind. They won. Today their farms are undergoing rapid electrification; as contrasted with New York state, the small towns of Ontario are prospering.[1] Woodstock, for example, with its twenty-eight different industries all using electricity, which like the water supply is publicly owned and distributed, is growing with its roots in its own ground—not a one-industry mushroom boom town, but a sort of manor town to the surrounding countryside. Like scores of other towns within the Hydro region, it combines within itself and its immediate rural environment the opportunities for a balanced city and country life, of diversified industry and indigenous culture.

Now contrast with the wide spread of cheap electricity in Ontario, with its balanced development of town and country, the condition of our middle Atlantic states, of our industrial states generally. With us the industrial metropolis has dominated large scale electrical development. Our greatest electric generating stations have been built in already over-

1. See articles of Sir Adam Beck and Martha Bensley Bruère in Giant Power number of *Survey Graphic,* March 1924.

crowded manufacturing centers. The influence of this policy has extended even to the American side of Niagara where hydro-electricity generated at the Falls, instead of being spread out over the state for a radius of two hundred and fifty miles as in Ontario, is principally consumed in a few cities and factories clustered near the source. The main reason for this practice, apart from the fact that our seaboard cities are the funnels through which our agricultural and manufactured surplus flows out to Europe, is that the steam engine built our manufacturing mammoths with coal hauled by rail from the mines in the days before high-voltage, long-distance electrical transmission had taken form even in the dreams of the engineers. Instead of placing the generating stations at the mines, as Ontario of necessity placed hers at her primary source of water power, we have built ours where they could play second fiddle to the steam engine. Among the largest electric power stations in the world are those of New York, Cleveland and Chicago; and practically all power generated in these metropolitan plants is used within their municipal boundaries. Until this arrangement is reversed, until our primary power stations are placed at the mines as well as water falls and electrical current is evenly distributed over wide areas, regional planning will remain without its essential economic foundation and technical framework. For, it must always be remembered that except on the Pacific coast our major source of electrical energy is not water but coal; the bituminous coal seams of Pennsylvania, West Virginia, Ohio, Kentucky, Indiana and Illinois are our Niagaras.

It is an interesting sign of the times, and one which social workers and social reformers generally might well note with humility, that it is a mechanical engineer who has most clearly seen the fundamental interdependence of giant power and regional planning, and the far-reaching social implications of both. Morris L. Cooke, director of Pennsylvania's Giant Power Survey, invented the term "giant power" for the special purpose of focussing public attention upon the social opportunities and dangers latent in large scale electrical enterprise. The earlier prospectus of "superpower," as interpreted by its leading proponents, has for its primary aim the piling of power upon existing power in already congested centers. In transmitting the report of the Giant Power Survey

Board to the General Assembly of Pennsylvania, in March, Governor Pinchot, who has interpreted Giant Power to the public, said:

Superpower is the interchange of surplus power at the ends of the distributing wires of each system. Its principal object is profit for the companies—not benefit for the public—and it is on the way to being realized with a rapidity which it is difficult to understand. . . . Giant power and superpower are as different as a tame elephant and a wild one. One is the friend and fellow worker of man—the other, at large and uncontrolled, may be a dangerous enemy. The place for the public is on the neck of the elephant, guiding its movements, not on the ground, helpless under its knees.

With giant power stations at the mines instead of at the heart of great cities, and with an integrated and not merely an interconnected system of transmission lines, we shall be able to follow, and with our ampler resources, improve upon the example of Ontario.

But the desired social results will not follow automatically the construction of mine-mouth electric stations. They will need for their realization constant and intelligent planning. The public will need not only to be on the neck of the elephant but also to have its wits sharpened to make the beast do what it wants. Regional planning must go before giant power, if giant power is to be a region-builder and not like steam power a wastrel of our human and economic resources.

Regional planning is distinguished from city planning in much the same way that giant power is distinguished from superpower. Just as superpower would pile mechanical energy upon existing mechanical energy instead of giving it wide distribution, so city planning in the narrow sense tends to widen the girth of big cities and so enable them to fatten and grow bigger. Regional planning approaches the problems of the great cities themselves not from within but from without, through the small town and the farm. The logic both of regional planning and of giant power points to the farm, the small town, the countryside as the first points of attack.

This accounts for the fact that Pennsylvania's Giant Power Survey, after establishing the economic and technical advantages of large-scale electrical generation in the coal fields, goes thoroughly into the problems of rural electrification. Of our 6,450,000 American farms, less than 3 per cent have electricity from central stations. Only in California, where electricity is derived principally from water-powers far removed from the metropolitan centers, has rural electrification proceeded at a rate comparable to that in Ontario; there 27 per cent of the farms are supplied with electricity from central generating plants. In the United States as a whole we have made no serious effort to carry the fruits of modern electrical invention to the farms, although twice as much primary power is used by our farmers as by all our factories combined. But much of it is literally horsepower or mulepower—that is to say, relatively inefficient power because the tending of animals itself absorbs labor. Besides their upkeep is high and a great deal of their stalling and feeding will not wait upon the convenience of man. Nor are horses and mules handy about the house. They will draw plows and wagons, but they are not apt at cooking meals, dusting the floors and furniture, washing and ironing clothes. At best they are man's servants, not woman's. It is the women especially whom the isolation and hardships of farm life drive to the city or to insanity or both.

Contrary to the prevailing city notion, there is no group in our population that cling more tenaciously to their homes and their occupation than men and women who till the land. But because of the backward state of agricultural technique the demand for the best farms is keen. Land values are high and without modern mechanical facilities the struggle to work with profit and to win reasonable leisure is increasingly hard. Because of their tenacious love of the land men go great lengths to obtain these facilities. In Lancaster County, Pa., groups of farmers have pooled their small resources in order to build dams and harness local streams so as to get electricity for their houses and fields and barns. One of the first uses to which they have put their high cost electricity has been to pump enough water to enable them to install modern toilet conveniences. How primitive the technical equipment of American agricultural life still is appears from the fact that in highly industrialized Pennsylvania only 46,402 of its more than 200,000 farms have water piped to their farm buildings, and that the proportion of those that have even an approximation to modern sewage disposal in their homes is almost as small. Tens of thousands of farmers in the United States have installed individual electric lighting systems or motors driven by gasoline engines to get even a modicum of electrical service.

But the cost of current so generated is almost prohibitive. Only exceptionally prosperous farmers can afford it. Of the 202,250 farms in Pennsylvania, 178,666 are without electrical equipment of any kind and only 12,452 have public utility service. On a liberal calculation, only 20 per cent of the total land area of the state has electricity within reach in spite of the fact that the world's greatest supply of fuel lies within its borders. Almost half of all the electricity used in Pennsylvania is generated and principally consumed in the Philadelphia and Pittsburgh metropolitan districts. Under a giant power system it would be economically feasible to carry electricity in five years to half the farms of the state, to 75 per cent of them in a decade—and until this is done the balance between rural and metropolitan life of the regional planners' dream will remain principally a dream.

These time estimates of five and ten years are based not only upon the findings of Pennsylvania's Giant Power Survey, but also upon actual accomplishments in certain European countries. The quandary which regional planning aims to resolve—abandoned farms and declining small towns on the one hand, overcrowded cities on the other—is not uniquely American; the older agricultural and industrial countries of Europe have known it, have wrestled with it, face it still. But some of them, like Ontario on our side of the water, have gone much further toward solving it than we. And they have found the wide distribution and social control of large scale electrical service the greatest single aid to its solution. Bavaria,[2] for example, has an area about two-thirds that of Pennsylvania; but it has a million or more acres under cultivation. Bavarian farmers, their wives and children, were growing restive under the economic and physical hardships of farming. The old home-loving generation was perturbed, the government was concerned. Electrical generating stations received public assistance, farmers' cooperative societies were helped to build and operate distributing systems. By 1921, a little over one-half of the rural homes in that stronghold of ancient customs and folkways

2. For the social facts and statistics in this paragraph I am indebted to the article on The World's Experience with Rural Electrification, published by Harold Evans, counsel, Rural Electric Committee, Pennsylvania Council of Agricultural Organizations, in the *Annals of the American Academy of Political and Social Sciences*, March 1925.

had electricity; within five years it is planned to carry electrical current to every farm. Denmark has an area little more than twice that of New Jersey or one-third that of New York. Three-fifths of the population live in the country, three-tenths follow agriculture. Before 1918, electricity there, as with us, was a city luxury. But the spirit of agricultural revival, as all the world knows, was strong in the little kingdom. Today, one-half of the farms are electrically equipped, and it is planned to bring every farm within the electrified zone within ten years. In Sweden with her area of 173,000 square miles—about equal to that of New England and the Middle Atlantic states—60 percent is forest, only 9 per cent arable land. Yet she has as much improved farm land as Pennsylvania, about 12,000,000 acres. Ten years ago rural electrification was practically unknown in Sweden. Her farmers' sons and daughters had their eyes turned to the cities and across the sea to Wisconsin, Minnesota and the Dakotas. Today 40 per cent of the 9,500,000 acres under tillage has access to electricity and the service is being extended. In these countries the romance of invention, craftsmanship and economic enterprise is again preparing to flower on the farms and in the country-side towns.

What electricity can do for the farm when it is obtainable in quantity and at reasonable rates from a central station is shown in the record of a single Pennsylvania farm reported by Professor R. U. Blasingame of Pennsylvania State College. Levi H. Brubaker owns a farm of 133 acres in Lancaster County. With the coming of factories to the neighboring town, he confronted the usual competition for field and household help. Without electrical equipment he could give neither steady employment nor the wages demanded by skilled labor. To meet the situation he electrified his farm and organized it on a factory basis. He divided it into two sections, each of which he subdivided into three fields. Each section he runs on a three year rotation—1, potatoes, wheat and alfalfa; 2, tobacco, wheat and corn. By using electricity to spray and grade his potatoes, thrash his wheat, cut his ensilage, and generally to substitute machine for hand work, he is able to keep three men steadily employed the year round, to pay them high wages and to do without extra seasonal labor. If electricity were cheaper he might adopt the manless electric plow used in some parts of Germany and in experimental use at Iowa

State College. Indeed he might consider the electric drying of his hay and alfalfa, a practice developed in Bavaria and other European countries, and so largely increase the yield of his fodder ground. As it is, electricity has not only revolutionized his agricultural practice but, unlike the horse and mules of fading memory, enters the house, cooks the meals, dusts the floors and furniture, washes and irons the clothes, pumps water in abundance and in a score of other ways makes life worth living for his wife.

So much for one farm. When regional planning and giant power have done their work, what kind of world will they have fashioned? Any attempt at prophecy that went beyond the limits of actual achievement in Ontario, California and Europe would inevitably fall into as stilted and artificial a pattern as More's Utopia. No amount of expert planning or mechanical equipment can do more than create an environment in which the human spirit shall have maximum freedom to develop its potentialities. We know that both the lop-sided industrial life of our slum-breeding cities and the hard, stark, culturally atrophied life of the isolated farm and small towns make rounded education and spiritual development impossible. Effective regional building, by establishing a vital, organic, functional integration of the farm, the small town and the financial metropolis, should correct the present abnormalities and diffuse the advantages of each. By carrying industry closer to the farms, and drawing the farms closer to the industrial centers, by opening the windows of the cities to the fresh air of the countryside and infusing into the farms and small towns the nervous energy with which our machine-geared cities are oversupplied, it should restore to our mechanized civilization the diversified occupational and cultural opportunities of the earlier household and neighborhood economy. It should stabilize and enrich community life, and so prepare the ground for new folkways and indigenous customs, for the flowering forth of new community visions of the good life which are of the essence of religion.

All these things are within our reach. But who can say whether as a people we have the capacity to grasp them?

9 The Road to Good Houses

Henry Wright

The housing problem is still associated in our minds with the slums of
the big cities. How could the tenements of the poor be made sanitary
and reasonably safe, we asked—and the last generation made its fight
for restrictive codes to prevent the worst evils of overcrowding and
filthy living from appearing in the new quarters of our cities.

But the housing problem could not be kept in the slums; it has become universal. We still cling to the ideal of one home for one family,
but statistics in the United States show that there are 1.8 families for
each separate house; and the dwellings the majority of us must now accept are neither desirable nor satisfactory. New quarters of our cities
are scarcely in existence before they begin to "run down." We are irri-
tated by this discovery and put the blame on the high cost of materials
and labor "since the war," or on the high cost of financing houses; but
while these factors are real, they are not the essential source of our difficulty.

Let us pause a moment and see where we stand. In housing we are
torn between an intolerable reality and an impossible ideal. The reality

Reprinted with minor changes and without illustrations from *Survey Graphic* 7
(May 1925): 165-168, 189.

is that we are steadily being crowded into smaller quarters; and that the tenements and multi-family houses which people in "progressive" centers live in do not appeal to us as permanent homes. The noise, the lack of privacy, the incessant consciousness of neighbors, the bleak outlook from the windows are things we put up with because we prefer them to the present alternative—the hasty breakfasts, the dreary hours of commuting, the abbreviated third act of the play, and those other little discomforts which are the price we pay for an escape to Suburbia.

All the while we are lulled by the fancy that we will some day be able to realize the home of our dreams. We see it pictured in the house and garden periodicals and in our Sunday magazine sections; we hear it praised and boosted in Better-Home weeks and in Own-Your-Own-Home drives. It is the dream of a picturesque house standing free and independent on its own plot—a whole country estate if we have luck, but at any rate an independent and isolated plot. While we have learned to adjust ourselves to the bare utilities of the apartment, while we take a little pride perhaps in the disappearing kitchen and the disappearing bed, and are only waiting for some ingenious person to perfect the disappearing baby, no one must meddle with our Ideal Home!

Twenty or thirty years ago most of our suburbs could boast well-shaded streets and quiet lawns; and the dream was, for a brief time, not altogether hopeless. Today conditions have changed. In pursuit of the ideal home people use the automobile to escape beyond the borders of the city and beyond its restrictive building codes—and accept the inconveniences and often risk the dangers of bad sanitation and an inadequate water supply. With the housing shortage in our larger cities the small house has again appeared as an appreciable factor in the amount of housing available, but in respect to quality and desirability, the value of this trend may be seriously questioned. Within the limits of New York City no less than fifty miles of new small frame houses have been built, in long monotonous rows, with a single repetitive design, closely crowded together on poor land, usually without proper public facilities or fire protection, and often with the barest provisions for health and sanitation. Practically no recreation areas have been set aside in these districts. The houses are of the flimsiest construction and the cost of up-keep will be excessive and will fall on purchasers just when they are least prepared for it.

In Philadelphia with the relatively low grade and low cost row-house type, which has so frequently been cited as a distinctive advantage in that city, housing facilities are quite as far behind needs as elsewhere. In St. Louis areas set off and restricted for protected single family houses remain relatively unoccupied while those devoted to the multi-family house are being rapidly filled in. Even in Los Angeles with its influx of foreign wealth the erstwhile "bungalow" is being abandoned in much new building, and replaced by the efficiency apartment and apartment hotel.

It will no doubt be a shock to most home-seekers to be told that their ideal is impossible, and that it is precisely what stands in the way of any improvement in our housing prospects. But by our insisting upon building on the outskirts of our cities as if we were solitary Robinson Crusoes, we lose the genuine advantages of city life and civic cooperation, and before we know it we have lost the solitude at which we have been aiming. The fact is that our ideal home dates from a time when the costs of a house were all above ground. We have not adapted that ideal to the present condition, wherein 25 percent of the cost of a house derives from the things that the community, not the individual, provides. On top of this, an additional 15 per cent to 20 per cent is buried in costs and services other than the actual building itself. We cannot solve our problems individually and in piecemeal fashion any longer; for the determining factors are outside our hands.

Our whole individualized process of home building at present is wasteful and extravagant. First, the land is taken out of agricultural use and is opened up, divided and sold—usually long in advance of its actual use. Someone must bear the waste and the carrying charges; both elements could be minimized under a community plan. Then by scattering the development of new streets and sewers and mains instead of opening them up hand in hand with the actual building of houses, the expense of municipal services and the cost of home sites is increased for the whole community. Since the eventual use of the neighborhood is not provided for in the beginning, even in so-called zone plans, streets are conventionally built on a scale which would eventually serve commercial purposes—another waste, for permanent residence areas may be served by narrower and more lightly paved streets than commercial areas. Building houses individually takes an extravagant amount of land; yet it provides neither sufficient garden-space nor privacy. In fact, with the usual multiplication of walks, passageways and driveways between detached or semi-detached houses there is continual noise, confusion and dirt, and a negligible quantity of useful space remains, particularly when the addition of a private individual garage takes up the last remnant that might be used for children's play.

The combined result of all these forms of waste and extravagance is reflected in the neighborhood. Many desirable things are overlooked or neglected because of increased cost; playgrounds and parks, for example, are seldom provided for, and if they are added later they are curtailed because of their mounting expense. Facilities for telephone service, gas and electricity may likewise long be inadequate, and when all these things *are* completed, the community becomes too expensive for the average family to bear the burden. As a result changes occur; either the poorer families are driven out, or the neighborhood "runs down"; perhaps lodgers and small businesses are brought in to help carry the load. The city may indeed attempt to bear the cost of elaborate municipal services to outlying neighborhoods that cannot meet their share; but this process cannot be kept up indefinitely.

The eventual fate of the extravagant neighborhood is to be added to those ill-kept and blighted districts which occupy the intermediate areas of our extending cities. In the expansion of the town from the center outward, the plain man is attracted to the edges by the prospects of an individual home; he wakes up to find himself in the midst of a slum. So the development of the city becomes a perpetual game of leap frog, in which the city consecutively destroys its border developments, leaving a wake of sordid, decaying areas, heavily taxed out of their original use, and on the point of being converted into the intolerable reality of the high apartment house, or the equally crowded tenement!

Meanwhile our practical builders go on producing substitute dwellings which fit our purses if not our desires. Since we have not yet learned to cooperate intelligently to secure privacy, gardens, sunlight and space for children to thrive in, the builder of the apartment house enables us to "cooperate" in a single structure, deprived of most of these things, but big enough to support the heavy load of taxes for municipal utilities.

Here the benefits of cooperative living and comprehensive architectural design are reduced to a minimum; not because a multi-family dwelling is necessarily inferior to a single-family dwelling, but because the design of such buildings is subordinated on the whole to a single motive—the most intensive use of the land, with a maximum yield of profit.

What is the alternative? The real choice is not between the "rent-barracks," as the Germans call the tenement, and the isolated House of our Dreams. The real alternative for most of us, as our wants become more complicated and as community costs go up, is between the rent-barracks and community planning.

We build and work as if we were lonely "monarchs of all we surveyed" —and achieve dull uniformity. Community planning, on the other hand, is a method of achieving individuality by learning to work in common. The contrast . . . between the rows of individual houses, done in the American style, and the spacious well-planned groups of the English garden city is essentially not a contrast between two countries, but between two different types of planning. The few American examples of such community development, though perhaps they lack a little of the charm of the more practiced English tradition, are just as superior to individualistic chaos as the English plans.

There are many opportunities for intelligent economy in such team-work. In small detached houses, to begin with, the cost of outside connections is often fully half the cost of plumbing and fixtures within the home. Contrast this with English progress in building low-cost homes for the worker, in which these accessory costs, by a system of combined drainage, have been reduced to 25 per cent the cost of individual service. This is typical of the whole process of community planning. Thus the cost for land and public services in present English community planning practice, under government regulation, has been reduced to less than 10 per cent of the cost of the dwelling, as compared with about 25 per cent with us. The net result of present English practice has been to produce these houses of permanent brick construction on a basis which is relatively more favorable than the usual flimsy frame houses in this country. In fact, the workman's home in England has been so studied and perfected in plan and economies of service that it has become the standard of home-building for all classes.

It is important to realize that these gains are not gains due solely to better financing or large scale production, though these are important factors, nor has the standard of living been pared down at any point. What has made the results so different from ordinary mass production has been the coordination of the entire process of planning both the house and the neighborhood so as to take fullest advantage of community methods. As a result each tract is supplied at the outset with its local park and playground; streets are proportioned to use and located with reference to service, rather than to the mere production of saleable front feet of land.

We have tested these gains in various isolated experiments in America, but progress has been discouragingly slow and limited. Here and there small groups of houses have been adjusted to site and group economies in roads, garages and minor community features, as in Roland Park, Baltimore, and St. Martin's, Philadelphia. The advantages of well-related planning were demonstrated in a number of the large housing developments carried out before and during the war. Unfortunately there was no opportunity to give the results an adequate test. The best example of utilization and management of these developments is probably that of the Bridgeport Housing Company. Here a wide variety of single, double and multi-family houses have been used on a leasing basis which approaches home ownership in the degree of community interest it encourages, while at the same time providing a desirable degree of elasticity in the adjustment of housing space to family needs and aspirations. Once the notion of tenancy is split off from what too often automatically accompanies it—badly planned living quarters—we may discover that our emphasis on home-ownership stresses only the virtues of that plan and does not reckon with its disadvantages. We must attempt to make the home itself stable and secure, so that a residence district will not always be threatened with increasing rents, increasing taxes, and a more intensive kind of use; but we need not regard the normal form of ownership as necessarily that by an individual family. The corporate form of ownership, such as that devised by Copartnership Tenants Ltd. in England, is just as stable; and it corresponds more nearly to the form we have found necessary in other branches of industry, involving a large initial capital outlay, whether run on individual or cooperative lines.

In the Sunnyside development at Long Island City, the City Housing Corporation has put into practice, under typical American conditions, a number of the economies characteristic of community-planned housing, building houses for people with a family income of $2,400 to $3,000 per year (see *The Survey*, November 15, 1924).

The first economy consists in obtaining a sufficiently large parcel of ground to be treated as a unit, and not to be opened up in advance of use. Unfortunately at Sunnyside this economy was only partial; we were not able to avoid the wasteful street system already laid down by the city. The next economy grew out of grouping the houses and apartments. By this means many types of dwellings and modes of construction have been woven into the experiment; the individually owned house, the cooperative apartment, and the rented apartment; and these differences in function serve as the basis for differences in design. Planned housing of this kind is able to achieve the sort of honest individuality that comes from performing adequately one's own part in a larger whole; each house is, as it were, a good private citizen, with its individual entrance, its individual porch, its individual drying green, its complete sense of privacy, and at the same time it performs its civic obligations—it supports a park, a playground, a tennis court, swings, slides, wading pools. Above all, no house attempts to shout down its neighbors by reason of special size or style.

In such experiments we have already gone a considerable distance towards meeting the hidden costs of housing; we have been able to put more into gardens and playgrounds and into a substantial type of construction because we have wasted less on paving, on fences, on unusable ground; because we have been able to avoid the high costs of special fireproof construction which is imperative in more crowded quarters, and because we have eliminated the speculative profits of the builder who aims to give as little as possible for as much as possible. In the space of twelve months, 128 houses have been completed and occupied at Sunnyside; a second unit is nearly ready; a third is under way.

That community planning is not contrary to all the instincts and desires of the American people is shown, I think, by the degree of success that has attended these scattered experiments. If we barter our will o' the wisp Ideal Home for the real freedom to design and build complete communities, we may achieve in common what the majority of us will never succeed in achieving separately.

New Towns for Old:
Garden Cities—What They Are and How They Work

C. B. Purdom

England has two garden cities, [Letchworth and Welwyn] . . . .
   There are many schemes in America and England, and in most other
countries of the world, that are called garden cities and possess, many
of them, some features of the garden city; but none of them possesses
its distinctive features. . . . Many so-called garden cities are housing or
suburban developments, good in their way, some of them very good indeed, but with no direct connection with the garden city beyond what
they owe to it in site-planning and so forth. Ebenezer Howard's garden
city scheme, as first described in his famous little book *Tomorrow*,
published in London in 1898, is that of a new self-contained town of

Reprinted, with omissions, from *Survey Graphic* 7 (May 1925):169-172. Unlike
the other articles reproduced here from the special Regional Planning Number of
Survey Graphic, this one was not written by a member of the RPAA. C. B. Purdom wrote many books about Ebenezer Howard's garden city proposal and was
among its most enthusiastic propagandists. A common interest in the garden city
concept unified those who attended the conference for which the RPAA prepared this special issue. Purdom, at the time, worked as finance director of Welwyn, the second garden city developed under Howard's supervision in Great
Britain. He was also executive of the International Garden Cities and Town Planning Federation—a body with whom the RPAA became formally affiliated in
1923. This heavily cut version of Purdom's article serves primarily as an introduction to the following selection by Alexander Bing.—Ed.

thirty thousand inhabitants, with a wide agricultural belt surrounding it, which he suggested should be built to show how cities should be laid out and developed in the future. Mr. Howard's idea was to start city reconstruction, not in the middle of the congested and slum areas, but right away in the open country, so that industries and their workpeople, and the public at large, should have an alternative to staying in the cities, or even to living in the suburbs. He thought that if a good working example of this sort of city building were carried out, people would see its merits and a new direction would be given to city planning and development. There were two leading ideas in Mr. Howard's mind; one was that town and country interests would be combined in this system of comparatively small industrial town centers; the second was that improved values provided a certain financial basis for the scheme . . . . The originality of the garden city idea, the fact that it aims at putting an end to the present system of city expansion, replacing it by a more scientific method of city planning, accounts for the obstacles in the way. Established interests are against it as they are always against anything new. But the overwhelming difficulties of the great cities' slums, traffic congestion, high rates [taxes], and many others, make it inevitable that some remedy must be found, and the smaller cities, observing the straits to which undue expansion has brought the great ones, must seek for some way of avoiding them. Zoning and city planning are becoming popular, but something more constructive, something that touches the fundamental structure of cities is required. This is found in the garden city idea.

Just what is that idea? It may be summarized in the following terms:

A garden city is a town, that is to say, a distinct civic unit, having the political and economic characteristics of towns in the present day. A garden city is not a village, not even a large village, nor a housing scheme, nor a suburb. A village is essentially a rustic community, while the essence of a town is urbanity; it is a center of culture and manners, which means a variety of population providing opportunities for education, entertainment and social life.

A housing scheme is for a class, while a town is for all classes. A suburb is an appendage to a town, an incomplete thing, necessarily lacking the unity that a town must have.

A garden city is a town planned for industry and healthy living. Not
merely a town, but a town designed to fulfill its functions. If a town is
to be a center of industry and commerce—one of its main functions—
there must be design in its physical structure. Towns should be designed for the industry for which they are best suited, and the industrial
areas should be placed where they serve industry best and fit in with
the scheme of the town as a whole. Towns are not only for work, but
for life, and healthy living conditions, among which may be placed the
physical amenities of life, must be provided. The garden city therefore
is conceived of as a town functioning as a whole.

*A garden city is a town planned for industry and healthy living of a
size that makes possible a full measure of social life, but no larger.* This
is where the garden city idea strikes directly at the current method of
town growth. There is popularly supposed to be no limit to town
growth. Yet without some idea of size, of a limit to growth, design is
impossible, and planning is out of the question. The absurdity of most
city planning is that it is a mere physical extension of towns devoid of
any ideal of town life and any real science of town construction. Until
city-planners can answer the question (or have it answered for them):
What is the proper size for a town? they are bound to plan empirically,
without science. And so everything suffers and will suffer in town building; for neither public buildings, nor roads, nor public services of any
kind, nor commercial areas, nor industrial sites, can be adequately
planned until the limits of the town are settled. For practical purposes
a limit is always assumed; but the limit that is adopted has no basis in
fact, and may vary for different purposes and with different persons.
This is the most important of all city planning questions, and deserves
the attention of economists.

In connection with the garden city formula the size of the town is
taken to be that required for the full development of social life. This
should not be regarded in a narrow sense, for by social life is meant all
the activities of a community, including education, entertainment, industry. A due balance must be observed between these activities, and
it should be remembered that towns are not to be regarded as isolated
units, but as associating together for the attainment of larger objects
than a single town could reach. So that the garden city idea of town

development is that of a series of inter-related and distinct communities, replacing the conception of the gigantic city of today.

A garden city is a town, planned for industry and healthy living of a size that makes possible a full measure of social life, but no larger; surrounded by a permanent rural belt. In other words, town and country made one; the town including a central built-up area together with a surrounding rural district. The agricultural belt is the actual means by which the size of the town is limited. It protects the town from other towns, it brings the agricultural industry in contact with urban life and industry, and establishes agriculture as an element in town economy. In all countries the rural problem is no less urgent than the problem of the cities. The separation of the great mass of the population from agricultural pursuits, and the weakening of the rural districts by the over-concentration of population in the towns, are everywhere regarded as great evils. The solution is to be found in spreading the organization, financial opportunities, and social life of towns, over a wider area than is at present covered.

Finally: *A garden city is a town planned for industry and healthy living, of a size that makes possible a full measure of social life, but no larger, surrounded by a permanent rural belt, the whole of the land being in public ownership, or held in trust for the community.* The land on which the town is placed should be held in the public interest, so that the land values are socially enjoyed. This is the economic basis of the garden city. It is a well-known fact that land values rise with population; the garden city, founded on agricultural land, has its land values as they are created, reserved for the community. An idea of widespread effect, simple in its operation, fair and reasonable in its incidence, and disturbing to no vested interests. At the two garden cities the companies owning and developing the land are private enterprises; but the dividends and interest paid on the capital are limited in amount, and the balance of the revenues has to be devoted to the town. The matter cannot be dealt with here at length, but it is obviously the most important element in the garden city idea. For a garden city might well be defined as the development of a town on the economic basis provided by the systematic and deliberate creation of land values, the profits on which form part of the town's revenues.

Enough has been said to indicate the wide bearing of the garden city idea. It may be considered to be practical idealism of a most effective kind, an ideal conception of city life that has a proved economic basis.

11 New Towns for Old:
Can We Have Garden Cities in America?

Alexander M. Bing

The creation of new towns—whether the motive be semi-philanthropic as in the case of limited dividend companies, or purely commercial, as when they are built by a large industrial corporation or a real estate operator—is no small task. There must be organizing ability, substantial financial resources and business judgment; there should be, as well, a desire for aesthetic and social achievement. We have missed some wonderful opportunities in America to blaze the way for better things. When Gary, Indiana, was built, for example, there was abundant organizing ability and financial strength. But there was no effective desire for either aesthetic or social achievement. In other cases in America the artistic ideal has been carried out splendidly, but business judgment does not appear to have been as keen. Unfortunately where one of the necessary elements has been present, one or more of the others have been lacking.

The presence of the International Garden Cities and Town Planning Association in America for the first time raises the question sharply—are conditions in America suitable for a garden city experiment? If they are, do we who possess the energy and ability to do so many wonderful

Reprinted from *Survey Graphic* 7 (May 1925):172-173, 190.

things, possess also the idealism and organizing force that must be combined to make it successful?

Let me enumerate briefly some of the factors which must be united to build a successful garden city. In the first place there are the requirements for a proper site. These include a sufficient area of undeveloped inexpensive land—from two to ten thousand acres. For the proper handling of freight this land should be on a trunk railroad with good automobile roads leading in several directions. It should also be reasonably near one of the big cities. Healthfulness, a good source of water supply and a certain amount of natural beauty are required. The nature of the topography should lend itself to easy and inexpensive land development over a considerable area. A central portion of level land with surrounding hills in the distance, some wooded areas and a stream and lake would make an ideal combination.

These requirements can undoubtedly be met in America, although it is more difficult to fulfill them near a city like New York, than it is in the neighborhood of London. It can safely be said, however, that our failure to initiate a garden city experiment is not due to the scarcity of suitable acreage.

When we come to the financial requirements for our American garden city, the answer is not quite so simple. There is obviously no lack of capital for the ordinary commercial enterprise. But the possibilities for social usefulness in pointing the way, if not in achieving better methods of community planning and organization, will not be realized if the proposed garden city is to be built with the sole object of profit making. Such an enterprise should rather be undertaken by a limited dividend corporation. It must be confessed that we have been backward in the organization of such companies. Philanthropic foundations of a magnitude elsewhere unknown are flourishing in America. But the business enterprise which, to achieve a social end, voluntarily limits its return to investors has not in the past made as strong an appeal in America as it has in Europe. There is no reason, however, to believe the American public will not respond to an appeal of this kind. There is also reason to hope that, some day—let us trust in the not far distant future—the existence of these philanthropic funds will constitute an element of strength for properly conducted limited dividend corporations. It seems reasonably certain that with all the wealth there is in this country, financial resources can be procured to make possible the building of a garden city along limited dividend lines.

It should be pointed out however that in America a very much larger amount of capital would be needed than in England. Letchworth was started with less than half a million dollars. Its development was much handicapped by this inadequate financial strength, and its growth on such slender resources would have been unthinkable had it not been for the English system of building on leasehold land, and for the fact that for many years housing enterprises have been subsidized in one way or another by the British government.

In America a short-lived tax exemption has been our only form of government housing aid. If a garden city were to be projected it would be essential to have sufficient capital on hand to do most of the building of homes, factories and public utilities. A certain amount of financial assistance would probably be forthcoming from industrial corporations wishing to locate in the new community, but success might be jeopardized unless the garden city company had complete financial independence.

Furthermore, the success of land development enterprises depends perhaps to a greater degree in America than in England upon reasonable speed in the prosecution of the work. Taxes and interests on the cost of vacant land and public utilities accumulate rapidly. Even though a large amount of increased value results in the process of development, this increase will be absorbed by carrying charges unless the development can be carried out rapidly. Letchworth, in the days of its first growth, was favored by the lower interest rates then prevailing in England. In this respect Welwyn, the more recent English experiment, has been less fortunate. Both, however, received large amounts of money from the government at low rates of interest; such aid could not be expected in America. The financial problem does not seem insuperable, but it is a major difficulty.

The exact amount of capital required to make a success of such an experiment would vary in different localities and would depend upon the size of the city to be created. Between ten and twenty-five million dollars would probably be needed.

The third requisite for success is technical and organizing ability. The latter America possesses in abundance. As for technical skill, England has probably had more experience than America in town and community planning. But war housing as well as a number of large private enterprises have shown that we are not without skill in this important professional service nor can there be any doubt as to the ability of our technicians to adapt themselves to the problems which the new experiment would present.

We now come to the internal arrangements of the town itself. It would be desirable, if not essential, to make at least tentative arrangements in advance with industrial companies who would be ready to occupy sites in the new community. Given the rapid expansion that has taken place in many of our industries, it would not seem difficult to find such corporations. Whereas in the ordinary town an industrial corporation would face the difficulty of finding homes for its workers, in a garden city these homes would be provided. Not only would the industrial corporation be relieved of one of its major problems, but the housing available would be of a very superior kind, in ideal surroundings, and offered at moderate prices. Other necessary conditions, such as transportation, accessibility to a big city, climate, etc. being fulfilled, there is no reason to doubt that very favorable arrangements either as to the lease or purchase of land could be made with industrial corporations. But in order to eliminate possible delay, it would be desirable not only to make arrangements in advance with a number of industries, but, if possible, to begin the erection of a plant at the same time as houses and schools are being built.

Here arises a very real difficulty—the provision of inexpensive homes for common labor. In older communities it has been the practice to house those who are lowest in the income scale in left-over buildings, those that better paid workers would consider undesirable. New houses cost more than the unskilled can afford to pay. But in the new community there will be no left-overs. Everything will be fresh and new. Will not living accommodations be too expensive for unskilled workers? In England this difficulty has been largely met by government subsidy of one kind or another. In America we could not figure on assistance of this kind. Large quantity production, cheap land and the various economies that would result from the building up of the community in accordance with carefully drawn plans would help somewhat to reduce costs. It might also be possible to give the unskilled worker the benefit of at least a part of the increment which the development of a farming area into a large, flourishing community would bring about in the business portions of the city. Public utilities, the control of which would be kept by the garden city company, would probably be very profitable. Perhaps a portion of these profits could be used to reduce the housing costs for the lowest paid workers. A type of dwelling (similar to some of the houses that were built during the war) might also be developed to permit the subletting of rooms under better conditions than those which exist in a house or apartment not specially designed for the purpose. This idea was used by Andrew J. Thomas in his recent operation at Bayonne; a room and bath is located at the entrance to the apartment so that it can be leased to a roomer without disturbing the privacy of the home. It might also be desirable to give a partial tax exemption to houses whose value or rent per room was less than a given amount. In one or all of these ways it might be possible to reduce housing costs sufficiently to meet this difficult problem. In the new community, moreover, the worker would live near his work and would therefore save the car-fare and fatigue incident to a long journey back and forth from home to the factory. Certain goods would probably be cheaper, and an opportunity could probably be given to everyone to cultivate his own vegetable garden.

On the other hand, the difficulty of providing a decent home within the purchasing power of the lowest incomes would be somewhat increased by certain American habits. We are used to cellars and usually demand them. In England a cellar is dispensed with. We are accustomed to central heating. In England and on the Continent this is quite unknown in the small house. Our workers are accustomed to much better plumbing than those abroad. Even among families of a fairly low income it is becoming more and more general to use automobiles and therefore to require some sort of a garage.

On the social side, it would probably be harder to create a garden city here than in England. Our population lacks the homogeneity which simplifies the building up of a new community; the number and variety of races would create obstacles. In England, the popularity of the co-operative store and the familiarity of the man in the street with cooperative methods has been of great advantage.

It is undoubtedly easier in England to capture some of the advantages of a new model town than it would be in America. But these considerations go rather toward proving the greater need for garden cities here than to indicate any fundamental bar to their creation. Even more than England or the Continental countries, we need the relief which a new and better type of town planning afford. The real solution of the housing problem does not consist in the slight improvements which can be made in house planning—desirable as such improvements are. Fundamental progress will come only when the attack is made upon the entire problem. This can probably be done through the creation of garden cities by very large limited dividend companies.

Whether all the elements embraced in the official definition of a garden city can be applied in the United States is problematical. The most difficult of these would be community ownership of the land, particularly since we are not given to long leaseholds. The fact that we can impose proper restrictions even when land is sold would make such a provision less necessary. The desire of English and Continental town planners to conserve the land increment for the benefit of the community could be substantially carried out if the company retained the ownership of all store property, renting it only for comparatively short terms. The residential land, if sold with proper restrictions, would never increase very greatly in value. The practicability of the farming belt, and its size, would depend very largely upon the location of the new community and upon the availability and value of the land. The protection which this belt of open land is designed to give is just as much needed here as in England.

There can be no doubt that a garden city experiment is desirable and practicable in America. Every large city ought to have a number of these new communities grouped conveniently around it, competing with each other to solve the social problems which underlie the business organization of community life. All this can be done on a business basis, that is to say, through the investment of funds. Their gift is unnecessary. But the investment should be on a limited dividend basis. The business success of English limited dividend companies can be more than duplicated over here. Profiting by their experience, and aided by the greater resources of America, such an enterprise ought to be a great financial success. If the tremendous energy and resources which would be mobilized for such an undertaking were to be harnessed to that abundant store of idealism which is latent in us, splendid results might be looked for.

In the feverish rush of our huge, stone-encrusted cities we must seek some relief for the great masses of the population upon whom the evils of city life fall with the greatest force. Is it not time that we, in America, gave the garden city a trial?

II The First Statewide Planning

"We have been to a large extent the creatures of circumstances; we have permitted external forces to shape our lives, without making an effort to see how far these forces conformed to useful human purposes. With the powers that are now at our command . . . we may reverse this situation."

—Report of the Commission of Housing and Regional Planning

Introductory Note

When New York Governor Alfred E. Smith asked Clarence Stein to chair a state housing commission, Stein balked. He told the governor that he would undertake the post only if the commission's responsibilities encompassed regional planning as well. Governor Smith conceded and Stein became the Chairman of the New York State Commission of Housing and Regional Planning. Aside from a number of important housing reports directed toward a constructive housing program, the commission conducted the first statewide regional planning in the nation: *The Report of the New York State Commission of Housing and Regional Planning* to Governor Alfred E. Smith (May 7, 1926). Like most planning reports, it was largely ignored. Then, forty-five years later, the state's planners produced a plan strikingly similar in its broad outlines to the 1926 report. Realizing the ironic resemblance, the planners belatedly acknowledged that the commission's report "was ahead of its time."[1]

Mumford and MacKaye, among others, conducted studies for the commission. And although initially reluctant, Henry Wright eventually contributed the essential ideas and his distinctive illustrations to the following report.

1. New York State Office of Planning Coordination, *Development Plan—1,* (Albany, January 1971), p. 5.

Copies of the commission's report, complete with its illustrative maps, are rare; the state printed only a thousand of them. While this certainly contributed to the surprising obscurity of the commission's work, the report's radical message may not have inspired the state to further publicity. The report demanded massive public intervention in the private market. If the state actually implemented the commission's recommendations, urban property values would have been seriously undermined. During the booming twenties such ideas encountered strong and unified opposition from the business community.

The report actually falls short of being a final plan for the state, as its author admits. But it exemplifies the principles and methods of regional planning as the RPAA thought they should be. Despite the report's specific focus on New York State, the basic information describes the situation throughout the United States. As a demonstration of the RPAA's planning theory, the report continues to be relevant.

12 Report of the New York State Commission of Housing and Regional Planning

The ever-increasing concentration of population in cities and towns and the continuous depopulation of the countryside have given rise to problems in both city and country in which the State as a whole has a vital interest. The onward march to the city has resulted in rising urban land costs, a consequent intensification of land use which, in turn, further increases land costs and requires still more intensive use of the land. This unending cycle has already so over-burdened public facilities that every growing city must finance new public improvements in a measure far beyond its ability, with a resulting breakdown in street traffic and transit facilities, in public school equipment and all other public services. Attempts to relieve street congestion by widening streets and resort to mechanical devices serve only to exhaust the city's tax revenue and increase congestion still further. The staggering cost of needed rapid transit facilities is met by sacrificing schools, parks and playgrounds and even this offers no relief. The experience of New York City in subway construction demonstrates that by the time new subways are com-

Reprinted, with minor editorial changes and roughly half the original illustrations, from the State of New York, *Report of the Commission of Housing and Regional Planning to Governor Alfred E. Smith* (Albany: J.B. Lyon Co., 7 May 1926).

pleted they are already inadequate. They also serve only to develop new sources of congestion at the center.

The problem of the country is equally vital. Every year thousands of acres of land hitherto cultivated are abandoned to weeds and brush. Within the past forty-five years 5,700,000 acres of farm land in New York State have been withdrawn from cultivation. While the heaping of population into New York City creates the highest land values in the world, within a hundred miles of the lower tip of Manhattan land may be bought for unpaid taxes.

The unplanned, uncoordinated development of the past has given us the problems with which we are wrestling today. While the old forces that have shaped the present State are still operating, new forces have come into being to dominate the future. These new forces may be left free to alter the present mould without direction and without control. On the other hand they may be intelligently controlled. They may be directed toward a more effective utilization of all the resources of the State and thereby profoundly affect the future movement of population.

Two years ago the Commission of Housing and Regional Planning began this preliminary study of the relation of the resources of the State to its economic history. This is no academic study. Its purpose is the practical one of preparing for the future. This report is not a plan. It is a collection and analysis of some small part of the final data that will serve as a basis of future planning. In this study the Commission has attempted to ascertain and measure the forces which have shaped the present State and to evaluate the new forces which are now altering the present mould. Its purpose is to find a basis for a plan for the future development of the State. A plan of the State is not a thing to be willed into being by any one man or Commission or power. It is the result of many forces—physical, economic and social. Although it must rest on the unchanging physical conformation of the State, it is subject to constant revision as a result of changing habits and economic relations of men, and of their ability, through better understanding or invention, to harness nature to their need.

In carrying forward its studies the Commission has been more and more impressed with the need of a permanent agency for planning the physical development of the State. At the present time several State departments are engaged in the preparation of unrelated plans. Coordination may best be accomplished by a planning board in the Executive Department.

The Commission recommends the establishment of such a board with the personnel composed of the heads of the several State departments charged with the expenditure of funds appropriated for permanent public improvements, and representatives of planning boards created under chapters 267 and 539 of the Laws of 1925.

Forces Which Shaped the Present State

In little more than a hundred years the State of New York changed from a scattering of pioneer settlements in the virgin forest to a highly organized industrial community. Into that relatively brief period were crowded the stages of development which had taken centuries in the Old World. Various resources were exploited in response to the economic needs of different periods. One industry followed another. Population flowed and ebbed until the State we know today was produced. If we can lay the ground-work by seeing the natural features of the land to which the settlers came, if we can trace broadly the migrations and activities which ensued and if we can discover the causes for the changes which have taken place, we shall be in a position to know more about the future and how we may mould it.

The Natural Conditions
The Physical Conformation Topographically New York appears as a clear frame-work of hills separated by a great L-shaped valley system (Figure 4).

The latter is a belt stretching eastward from Lake Erie along Lake Ontario across the center of the State to the Hudson River which, with its bordering low lands, reaches southward to the sea. Connected with this system is an off-shoot continuing northeastward along the St. Lawrence River, while another strip of low land lies east of the Adirondacks, extending the Hudson Valley by way of Lake Champlain to the St. Lawrence and Canada.

Rising from these valleys are three great hilly regions, the Adirondacks isolated to the north, the other two joined to form a series of mountains

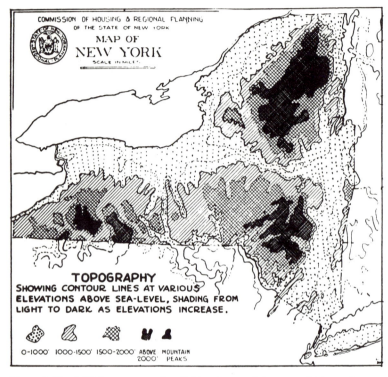

Figure 4. The 1000-foot contour line divides the state into areas which may be roughly contrasted. The lower regions form a system of connected valleys. The upland regions are grouped in three sections: the Adirondacks, the Catskills and the Alleghenies. The principal activity, manufacturing and agricultural, is found below the 1000-foot level. The valley system has had a far-reaching influence upon the development and changes which have occurred in the state.

and uplands along the southern border of the State from its western boundary to the Hudson River Valley. This great range is divided at its center by the narrow Susquehanna Valley which separates the Allegheny plateau in the west from the Chenangos and the Catskills in the east. In the extreme west the Allegheny River and in the east the Delaware make smaller and less important breaches in this wall as they flow southward.

The 47,654 square miles of the State are divided almost equally between the valley land or plains, the rolling upland, and the mountainous areas.

This physical conformation is the unchanging background to all the stages of development. Originally the State was covered by forests abounding in game. These widely distributed sources of wealth have largely disappeared. The richest areas now coincide with valleys and plains, the uplands and mountains being poor in resources capable of direct utilization.

The Great Valley The great valley L and the St. Lawrence offshoot are the regions most favorable to agriculture. In them are found the most fertile soil and the longest growing season. Though New York is not noted for mineral wealth, the most productive mines, wells and quarries, such as they are, are located in the low-lands.

Highland Reserves The highlands in turn contain the greater part of the still remaining forests. However, their importance is not limited to the service of their lumber. It will be noted that the mountain regions are, with the exception of that part of the Hudson Valley in the southern corner of the State nearest the sea, the areas of heaviest rainfall. If the uplands were wholly denuded, the heavy rains would wash down them rapidly and create floods in the valleys. The snows would melt more quickly in the spring. Between rains the rivers would shrink and the lower regions would suffer drought. Thus the forests regulate the delivery of water to the rivers which freshen the valleys.

Key Position for Trade As important as the configuration and resources of the State itself is its position with regard to surrounding regions. The natural trading routes which traverse it at an early date gave New York a key position. If we look at a map of the Atlantic seaboard, New York appears as a link joining New England on the east with the Great Lakes and Pennsylvania on the west. Two chief routes cross the State, one east and west, the other north and south. The first runs from Lake Erie across the central valley belt past the present site of Albany to New England. The second leads from Canada and the St. Lawrence by way of Lake Champlain and the Hudson River to the sea. The mountains along the Pennsylvania border prevent easy north and south travel west of the Hudson, except where they are broken by the Susquehanna River. The Green Mountains and the Adirondacks in the north, the Hudson and the Catskills in the south, discourage east-west travel except along the valley belt.

The key position and the trade routes supply the main reason for New York's first importance rather than the natural resources within the State.

Early Development

Fur and Trading Posts The ease of communication in eastern New York made possible an early development of the fur trade. The center of this activity was the junction of the natural routes in the vicinity of Albany. Trapping and the barter of hides and pelts was the first industry of importance in pioneer days and continued to stand high throughout the eighteenth century. In the five years from 1717 to 1722 furs shipped from the port of New York accounted for 15 per cent of the total exports, being valued at £47,867.

Lumbering, Rivers and Settlement After furs, the most extensive natural resources of the State were the forests. They have proved the only exhaustible resource of great importance. Lumbering proceeded steadily from the first settlement in 1620, overtook fur trading in value and then retained first place among the industries until about 1850. The accompanying maps show the progress of deforestation (Figure 5). Even more than the trapper the lumberman was dependent upon the natural water routes for transport. Lumbering operations followed the valleys.

The establishment of lumber camps and saw mills determined the sites of the earliest settlements. By 1810 there were nearly 500 of these settlements. Some were abandoned early, some became important towns and were later abandoned, some still are important, though the timber which created them has long been gone. Fully three-fourths still appear as names on the map.

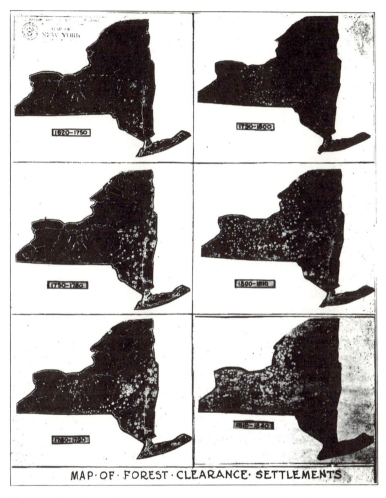

Figure 5. The primeval forest once covered the entire state. The white dots represent lumber camps and sawmill towns established during six periods from 1620 to 1840 and show how the forests of the state were gradually cleared away, leaving only one large timber area in the Adirondacks and smaller areas in the Catskills and Alleghenies.

Land and Independence Pioneers following in the wake of the lumbermen or clearing the land for themselves, established farms. The pressure of people was toward the land and independence.

The self-sufficiency of each family unit was so complete that in a letter to the Lords of Trade written in 1767, Governor Moore imagined it would last forever:

The custom of making Coarse Cloths in private families prevails throughout the whole Province and in almost every House a sufficient quantity is manufactured for the use of the Family, without the least design of sending it to market. . . . The price of labor is so great in this part of the world that it will always prove the greatest obstacle to any manufacturing attempted to be set up here, and the genius of the people in a Country where every one can have Land to work upon leads them so naturally to agriculture that it prevails over every other occupation.

Despite the high wages offered it was impossible to keep laborers in the towns. As it now seems perfectly natural to us that the sons of farmers should drift to the cities, so in that day it was the natural ambition of the townspeople to get out on the land. The population was widely distributed over the whole State.

Self-sufficiency of Farms Farms were established in regions that were later to become unprofitable for agriculture (Figure 6). It must be remembered that they were not unprofitable then. The change was due partly to the rapid exhaustion of the shallow soils of the higher, hilly districts. But there were other factors. Working on land already cleared by lumber operations, even though not especially fertile, often gave more immediate yield than expending the time and labor necessary to cut off the virgin forest in a district of richer soil. But the chief reason that some farms became unprofitable lay in the changed economic status of the farmer. When each family supplied practically all its own needs from its own efforts, when men wore homespun clothes and homemade shoes, used wooden pegs instead of nails to build their barns and shaped their own axe handles, even a poor farm could achieve economic independence. This was all that was desired.

Crops at this time were not converted into cash, but were used by the farm itself. For this reason there was no such thing as a profitable or unprofitable farm. Farms were simply more or less prosperous. The dif-

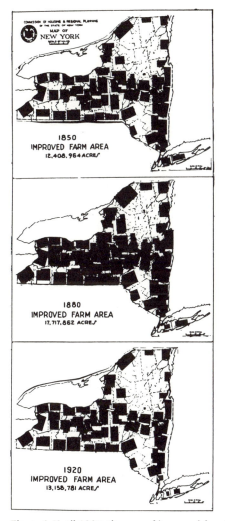

Figure 6. Until 1880, the area of improved farmland increased steadily. Then the vast areas of fertile land in the West made accessible by rail and water and the emergence of a national economy of interdependence forced an abandonment of improved farmland which in 45 years has amounted to 5,700,000 areas. (U.S. census.)

ference between a poor and a good farm was that one required more labor than another to support a family. In later years it was the necessary conversion of crops to cash with which to buy the manufactured products of the cities that brought the idea of profit and loss into farming. This change in the status of the farm has been gradual and is not even now complete.

Scattered Local Industry Meanwhile as the farms spread small local industries were built up in the villages, because the cost of transportation made it unprofitable to carry away the raw materials to distant centers and ship back the finished product. Saw mills already existed from the lumbering days. Others were built. Where grain was grown grist mills ground it into flour or meal. By 1825, 2264 such mills were scattered over the whole State. In the same year 1584 carding machines and 1222 local fulling mills prepared wool for the home looms or finished their product. Tanneries used local bark and hides. All factories which depended on power were of necessity located on streams where waterwheels could be installed. Local industry was part of the economy of the farm and not a thing separate. The farmer paid a fixed proportion of his grain and hides for the services of the miller and tanner. He did not pay money. It is only in relation to the outside world that local industry was on a money basis. Little by little canals were built forming a veritable network over the State, so that by 1840 or 1850 farm products could be transhipped and brought to tidewater at New York City. The Erie Canal, completed in 1825, was the backbone of the system which left practically no arable land in the State more than 20 miles from one of its branches. Stretched across the central valley belt, the canal joined Lake Erie with the Hudson. However, more commerce was carried on inside the State, not across it from outside regions, until the middle of the nineteenth century.

Spread of Population In the early days the population hugged the Hudson Valley, centering in its upper reaches and rapidly fanned out across the State, following lumbering, farming and local industry.

In 1790 the Hudson Valley and Long Island contained all but 17,000 of the State's 343,000 population. It is interesting to see that at that time the upper Hudson was more important than the lower Hudson or New York City. In the upper valley were 139,000 persons, with only 118,000 in the lower valley, and 69,000 in New York City and Long Island. Manhattan at the mouth of the Hudson was of course a trading center, important as a seaport both in foreign and coasting trade.

Between 1790 and 1840 the total population grew from 350,000 to about 2,400,000. It was more equally distributed over the State at the end of the period than at the beginning. In 1790 almost 80 per cent of the people lived on farms. From 5 to 10 per cent lived in villages of less than 2,500. A somewhat smaller number lived in larger towns, while about 10 per cent lived in what is now Greater New York. Throughout this early development men sought the resources which were most conveniently recoverable, without thought as to the future of the State. They were primarily interested, not in building up a community, but in pursuing their livelihood as best they might. They filtered in on the fur-trade routes. They followed up the rivers for lumber. They settled in cleared spaces. They started local mills to serve the farmers. Thus was passed on to the children of the pioneers a region chiefly agricultural, with many small, self-sustaining rural communities and a growing commercial center at the southern tip of the State.

Complete Noncentralization The whole period to 1840 was characterized by almost complete noncentralization, with small, self-sufficing communities scattered throughout the State—each raising its own food and manufacturing the greater part of its own necessities.

Yet already forces for change were making themselves felt.

Statewide Growth: Epoch One

Growth of Farms and Cities In the years that followed 1840 two distinct population movements are apparent. The first is a continuation of the movement already discussed, the movement to the soil. More and more land was brought under cultivation. The rural population and the farm acreage of the State continued to expand until 1880 when they reached their peak. Long before this growth had ceased, the second movement, the drift to the cities, began. Already in the early years of the nineteenth century the trend toward centralized manufacturing and concentration was manifest. By the early forties it had become a factor of primary importance in the life of the State. For four decades these two opposing tendencies continued side by side. This period we will call epoch one. What happened from 1880 to 1920 when the farm land steadily decreased and the cities grew with increasing speed will be discussed under epoch two.

Extinction of Forests Epoch one saw the exhaustion of the profitably exploitable timber resources. The development of the canals made possible the rapid clearing of land and gutting of the forests all over the State. The number of saw mills increased from 4,300 in 1820 to nearly 7,000 in 1835. By means of this rapid exploitation of the forests New York maintained first place among the timber-producing States of the Union until 1850. During the next ten years it had dropped to second place and thereafter declined rapidly.

The lumber industry was carried on without reforestation. When it had cut over the virgin growth it therefore ceased to be. The men it had employed were forced to join the growing mass of workers in the towns or settle on farms.

From 1840 to 1880 the acreage of improved farm land grew steadily from 10,500,000 to 17,700,000. Yet the population grew faster, so that the per capita areage dropped in these forty years from something over four to something under three and a half. By 1850 the State to an important extent had become dependent on other regions for its food supplies. This dependence grew at an increasing rate.

Transportation and the End of Self-sufficiency The development of the canals and more especially the building of the railroads made it possible to market profitably in New York the products of the fertile areas being opened up in the West. By the same means the manufactured products that were made cheaply in great manufacturing centers could be distributed far and wide by an improved technique.

The cities of New York State and those in neighboring States became the factories for the whole country. The state as a whole changed from a self-sufficient unit to a specialized part of a highly complicated economic empire. As this took place the scattered local industries found themselves unable to compete. Their gradual disappearance and the growing specialization within the State itself was an incident in the development of interdependence throughout the nation.

After canal and railroad had made travel easy across the State, an increasing flood of emigrants went on to the fertile plains of the Ohio and Mississippi Valley. As they established themselves their products began to come back for the more populous East or for Europe; in exchange for these products the manufactures and special resources of the East and of Europe were shipped to them in turn. Before 1850 the intrastate traffic on the Erie Canal was larger than that destined for the West or coming thence, after 1850 the reverse was true.

Steam and Concentration The growing importance of steam driven machinery both enabled and dictated this change in the economic structure. Already in 1840 this new motive power was coming into its own. When water wheels were the chief source of power, industry was of necessity scattered about the country (Figures 7 and 8). Between 1870 and 1880 steam passed water as the motive power in the industry of the State, having 235,000 as against 219,000 developed horse-power. Steam demanded that factories be located where fuel was easily obtainable, along the railroads or canals. Steam made larger machinery and increased production possible, forcing industry to seek wider and wider markets, and to fetch its raw materials greater and greater distances. Manufacturing thus came to be concentrated in those areas where transportation facilities were the best.

Transportation and Growth in Valley L Even before the railroads were of importance this requirement was met in the great valley L, which coincided with the main lines of the canal system (Figure 9). When in 1865 the combined tonnage of the railroads equalled that of the canal, the valley was still better served as regards transportation than any other part of the State. Factories crowded in. Towns sprang up and grew. So great was the influence of rails and coal that by 1875 the canals serving intra-state traffic, away from the railroads, began to lose their business, and one by one they were allowed to fall into disuse.

In 1810 textiles were principally made on the 33,000 looms in the homes, but factories were beginning to get their foothold. At that time 26 cotton mills were located in 15 counties with a total of over 12,200 spindles. Together with the 124 hat and 51 nail factories of the period these forerunners of modern centralized manufacturing were established in the towns.

The growing concentration of manufacturing is indicated by the increase in population in the towns. The cities of the great valley L grew rapidly (Figures 10 and 11). In 1875 this strip which represents about 20 per cent of the area of the State, held as many people as all the rest.

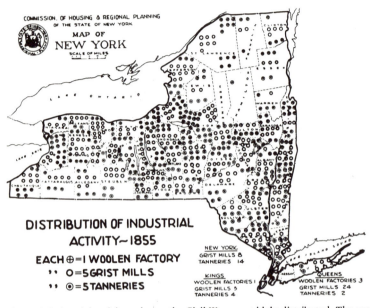

Figure 7. Industrial activity prior to the Civil War was widely distributed. The production and distribution of goods were localized, making each community virtually self-sufficient. (N.Y. State Census, 1855.)

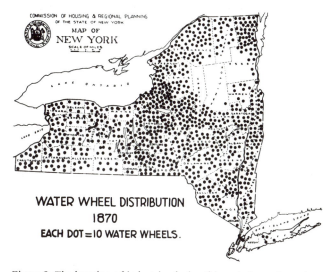

Figure 8. The location of industries during this period was dependent upon local waterpower development. (U.S. Census.)

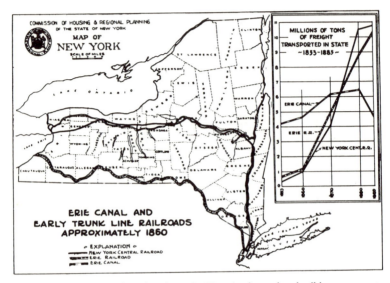

Figure 9. With the opening of trade to the West, both canal and rail improvement were developed in its interest. Lateral trade routes were neglected and even abandoned, as a result of which many districts otherwise favorable for industrial development fell into disuse.

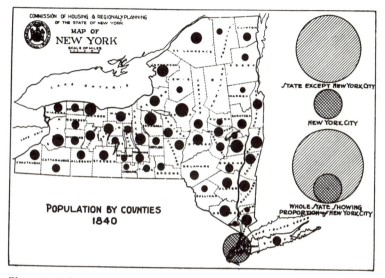

Figure 10. Relative population concentrations of New York in 1840. Comparison with Figure 11, which shows the 1860 distribution, indicates the influence of favorable transportation along the route of the Erie Canal. (U.S. Census, 1840.)

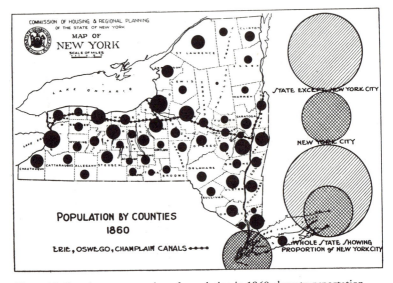

Figure 11. Growing concentration of population in 1860 along transportation routes in the valley belt. (U.S. Census, 1860.)

New York City, the Nation's Port We must not forget the importance of commerce as well as of factories in attracting population. New York City became the ocean terminus for a large part of the nation; it was at the same time closer to Europe by sea, better connected with the great West, and a better port than any other on the coast. The period of its most rapid rate of growth was from 1820 to 1860 when it changed from a city of 120,000 to a metropolis of 1,200,000. In 1840 it held 16 per cent of the population of the State. By the end of epoch one it was 38 per cent. Since that time New York City and the valley belt have accounted for nearly all the growth of New York State.

The factors dictating these changes in epoch one we shall find increasingly dominant throughout epoch two.

Urbanization: Epoch Two

Epoch two saw the complete breakdown of the independent economic units that composed the State. The city became the dominant organism, supplemented by the specialized farm. In studying this period, regional planning is primarily concerned with the reason for this change and its influence on the way of life.

Abandonment of Farms and Specialization Epoch two is marked by the steady abandonment of farm land, improved acreage decreasing faster than unimproved. In 1880 58 per cent of the acreage of the State was improved farm land. From this date to 1920 it fell to the 1850 level or 43 per cent of the total. Improved land was abandoned at the rate of 100,000 acres a year. The path of the shrinkage did not entirely retrace the path of the growth. There was less farm land in the Hudson River Valley than there was in 1850, and more in the western counties, especially along the Ontario frontier.

Important changes in the character of farming have taken place as well. Early in epoch one there was little specialization. Farmers in most regions raised mixed crops including much grain, and kept all kinds of live stock. During epoch two farmers specialized in dairying and in western and northern counties in fruit raising. On the other hand, in 1840 there were about 5,000,000 sheep in the State. In 1880 this had dropped to 1/3 and in 1920 to 1/10 of that number.

Competition and the more modern methods led not only to specialization but the abandonment of the poorer soil. The local market gave way to a wider one in which the cheaper products won out. The productivity of the better soil was increased, not so much land was needed for a given output; the better land could get along with fewer laborers per unit of product.

Disappearance of Local Industry Thus the local industries found their markets disappearing. We have already pictured the wide distribution of small saw mills, woolen factories, grist mills and tanneries at the beginning of epoch one. Figure 8 shows the wide distribution of water wheels in 1870, 7700 of which furnished the power for local industry. Epoch two was characterized by the abandonment of most of these local manufactures, and the concentration of larger and larger plants in the cities which sprang up in the L valley system.

The effect of these changes is shown most vividly in the population movements. The total population of the State was growing rapidly throughout both epochs but there is another important part of the story.

Decrease of Rural Population Let us analyze this growth first by counties. Between 1830 and 1850 every county in the State but one increased in population. Between 1910 and 1920, on the other hand, more than half the counties of the State decreased in population. In practically every decade between, the number of growing counties was fewer, and the number of shrinking counties was larger. . . . We see a state with gradually concentrating population.

. . . In certain counties . . . the population of the county as a whole increased but the growth took place entirely in the manufacturing centers, while the agricultural population declined. There were no such counties from 1830 to 1850. Three of them appear from 1850 to 1870. Between 1910 and 1920 there were eleven. . . . This shrinkage of the rural population which began in 1860 was so great that by 1920 there were fewer people living on farms and villages of less than 2,500 than there were in 1820. There were fewer people living on farms—leaving out the villages—than there were in 1810.

Growth of Urban Population in Valley L The two maps in Figure 12 comparing 1850 with 1920, and showing the proportion of the inhabitants of the various counties living in large cities present the picture in

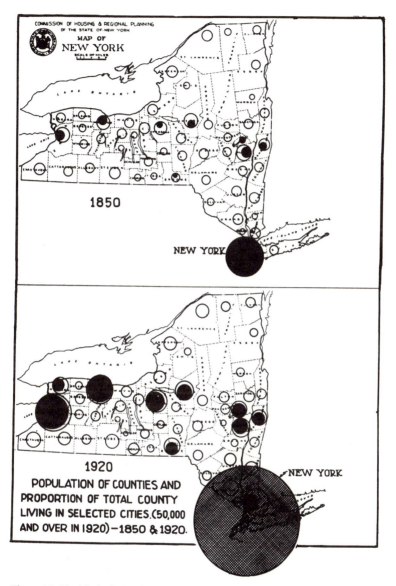

Figure 12. The black circles show the location of the eleven cities in the state having over 50,000 population in 1920. Their growth from 1850 to 1920 amounted to 680 percent and was 86 percent of the net growth of the state in that period. All but one of these cities lie in the valley belt.

another way. Eleven cities, each having a population of 50,000 or over in 1920, account for 86 per cent of the net growth of the State in these seventy years. They are New York, Buffalo, Rochester, Syracuse, Albany, Utica, Yonkers, Schenectady, Troy, Binghamton, and Niagara Falls.

All these cities except Binghamton lie in the great valley L. This belt which in 1875 contained only as many people as the rest of the State, in 1920 held four times as many. Its growth has been more and more rapid: In 1890 it contained but 68 per cent; in 1920, 80 per cent (Figures 13 and 14). The drift of population was not merely from country to city, it was from the rest of the State to the valley system—where most of the big cities established themselves.

Among these urban centers in which occurred the main population growth of the State, New York City takes first place (Figure 15). The expansion of the metropolitan area is the most striking example of concentration. In 1790 there were about 50,000 people in New York City, or one-eighth of the nearly 400,000 people in the State. In 1925 New York City, with its nearly 6,000,000 people, accounted for 53 per cent of the population of the State. All through epoch two New York City had a larger population and grew faster than all the other cities together.

The reasons for these changes are not far to seek. They lie in an intensification of the tendencies of the machine age. In the fifty years before 1921 the total horsepower of prime movers in New York State factories increased 900 per cent. Water was the principal source of power until 1879, steam until 1921, and now electricity has passed both and is 25 per cent more important than steam.

Meanwhile the primary horsepower per wage earner increased from 1.52 in 1899 to 2.84 in 1923. This means that larger and larger machines were being operated by one man. The per capita production grew, and per capita buying power and demands increased. The present number of wage earners in the factories of the State of New York, if they were to revert to the methods employed in 1899, would require over a million additional wage earners to maintain the present productivity, and these additional wage earners could be neither fed nor clothed without reducing the present living standard.

Self-Sufficient Farms in 1840 The way of life for the majority of the inhabitants of the State could hardly have changed more completely than be-

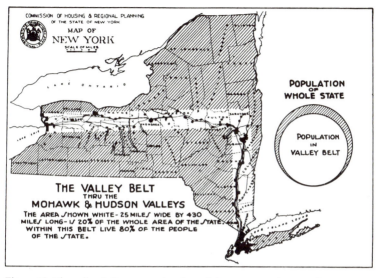

Figure 13. The valley belt or central region of the state contains over 80 percent of the total population. (U.S. Census.)

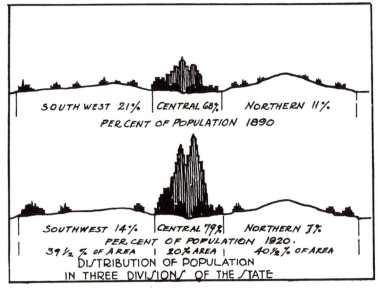

Figure 14. Geographic shift in population distribution from 1890 to 1920 reflects growing concentration in the valley belt.

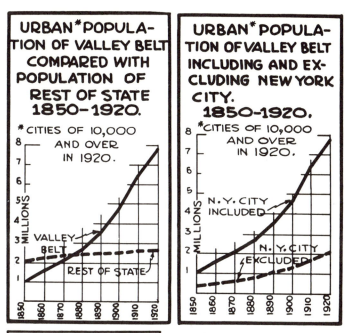

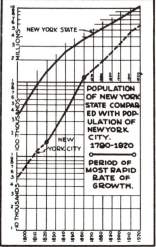

Figure 15. The changes previously discussed brought about the concentration of population in the valley belt and New York City.

tween the beginning of epoch one and the end of epoch two. In 1840 the typical citizen lived in a small almost self-sufficient rural community, about 500 of which were scattered all over the State. He might be on a farm, raising crops and tending animals, taking his wheat to the grist mills, his hides to the near-by tannery, his wool to the small carding, spinning and weaving plants which came to supplant clothmaking in the home. When he shipped his products to any distance, he would use the canals. The life had hardships and uncertainties of its own; it was rigorously simple and knew few luxuries. Both its advantages and disadvantages were quite different from those which we now know.

Gradually this society was broken down. The farmer began to want the manufactured products that the cities were increasingly able to supply. To meet these new needs he was forced to sell his products and change to a cash crop basis. With the development of the railroads he found the fertile lands of the West often able to undersell him even in cities near at hand. He naturally came to specialize in crops for which his land was best fitted or products with which the West could not compete. The process was carried so far that at the end of epoch two many farmers were buying staple food from the West for their own use, while they sold practically all their own products to the cities. Through the purchase of store clothes and farm machinery, of telephone service and motor cars, the farm was changed from an independent economic unit to an integral part of the specialized industrial system. Farms were no longer merely prosperous or unprosperous. They were profitable or unprofitable. **The Crowded City in 1920** Many of the farms that had been established on the poorer land were unable to compete when farming was put on this basis. These were abandoned and are still being abandoned. The population they supported was forced to move out to the fertile lands of the West or go to work in the factories of the growing towns.

At the end of the second epoch the typical citizen dwelt in the industrial center; he worked in a factory or an office with ever growing hordes of fellow employees and with automatic machinery always increasing in complexity. He lived often in congested tenements. His food and water supply came from greater and greater distances. Meanwhile many of the farmers found themselves hanging on to land no longer profitable. Their local markets had dried up. Only those who could ship to the cities continued to support themselves.

Such was the situation in New York State when, in 1921, electricity passed steam in importance as a motive power and the automobile had supplanted the railroad for many important classes of traffic.

New Forces Shaping the Future

We have seen that the social and economic organization of the State has passed through two periods. First there was scattered, small-scale industry serving local markets. It was the period of the water-wheel, hand-driven tools, the wagon road and canal and the town. Then came the age of steam, the machine, rail transportation and the city. The small plant gave way to the modern factory, sales forces canvassed the national market, the town declined, the city rose. In New York State the topography which determined the location of rail transportation forced almost all of the growth into one narrow valley that extends from Buffalo east to Albany and thence south to New York.

Electric Power and the Automobile Within the current century new forces have come into being: Long distance electric transmission and motor transport are among the most important. These are capable of altering the life of the people of the State in as striking a manner as did steam and the railroad. Electric power, made from the energy of falling water or at great central coal-burning stations and carried long distances at low cost, opens new possibilities of more available energy in the same way that steam did in an era of water-wheels. The automobile, motor bus and truck may have quite as marked an effect on industry as had the railroad.

Long distance transmission of electric current should make possible the introduction of technical methods that result in the production of cheaper energy. Large scale generation is itself more economical. At the same time it allows the recovery of valuable by-products that are lost in the small plant. The plant may be located at the coal mines or source of water power. The cost of transmitting electrical energy is much lower than that of shipping the equivalent energy in the form of coal. Furthermore the interconnection of generating systems allows the exchange of current between widely separated areas, thus equalizing the load and reducing the effect of a break-down that is a hazard in the case of local generating stations.

Supplementing Steam by Electricity Electrical energy therefore has the technical and economic possibility of supplanting local steam power. Figure 16 indicates the trend in New York State. Now the primary horsepower of motors driven by electric current is greater than the power in steam plants and steam power is actually decreasing.

Electric Power and Decentralization The introduction of electric power and particularly the development of its long-distance transmission have tremendous possibilities of influencing the social and economic pattern. When factories depended on steam power, the machinery had to be located near the boiler. The boiler in turn could only be set up where coal could be delivered cheaply, that is, at tide-water or on a railroad. When local electric generation began, the driving belt was lengthened. The power station needed to be on a railroad siding or tide-water but the factory was free, so far as its power requirements were concerned, to locate within the distributing radius of the station—a matter of miles. Now comes transmission for hundreds of miles. The generating station may be at a source of water power, the mouth of a coal mine or any other point where coal and water may be cheaply brought together. The power requirements of the factory place no practical barrier to its location anywhere. It may have energy at almost the same cost inland or at tide-water, in the valley or the highlands, at the rails or in the country.

The Motor Car and Decentralization Within the last fifteen years the motor vehicle has become an important means of transport. This year there are about 2,000,000 motor vehicles in New York State—more than one for every six persons. As a result of motor traffic there has been built up a net-work of hard surfaced roads, miles of which are added every year. The present projected highway system will embrace 14,000 miles of improved road in ten years. Thus we have an entirely new transportation system. Unlike the railroads it can extend as a net over large areas. It is flexible and capable of quick adaptation to new routes. Furthermore, roads may be built with a sharper grade than railways and therefore hills present less of a barrier.

The influence of motor transport has not yet made itself fully felt. The changes which it may introduce in social and economic life are very great. Factories which formerly located on the rails may now make short hauls of both raw materials and finished product by motor. Estab-

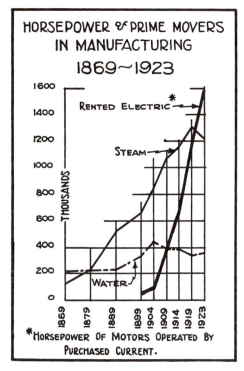

Figure 16. Industry is no longer either limited in its location by the uncertain supply of local waterpower as in Epoch I or tied close to the railroad for its coal supply as in Epoch II. The purchase by industry of electric current from central stations is the most important factor in opening opportunities for the better location of industry and people. (U.S. Census.)

lishments which were held to congested centers by the proximity of an existing labor supply may now draw workers who come in their cars or buses from greater areas. People themselves may be freed from crowded districts and enabled to get to work from suburban regions.

Enrichment of Farm Life Finally both electric power and motor transport remove certain of the objectionable features of farm life. Good roads and the motor break down the isolation of the farm. The motor also extends the area over which farms may serve urban centers with perishable products. Cheap electric power lightens the drudgery of farm life. Certain of the forces which have driven people from the farms to the cities may therefore be removed.

These forces make decentralization possible. They do not compel it. Are there any indications that a redistribution of population is probable? What forces are at work that may lead to a reversal of the trend of population that characterized the last part of the nineteenth century and the early years of the twentieth?

Social Cost of Concentration The primary costs of intense city concentration are the loss of human values. New York City shows these costs in more exaggerated form than any other. To a lesser degree they exist in every other city of the State. With the passing of rural or small town life have gone natural facilities for recreation. For the open field is substituted the city street with its constant stream of traffic. For woods and mountains are substituted parks. An artificial recreation grows up: pool rooms, moving picture theatres, dance halls and a host of other good, bad and indifferent forms of commercialized amusement. The home has suffered; the shadows of pyramiding land prices steal across one window after another until in the characteristic tenement in New York City two out of three rooms are sealed in perpetual darkness or twilight. The narrow canyons keep out not only light but air.

The reaction against these conditions is shown in the pressure to escape to suburban life. For the wealthy, the town and country house has long been familiar. The year-round suburban homes of salaried and professional men have been rapidly increasing in number. Since 1920 one of the most marked movements of population has been the attempted escape of the artisan from the congested center to new developments in outlying areas.

Economic Wastes of Congestion These costs are imponderables. They have exerted less influence on our development than the economic forces making for concentration. It is possibly indicative of future trends that congestion breeds economic resistance to further growth and has raised physical problems that so far defy solution. The Commission has already shown that land prices increase more rapidly than population and that to maintain the high land prices more and more intensive use must be made of the city land. An industry in a large city can only compete with plants in smaller cities if the city yields some compensating advantages. The lower land prices of the small center give it a great competitive advantage. As the city grows it must inevitably lose some industries which thrived while the city itself was smaller.

Transportation of both persons and freight becomes increasingly expensive as the city grows. The crowding on the New York subways is perhaps one of the imponderable social costs. But the increasing length of the haul is an economic fact whose consquences may be measured in dollars and cents on the tax bill. The congestion of city streets has slowed down the movement of goods. Street widening, one-way streets, non-parking regulations and elaborate traffic control are resorted to— and ultimately in the most congested area private, personal vehicular traffic is forbidden during the day. We are forced to ration the use of our street system. The larger city has higher per capita costs of government. These costs are in large part due to the assumption of new activities by the municipal government:[1] the provision of parks and playgrounds, extended duties of the health authorities. All of these costs must be absorbed in the cost of living.

Factors Impeding City Growth The large city can maintain its position only through an initially higher productivity that goes to pay for the excess costs of its operation. Any change in technique that breaks down this differential productivity operates against the large city.

It is apparent that there are new forces making for a change in the social and economic pattern. Long distance electric transmission and the motor remove certain of the limitations that forced economic ac-

1. See report of Commission of Housing and Regional Planning on Cost of Government, Land Value and Population, by Donald H. Davenport, January, 1926.

tivity into congested areas. The increasing costs of operation in the large city will impel certain industries to escape to smaller centers now that power and transportation are available there. Not all industries will be effected alike. But change is in the air. What will the pattern in the future be like? What pattern, that is allowed by the state of the technical arts, will carry with it the highest social values? How may the shaping of this most desirable pattern be controlled?

The Need of a Plan

The economic and social pattern is always in a state of flux. However, there are periods of unusual activity. For decades at a time there may be a marked drift in a particular direction. We now appear to be on the threshold of a period in which a strongly marked new trend will be established. Long distance electric transmission and motor transport offer potential release from the centralizing pressure. The apparently insoluble problems—physical, economic and social—that are raised by the pyramiding city may force a change.

Coordinated or Uncoordinated Development

In such a period the activities of a large number of bodies tend to shape the future pattern. The arrangement and location of transportation facilities is most important. A town becomes stagnant that has held a key position in one transportation system and is relegated to a less important position under a different system. Oswego was an important city during the period of canals. It was the lake terminus of the canal from Syracuse. It still has rail connection with Syracuse, but the rail service gives Oswego a relatively poorer position than did the canal. On the other hand, the Erie Canal made Buffalo the terminal for waterborne freight. In the decade during which the canal was completed (1820-1830) Buffalo increased in population 313 per cent. The development of large areas is now being controlled by the location of transmission lines. Again the location of a large industry may make a town, as when the General Electric Company located in Schenectady. Lackawanna is wholly a city by edict. So also the fixation of rates by public utility commissions has great influence. The uniform freight rate fixed to the harbor of New York has prevented a differential arising that would strengthen the competitive position of New Jersey harbor cities against the New York water front.

The problem therefore arises whether these activities shall be related to a general plan or shall be controlled only by the most proximate considerations. The uncoordinated economic planning that has characterized our past development neglects imponderable social values. A business man can only remotely concern himself with the conditions of life of his workers. Granted equal economic opportunity in two places, he may choose the one in which his workers may lead the fullest life. But he does not balance good homes against productivity. The aim of the State should be clearly to improve the conditions of life rather than to promote opportunities for profit.

Obviously there is need of a plan to which at least activities of the State shall conform. The action of the State will strongly influence some private developments. At this point the effective control by the State ends. The experience of planning organizations has indicated, however, that many individual business men are glad to call upon the knowledge of such authorities in developing their own plans. While such cooperative planning cannot be dictatorial, there is every reason to suppose that it will result in a healthier, better-organized social structure than we now possess as a result of our virtually planless development.

Growing Recognition of Need of Planning

Growing recognition of the need of intelligent direction and coordination of future development is evident in recent local planning activities throughout the State. An awakened interest had developed in problems of land utilization, in the control of traffic, of bulk, height and use of buildings, in the provision of adequate recreational and park areas in towns and cities, and in the extensive planning of physical improvements authorized by local, county and State governments. The past two years have marked unusual progress in city planning in Buffalo, New York City, Rochester, Utica, Syracuse, Schenectady and many of the smaller cities of the State. It is significant that in all this planning the dominant motive has been to plan not only the urban, but also the rapidly growing suburban areas where the immediate problem is becoming acute.

Planning activities in New York emphasize more and more the relation of the urban area to the suburban countryside and to the entire region. This regional point of view has not always prevailed in the initial stages of the city plan, but has been a logical outgrowth of local planning experience.

At first there has been a desire on the part of city planning authorities to shape the growth of the surrounding areas with relation to the growing needs of the urban center. The need for decentralization and the march to the suburbs has extended the city's influence into all the adjacent towns and villages. The growing influence of the city is responsible for a tendency toward urban domination of suburban life—a tendency which, though understandable, is laden with serious potential dangers. The desire of the city to impose its plan on the surrounding region has led to more than one attempt to extend the city's legal authority and planning control beyond the urban limits. In almost every instance this extension of authority has been opposed by the surrounding towns and by the county, and this opposition has been sufficiently influential to prevent the extension of municipal planning powers by the Legislature.

The opposition to the extension of municipal authority over surrounding areas is more than the familiar repulsion of urban influence. It involves the jealous regard for local autonomy, the objection to loss of any local powers now enjoyed, and the suspicion, sometimes justified, that the city plan extended will mean the loss of all those distinctive values, social as well as economic, which are characteristic of the surrounding area as a whole.

This apparent impasse, created by conflicting interests, demonstrates the ineffectiveness of obsolete forms of local government and the need for a type of government that can function regionally. This need has been emphasized by Thomas H. Reed, Director of the Bureau of Government of the University of Michigan. Speaking before the National Municipal League,[2] with regard to the problems of the Pittsburgh region, he said: "The most serious question which confronts students

2. Nov. 18, 1925. See Reprint, Vol. XV, No. 2, February, 1926, *National Municipal Review.*

of municipal government today is the development of some form of governmental organization through which these problems can be met. . . . Recognizing that there are certain governmental needs in the region which can be met only by some form of governmental organization extending throughout the region, there are three possible methods by which the extension of such governmental authority can be secured: First, by the creation of special authorities for each particular need (for example, the London Metropolitan Police District); Second, by the consolidation of all powers of local government throughout the region in a single authority; Third, by the establishment of regional government of limited powers leaving in existence the existing units of local government."

Although the first of these suggested methods has been most frequently used, and despite the recognition of the apparent advantages in efficiency and economy of the second method (that of consolidation of all local powers in a single authority), official regional planning in New York State has progressed through the cooperation of locally autonomous governmental units.

This method has been justified by more than its regard for prevailing local sentiment. It derives from a concept of regional planning dominated by an objective quite different from that of urban or metropolitan planning. This concept is expressed in the following words of Lewis Mumford: "The forces that have created the great cities make permanent improvement within hopeless. Our efforts to plan them lag pitifully behind the need when indeed they do not foster the very growth that is becoming insupportable. We are providing, in Professor Geddes' sardonic phrase, more and more of worse and worse. Not so with regional planning. Regional planning asks not how wide an area can be brought under the aegis of the metropolis, but how the population and civic facilities can be distributed so as to promote and stimulate a vivid, creative life throughout a whole region—a region being any geographic area that possesses a certain unity of climate, soil, vegetation, industry and culture. The regionalist attempts to plan such an area so that all its sites and resources, from forest to city, from highland to water level, may be soundly developed, and so that the population will be distributed so as to utilize, rather than to nullify or destroy its natural advantages. It sees people, industry and the land as a single unit. Instead of trying, by one desperate dodge or another, to make life a little more tolerable in the congested centers, it attempts to determine what sort of equipment will be needed for the new centers. It does not aim at urbanizing automatically the whole available country side; it aims equally at ruralizing the stony wastes of our cities."[3]

The conservation and the future development of the resources of a region to the end that an economic gain may not involve inevitable social loss, requires the preservation of all existing natural values both of the country and of the city. This does not mean the complete subordination of country to urban influence. It demands for the time being at least, the retention by local governments of all the powers which they now enjoy. But it further requires experience in cooperation and authority to act in concert with local governments.

One year ago, acting on recommendation of the Commission of Housing and Regional Planning, the Legislature amended the Municipal Law[4] to authorize any county or counties to establish and maintain out of local tax revenue a regional planning board to consist of representatives of the cooperating county and local governments. These boards are empowered and directed "to study the needs and conditions of regional and community planning in such county or counties and propose plans to meet such needs and conditions. . . ." Their function is advisory only, the appropriation for and the execution of plans being controlled by the local legislative agencies.

Acting under a special statute granting similar powers, the Niagara Frontier Planning Board was established April 9, 1925. The Niagara Frontier, comprising the entire counties of Niagara and Erie, lying along Lake Ontario, the Niagara River and Lake Erie, bordered on the south by Cattaraugus Creek and its gorge and on the east by the counties of Orleans, Genesee and Wyoming, covers approximately 1,550 square miles. It contains one of the most valuable natural resources in the world. The future importance of the region to the rest of the State and to the country as a whole cannot be overestimated.

3. *Survey Graphic*, May 1, 1925, p. 151.
4. Chapter 267, Laws of 1925.

The Niagara Frontier Planning Board was the direct outgrowth of pre-liminary conferences held in Buffalo and Tonawanda under the auspices of the Commission of Housing and Regional Planning in 1924. In September of that year a regional planning association was formed with a membership representing all of the cities, towns and villages in the two counties. By action of the association the official Niagara Frontier Planning Board took form without legal sanction in anticipation of legislation authorizing the establishment of such board and appropriations to cover the board's expenses. The board consisted of the mayors of six cities in the region and three representatives from each of the Boards of Supervisors of Niagara and Erie Counties. This board began to function with the cooperation of both local and county governments as early as November, 1924. With the enactment of the special statute a permanent chairman was elected, appropriations were made by the Boards of Supervisors of Niagara and Erie Counties to defray the expense of the Board for the first year of its operation, and a technical staff was appointed and located at Tonawanda. During the first year the Regional Planning Board has acted in a cooperative capacity as an intermediary between the State Council of Parks, the Erie County Park Commission and the State Reservation at Niagara in the development of a system of parkways for the region. The result of the studies of the board, in collaboration with these organizations, has been a proposed system which has been added to the map of the State Council of Parks after formal approval by that body.[5] The board adopted a program for regional planning study in the Niagara Frontier prepared by the Bureau of Housing and Regional Planning and has assembled data, prepared maps and investigated problems relating to and carried forward specific undertakings looking toward the development of a plan for the region as a whole.

Following the lead of the Niagara Frontier, regional organization has been undertaken in other parts of the State during the past year. A movement has been started looking toward the planning of the entire region comprised within the Genesee Valley.

5. For further details see First Annual Report of the Niagara Frontier Planning Board, 1925.

By action of the County Board of Supervisors of Onondaga County with Syracuse as a center, a Regional Planning Board has been established.

A Capitol District Regional Planning Association has been created through the cooperation of mayors, village presidents, and other official representatives of cities, towns and villages together with members of the Boards of Supervisors of Albany, Schenectady and Rensselaer Counties; and a Central Hudson Valley Regional Planning Association was recently organized. Both of these organizations are working toward the creation of official regional planning boards.

From the standpoint of metropolitan planning, the most important regional planning work in the State has been carried forward since 1922 by the Committee on the Plan of New York and Its Environs organized and supported by the Russell Sage Foundation. With the assistance of able technical advisors and planners this voluntary committee has undertaken the planning of a region comprising an area of 5,528 square miles, lying in three States and including about 400 organized communities, of which New York City is the center. This region, within a radius of 50 miles from the Metropolitan Center, in the words of Frederick A. Delano, Chairman of the Committee, "is tied together by common economic and social interests and by many problems not capable of solution except by united action of all authorities within the area." The purpose of the plan has been further described by Mr. Delano as follows:

"The plan being prepared by the Committee has for its general object the formation of the best form of development of areas within the region for industry, business, residence and recreation and the best system of circulation in connection with traffic and transportation. The plan must be comprehensive not only as to the extent of the area to be dealt with, but also as to the estimate of all the inter-related problems of community growth in the area." The Committee has already completed and published many valuable studies and surveys relating to physical and living conditions and has produced a series of monographs in connection with its economic and industrial survey, together with studies of the legal possibilities and limitations of the problem with reference to questions of zoning, city planning and the acquisition of land for public use.

Regional planning in the State of New York is already moving in the direction of a plan for the State as a whole. As has already been pointed out, local agencies control and will continue to control city and regional planning. It remains, however, to fill in the details of a State plan into which regional activities may fit and without which local efforts are likely to be checkmated. State bond issues for roads and other permanent improvements, if they are to be expended with greatest benefit to the State and local communities must be used with reference to a general plan.

Controlling Considerations For The Future
The State has a vital interest in planning. But what sort of a plan will be developed? What consideration must control?

The Commission of Housing and Regional Planning attempts in this report only to suggest certain board outlines in tentative fashion. A plan for the State cannot be mapped in advance in all its details and filed for reference. It must have life; it must grow. Only certain basic principles may be established to which the pattern will conform in its growth.

In planning for the future it might be assumed that on account of the greater flexibility of electric power and motor transportation on the one hand and the problems arising from concentration in large cities on the other, we would drift back into a situation much like that of epoch one, with small centers scattered all over the State. That, however, would be an unwarranted assumption.

It will be remembered that our survey of the State's resources showed that the most valuable regions for intensive utilization, even for agriculture, lie along the valley systems. Furthermore, decentralization of industry even under the new conditions cannot in most cases proceed far from the railroad trunk lines. So far motor transportation has tended to replace the railroad for local shipments and to supplement the short branch feeders of the railroads. What we must visualize is a civilization based on the valley pattern, but making a fuller and more intelligent use of it than at present. The uplands and mountains must also be employed as reserves of forest, for water catchment and recreation. No new conditions have arisen or are likely to arise that will make these areas fit to be primary centers of manufacture, farming or population.

The best utilization of the State must be governed by the physical contour and distribution of resources. Man cannot alter the main outlines of what nature has given him. Only by recognizing the basic natural conditions can he fit himself to exercise intelligently the control which he has over his own activities.

The more fertile soil and the most valuable geological deposits lie almost entirely in the areas below the 1,000-foot level—the L Valley, the Ontario shore, and the narrow strip east of the Adirondacks. In these regions climatic conditions are most favorable to agriculture. The composite map in Figure 17 shows clearly that farming as well as manufacturing and commerce belongs to the lowlands.

In planning for the future all these factors must be taken into consideration. The extreme scattering of population in epoch one involved an attempted utilization of resources much of which turned out to be low grade (Figure 18). In epoch two much of this area was abandoned (Figure 19). No new forces have developed that make its recovery for other than forestry seem desirable. In fact there are still many hundreds of thousands of acres of substandard land held in use for farming purposes that should be added to our forests (Figure 20).

On the other hand, a fuller economic utilization of the better regions of the State is possible today than was attained in epoch two, a utilization that will involve decentralization rather than concentration within the limits of the valley system. In conjunction with this development of the lowlands must come an increasing appreciation of the services which the uplands may render; the potentialities of new scientific lumbering, of a great playground for the millions who live in towns and of the water power stored in the hills. With such a development the State in the future may assume the general form suggested in the map of "Epoch three" (Figure 21).

A Broad Forecast

Certain portions of the State are admirably suited to form a complete social organism. The sort of development which should be anticipated may best be illustrated from the region bordering Lake Ontario and the St. Lawrence River. This is shown in Figure 22.

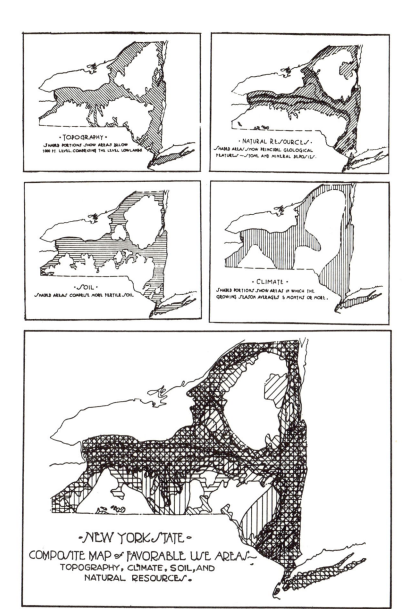

Figure 17. These maps show approximately the regional distribution of favorable agricultural areas and natural resources. Their superposition results in a composite of areas that are generally favorable for more intensive development.

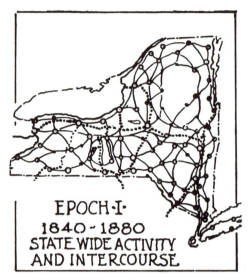

EPOCH·I·
1840 - 1880
STATE WIDE ACTIVITY
AND INTERCOURSE

Figure 18. Rapid development of natural resources; small towns economically in-dependent; industry served by local waterwheels and canal system; all widely dis-tributed over state. Toward end of period drift to new rail lines had set in.

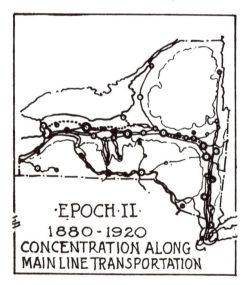

·EPOCH·II·
1880 - 1920
CONCENTRATION ALONG
MAIN LINE TRANSPORTATION

Figure 19. Development of central rail routes, change of industry to steam power and competition in agriculture of fertile west combine to concentrate growth in central valley belt and undermine the industrial prosperity of towns off main line transportation.

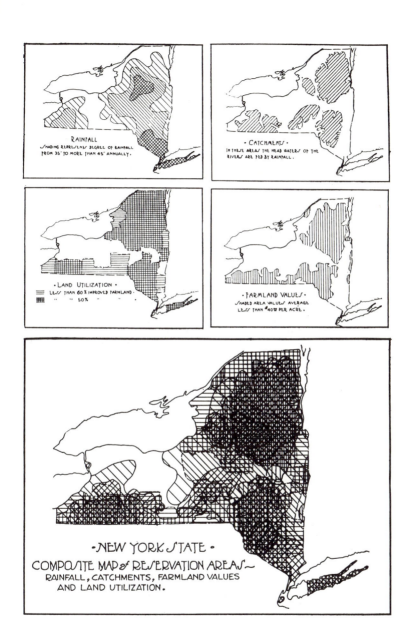

Figure 20. These maps show approximately the regional distribution of areas unsuited for agricultural and industrial development. Their superposition results in a composite of areas more suited for reforestation.

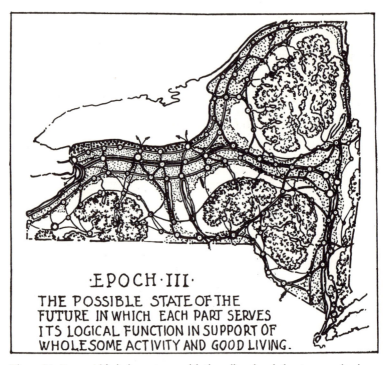

Figure 21. Comparable in importance with the railroad and the steam engine in determining the character of development in the second industrial epoch are the modern factors of the automobile, good road, and electric transmission line. These modern forces do not portend a return to the widely distributed development of the first epoch. Rather they will lend themselves to a more effective utilization of all of the economic resources of the state and to the most favorable development of areas especially adapted to industry, agriculture, recreation, water supply, and forest reserve.

FOREST RESERVE   DAIRYING
WATER SUPPLY   GRAZING   GARDENING·MANUFACTURING·ORCHARDS
HIGHLANDS · UPLAND PLATEAU · FERTILE PLAIN · LAKE

Figure 22. Visualized regional development of typical section of state extending from the shore of Lake Ontario across the fertile lowlands and rolling uplands, into the higher slopes of the Allegheny and Adirondack mountains.

From Niagara County on the west to St. Lawrence County on the east the low table-land along the water front has excellent soil and a mild climate. In this section of Monroe, Wayne and Cayuga Counties the average growing season is 170 days. A growing season of more than 160 days is found throughout this belt in all counties except St. Lawrence.

Large water power resources are found in the Niagara Falls and in the St. Lawrence and Adirondacks. The power in the last two is capable of operating extensive industry throughout the eastern part of this belt. The belt is served by the railroad, the Barge Canal and Lake Ontario.

At present the lowlands along the water front are devoted to fruit raising, the manufacturing cities are located in the table-land from 400 to 600 feet elevation. On still higher land are other farms. But though the general utilization of the region as thus described conforms to the ideal suggested, the actual development does not take full advantage of the great resources of the region. The district is not integrated. Cities like Rochester, Buffalo and Syracuse have grown to such a point as to introduce problems of planning, traffic and housing that might be avoided if smaller industrial centers were developed. The vast industrial and agricultural activity of which this entire region is capable must be related to the hinterland. The lower hills, rising 1200 to 1600 feet above sea level are favorable for dairying and grazing. The highlands should serve for forest reserve and water supply. Access to these and to the beautiful Finger Lakes section in the center of the State would provide recreational escape from the cities. With foresight and planning, such a region might take full advantage of all its resources and might provide a setting for a multitude of prosperous and healthful communities.

State Planning and Basic Needs

A plan like this is but a broad outline, simple in concept but complicated in application by a multitude of details and difficulties which are bound to modify its form and influence its accomplishment. The scope of the present investigation has not been sufficient to forecast, except in a most general way, the extent and nature of these problems. Yet, once the basic conception is accepted, certain projects fall naturally into place so that we may broadly suggest the more desirable developments.

For example, in the matter of agriculture the dependence of New York on the rest of the United States may be too great. For many years the State has not grown enough food to sustain its population. In many respects, as has been previously shown, it has become more economical for New York to rely on other States for products such as wheat, beef and mutton. But, with the steady increase in population, both within the State and outside it, with increasing transportation costs, and with development of all the best land elsewhere, this tendency may easily be pushed too far. Agricultural authorities have already pointed out that it has again become profitable to raise wheat within the State. With accurate knowledge of soils, climate and modern methods, and with proximity to the cities, New York farmers may little by little find it profitable to raise a larger proportion of the State's food.

But both agricultural authorities and farmers must base their operations, not only on knowledge of methods and soils, but on a logical arrangement of cities, farm zones and transportation routes. If, with a proper decentralization of city population, farming zones could be laid out near the cities, the farmer would have a better chance for a good living and a full life. The State might point out such opportunities to those who are still clinging to unprofitable uplands but do not know where to go unless it be into a factory.

The same principles hold true as to the utilization of forest reserves and the great water-power resources of the State. Their development is interdependent.

Water supply for the cities is intimately connected with the preservation of the forests, and with hydroelectric power, which requires dams, reservoirs and regulated flow. Coordination is necessary among the cities which are beginning to infringe on each other's regions of supply. New York City has not only exploited a large part of the Westchester watershed with the Croton reservoir, but has crossed the Hudson, reached into the Catskills with the Ashokan and Schoharie Reservoirs, and tapped the Mohawk watershed in upper Schoharie. There is now projected a tri-State development of the Delaware River for further needs (Figure 23).

The time is not far distant when we must make an allotment of the limited water supply among the large cities, and adjust it to the needs of hydroelectric power. This is an engineering task which cannot be

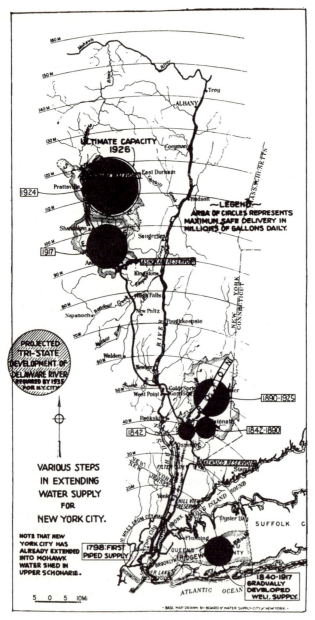

Figure 23. Diagram showing the progressive steps in supplying water for New York City. The most recent extenstion invades the Schoharie Valley, a region tributary to the Mohawk River above Albany.

successfully accomplished without reference to the State plan, having in mind the future distribution of population, with its power and water needs.

The location of public service utilities involves automatically the exercise of powers which must determine future use and value of large areas of the State. A wise control over the exercise of such power and a coordinated plan with respect to distribution of power and other forms of service is essential to the preservation of the State's interest in its own future.

A State Plan and Local Planning

Into this general scheme fit the plans and projects which various regions are making for themselves. The local region is the unit which must, in most cases, initiate action and carry out concrete details. A State plan will not attempt to limit this local action with hard-and-fast outlines; it would, rather, attempt to help the several regions solve their problems by bringing out the relationship of their special situations to outside conditions.

In local planning towns, villages and cities have found that they have many common problems which can only be solved by coordinated action, *i.e.,* by regional planning. So also these regional units will find that there are general problems which must be met by the joint action of neighboring regions: *i.e.,* by State planning. This broad plan and policy, whose need has been shown in this report, must grow from the experience and requirements of the integral parts.

The details of a State plan must be based upon accurate and comprehensive knowledge. The first requirement is a complete "land economic survey" such as that which is being undertaken in Michigan. An industrial economic survey is no less necessary.

In order to make the plan a living and growing thing, it must be contributed to and consulted by every important State department and by many private interests as well, whenever an important decision is to be made. The Park Council, the Water Power Commission, the Conservation Commission, the framers of taxation policy, the Public Service Commission, the highway authorities, manufacturers, bankers, railroads, power companies, local governments—all these and more should coordinate their activities because their decisions are related to most of the important planning problems and are actually interdependent. The achievement of such a coordination must be intrusted to some State agency close to the central executive who can keep in touch with all these varied activities and point out their relationship to each other and to the plan whenever a concrete problem arises. Without such an informed agency of liaison, coordination would be impossible. With it the habit of cooperation may be induced among the various authorities concerned, and the means of cooperation provided.

To broaden out the valley belt, to develop logically the undersettled regions, to give aid to farming and lumbering, to prevent further over-centralization in cities while assisting economy for the manufacturers by proper use of hydroelectric power, to coordinate water supply and to furnish a proper basis for local action—these are some of the objectives of a State plan.

The State has no more imperative duty than to foresee, to plan, and to assist in conducting such development. Up to now we have been too greatly at the mercy of blind chance and of our necessities. We have been to a large extent the creatures of circumstances; we have permitted external forces to shape our lives, without making an effort to see how far these forces conformed to useful human purposes. With the powers that are now at our command, with the technical insight and the social vision which the State can now summon to its service, we may reverse this situation: instead of being the passive creatures of circumstance, we may become more and more the creators of our future. By using nature and machinery intelligently, we can make them serve our human purposes. This is the final aim of the State plan.

III   Regionalism: Some Ends and Means

"Regionalism is only an instrument: its aim is the best life possible."
—Lewis Mumford

"A mechanical culture, such as ours, cannot sustain economic stability if allowed to drift with the winds of free competition and the unlimited pursuit of private profit."
—Stuart Chase

Introductory Note

In July 1931, four members of the RPAA—Henry Wright, Benton Mac-Kaye, Lewis Mumford, and Stuart Chase—delivered papers at the Round Table on Regionalism, a conference held at the University of Virginia's Institute of Public Affairs. Other members of the New York group also attended the conference, which the RPAA helped organize to gain public exposure for their ideas. The Round Table occurred at a particularly significant historical moment; well after the 1929 stock market crash but before the New Deal. What lends special historical importance to the event was that Clarence Stein persuaded New York Governor Franklin D. Roosevelt to address the gathering. Charles Ascher recalls Roosevelt describing the idea of a TVA in an off-the-record question-and-answer session that followed his speech.[1] Although no mention was made of that proposal, the speech itself made the front page of the *New York Times.* Others at the conference do not remember any reference to a valley authority but assume that the meeting may have influenced some of Roosevelt's presidential policies.

Regardless of whether the conference had this transcendent impact on national policies, it had real importance for regionalists at the time. Be-

1. Interview with Charles Ascher, 9 September 1974.

sides the public exposition of the RPAA's ideas, the Round Table brought many regionalists together for the first time, including southern regionalists like J. G. Fletcher and H. W. Odum.

Only two of the speeches are reprinted in this volume—Stuart Chase's and Lewis Mumford's. Mumford's speech encompasses the whole sweep of regional planning. It offers a particularly concise description of the region and its relationship to culture, the environment, and political institutions. He outlines a new ecological ethos about land use to replace the dominant practice of extracting whatever financial advantages the land offers and then abandoning it. And finally, in defining the regional planner's enormous task, Mumford constrasts metropolitanism to a new form that he describes as a regional city. This address was an important overture to his book, *The Culture of Cities,* which appeared seven years later.

Stuart Chase's speech deals with economic planning, an idea once again in vogue today. In his speech Chase predicted that little would come of the idea during that depression, although it would surface again during subsequent economic crises. His speech highlights economic planning as one of the essential tools regional planners will use to establish a new settlement pattern. Besides the obvious function of guiding investment to specific locales, economic planning could help set national or regional policies to insure that citizens receive a greater share of the wealth they help to create. Chase's government service during the First World War launched his lifelong interest in the social benefits of economic planning. As a member of the technical staff of the first American trade union delegation to the Soviet Union he studied the Gosplan, their first five-year plan. His favorable assessment of that plan appeared in *Soviet Russia in the Second Decade,* a book he edited with Rexford Guy Tugwell and Robert Dunn in 1928.

13 Regional Planning

Lewis Mumford

Regional planning is a name that covers, at present, a variety of different activities. It is important, at an early stage of the movement, that we should arrive at a common meaning. It differs in the extent of the unit covered from city planning, and since it includes urban areas as well as rural ones, it is another matter from country planning. At the same time, it differs essentially, as I shall show, from metropolitan planning, a type of planning which has at the moment taken over this useful word for its own special work. Perhaps the best way to define regional planning is to establish what is meant today by the "region."

The eighteenth century saw the decay and the final destruction of many types of corporate organization that had flourished in the Middle Ages. To the progressive minds of the eighteenth century, humanity was an undifferentiated mass of individuals: if they had any special historical and political identity in groups, it was that which they achieved as members of the state. The city and the region ceased to have, politically, their separate identity; they became in theory creatures of the state; and for purposes of state these natural groupings were often com-

Lewis Mumford, "Regional Planning," (8 July 1931, Address to Round Table on Regionalism, Institute of Public Affairs, University of Virginia), Avery Library, Columbia University.

pletely ignored. As a result of the revolution of 1789 in France, for example, the historic regions were broken up arbitrarily into a series of administrative departments, which ignored the historic boundaries and affiliations.

In the colonization of America beyond the eastern seaboard this habit of creating artificial boundaries, drawn on the map with the aid of the ruler, without regard for the actual possibilities of settlement and development, was driven to absurd lengths, partly by sheer haste, partly by ignorance of actual resources, and partly by political theories which sought to override the facts of nature. The new states, with their subdivisions defined by the section and the quarter-section, were drawn up without the slightest respect for actualities. Many of our states are even "defined" by river boundaries despite the fact, which the geographers of the nineteenth century were to establish, that the river is a highway and a means of intercourse, not a barrier; so that, except for temporary military purposes—an exception which the airplane has wiped out—it is the worst of all possible boundaries.

The great states of the world, still more their minor administrative districts, are the products of political forces and events which have only accidental relations to the underlying geographic, economic, and social realities. Their boundaries, their subdivisions, antedate for the most part our present scientific knowledge; they also antedate and ignore the instruments of communication and traffic that have made the world as a whole, for many fundamental purposes, a single unit.

Now, the human region existed as a fact, long before the political state as we know it came into existence. The region continued to exist, even though it was ignored and to no small degree frustrated by the prevailing theories of politics. But it needed the development of human geography to establish the region on a scientific basis. This was something that has taken place in almost less than a hundred years, thanks to a succession of able minds, Humboldt in Germany, Buyot in France, George Perkins Marsh in the United States, followed by Ritter, Reclus, Vidal de la Blache, Le Play, Herbertson, and Geddes—to say nothing of our own contemporaries in America like Fenneman, Mark Jefferson, and J. Russell Smith.

The geographer points out that mankind has not spread out in a formless undifferentiated mass, if only for the reason that the surface of the globe prevents this kind of diffusion. The major land masses divide naturally into smaller units, with special characteristics in the underlying geological structure, in the climate, and consequently in the soils and the vegetation and animal life and available mineral deposits. In each of these natural regions, certain modes of life have arisen in adaptation to the fundamental conditions: these modes have been modified by previous cultural accumulations and by contacts with other peoples, since no region is completely isolated from even distant neighbors, nor can it be, even in the most primitive stages of culture, self-sufficient: did not flint and jade and salt, even in the earliest dawn of history, travel thousands of miles and pass through many hands before they were finally used?

But the geographic environment sets a limit to the types of work that can be economically done, and predisposes favorably certain lines of activity; and this in turn profoundly modifies the social habits and institutions of the inhabitants. There may be mines without miners, just as there may be mulberry trees without the culture of silkworms; hunters may attempt to get a meager living out of an area that will yield a handsome living only to a high state of culture by irrigation and social effort: all these facts, which the ethnologist is quick to point out are indisputable; but in regions that have been settled over a considerable period, the underlying possibilities of the environment have been explored, and its uses are more fully exploited. Apart from its selective influence upon occupations, the region provides a common background: the air we breathe, the water we drink, the food we eat, the landscape we see, the accumulation of experience and custom peculiar to the setting, tend to unify the inhabitants and to differentiate them from the members of other regions.

These regional differentiations do not deny the facts of individuality or the facts of universality. As for the first, Marcel Proust, in the second volume of *Remembrance of Things Past*, has put the relationship with great clarity and intelligence.

Last of all, and even more general than the family heritage, was the rich layer imposed by the native province from which they derived their voices and of which indeed their intonations smacked. Between that province and the temperament of the little girl who dictated these inflexions, I caught a charming dialogue. A Dialogue, not in any sense a discord. It would not have been possible to separate the girl herself and her native place. She was herself; she was it also. Moreover, this reaction of locally procured materials on the genius who utilises them and whose work their reaction imparts an added freshness, does not make the work any less individual, and whether it be that of an architect, a cabinet-maker or a composer, it reflects no less minutely the most subtle shades of the artist's personality, because he has been compelled to work in the millstone of Senlis or the red sandstone of Strabourg, has respected the knots peculiar to the ashtree, has born in mind, when writing his score, the resources, the limitations, the volume of sound, the possibilities of flute or alto voice.

There are forces in existence, universal ones, which work in precisely the opposite way; these, too, are not excluded in the concept of the region. The lanes of international travel and trade, the spread of a universal religion like Mohammedanism or Christianity, or of a universal technique, like that of western science and mechanical invention, the existence of a common fund of ideas and interests tends to break down regional differentiations and to establish a universal basis for the common life. A regionalism that affected to ignore these forces would be absurd and stultifying for the presence of universal agencies does not wipe out the realities of regional life: it merely unites them to a greater whole. One must create an identity, a center of one's own, before one can have fruitful intercourse with other personalities. This holds true, too, for the relations between regions. It is only in the dangerous theory of the all-powerful and all-sufficing National State that self-sufficiency within political boundaries can be treated, as it now is, as a possibility; and it is only in war time that this mischievous notion can be even momentarily effectuated—albeit with great suffering to the underlying population.

While the recognition of the region as a fundamental reality is part of the achievement of modern human geography, the recognition of a closely knit inter-regional life is no less so: indeed, geography wipes away the notion of definite boundary lines as anything but a coarse practical expedient; since such political lines forget not merely one nature of the region itself, but the natural zones of transition and the highways of movement, which tend to break up such formal definitions.

During the last thirty years, there has gone on a steady attempt to define the major natural regions of the world and to study in more detail their human subdivisions; for, with the addition of man to the scene, the facts of history must be superimposed on those of geography, and along with the conditions of climate and topography and natural resources must be included those alterations in the environment which are recorded on our maps under the name of "culture"—to say nothing of these non-material transformations and accumulations which cannot easily be projected onto a map. There is still much work to be done in regional geography; but already its results are far enough advanced to show that our present political divisions ignore a good part of the major realities with which we have to deal. It is not an accident that in France, for instance, one of the early proposals to reapportion the political administrative departments came from the eminent geographer Vidal de la Blache.

The region then, as it is disclosed by the modern geographer, has a natural basis, and is a social fact. The term cannot without deliberately passing by all the work that the geographer has done, be applied to any large area. A city is not just a city when it is bounded by a circle with a five-mile radius, and a region when it is bounded by another circle with a fifty-mile radius. We obviously need some name to cover our large urban agglomerations, actual or possible; but "region" is not a happy one. Professor Geddes long ago suggested the name *conurbation* for a collection of cities forming a more or less continuous growth: but the term has not caught on, and until a better one can be coined, it would be as well to call such a collection a metropolitan area. Planning such an area, though its radius were twice as great, would still be metropolitan planning, not regional planning: it would be city planning on a large scale, and not regional development. Does this suggest that there are factors in regional planning which do not exist in metropolitan planning? That is exactly what I mean. Let us examine these factors.

The first different factor in regional planning is that it includes cities, villages, and permanent rural areas, considered as part of the regional complex. While metropolitan planning regards the surrounding open country as doomed to be swallowed up in the inevitable spread and increase of population, the regional planner seeks to preserve the balance between the agricultural and primeval background and the urban environment. Easy access on the part of the city resident to the country, equally easy access on the part of the country dweller to the city, are necessary to their culture and education. A type of metropolitan development which makes such intercourse difficult, tiresome, unfruitful, must, the regionalist thinks, be deliberately overcome. Metropolitanism is in fact another form of land-skinning. In the interests of urban growth, rising land values, opportunities for financial killings, it ignores the natural capacities of site and soil, and continues to spread a uniform urban layer over the countryside.

This urban layer lacks for the most part the cultural and commercial advantages of the central district of the metropolis quite as much as would a destitute rural area the same distance from the center: but the massing of population it creates tends to increase and bolster up financial values at the center. Regional planning, on the other hand, begins not with the city as a unit in itself: it begins with the region as a whole and it seeks to bring every capacity of the region up to its fullest state of cultivation or use. This does not mean filling up the land with an undifferentiated urban mass; nor does it necessarily mean, on the other hand, decentralization. But it may mean weeding out, by transplanting to more favorably situated centers, part of the population of the congested metropolises of today; since the assumption that they are bound to grow continually on the lines they have followed in the past is fundamentally an assumption that planning is impotent, except to facilitate results which would take place anyway without planning.

The second important factor in regional planning is its respect of balanced environment and a settled mode of life. The city growth and land colonization of the last century ignored both these factors of balance and settlement. We created the coal-agglomeration and the financial metropolis, seeking quickly to extract coal and iron from the soil, and to organize industry so as to produce a maximum profit to the investors; in the act of paying attention only to these limited ends, we forgot to create orderly, healthy, hygienic, and esthetically decent environments. While our cities produced pig-iron, textiles, coal, chemicals, money, in quantities the world had never seen before; they also produced an appalling amount of human misery, degradation, sordidness, which mocked all our fine pretensions to progress and enlightenment.

We produced an environment that in part—its inefficiencies were so great that one must stress this phrase—in part was good for machines and money-making: but it was not good for men. It was not a lively and educative and recreative environment. Art, culture, education, recreation—all these things came as an afterthought if they came at all, after our one-sided preoccupation with industry had ruined a great many of their potentialities, both in the life of the individual, whose health and intelligence had been sacrificed to material gain, and in the life of the community. When the pioneer had skinned the soil, he moved on; when the miner had exhausted his mine, he moved on; when the timber cutter had gutted out the forests of the Appalachians, he moved on. All these social types left rack and ruin behind them. The regional planner points out that no civilization can exist on this unstable and nomadic basis: it requires a settled life, based on the possibility of continuously cultivating the environment, replacing in one form what one takes away in another. Regional planning is concerned with provisions for the settlement of the country; and this settlement in turn implies a balanced use of resources and a balanced social life. Both these conditions are impossible in an unbalanced environment.

This brings us to the next important conception of the new regionalism: namely the regional city. What is the proper size of the city? That is a question that never occurred to anyone, apparently, except a few utopians, in the nineteenth century, although Aristotle and Plato both thought it of great importance, and the people of the Middle Ages, by their continuous schemes of urban colonization, certainly had definite notions on the subject, even if they did not pass into learned literature. It was Sir Ebenezer Howard who first suggested in *Tomorrow*, published in 1898, that the city had a natural limit of growth: that beyond this point it became inefficient, and that further growth must be taken care of as the beehive does—by swarming off, by colonization. We have not yet sufficient knowledge to say how many different types of city and satellite and village are appropriate to our life today, and what the limits of population in those various types are: but we can at least put the question to ourselves and suggest in what direction an answer lies.

The size of a city cannot, plainly, be defined by its actual or potential boundary lines; for anyone, with sufficient hardihood and a sufficiently large compass, could merely carry the method of metropolitan planning to a logical conclusion by describing a circle with a radius a thousand miles around Chicago and say that this was all potential Chicago territory, to be filled up by continuous growth from the loop outward within, say, a thousand years. No: the size of a city cannot be determined by a superficial area to be filled: it is related to the institutions and functions to be served. Primarily, the city differentiates itself from the rural area, from the market center by itself, and from the industrial unit, by the institutions which serve the cultural and educational life of the inhabitants. Farms, markets, industries are the basis of its existence: but its end, as Aristotle would have said, is the cultivation of the good life. A definite relationship can be established between the population and its civic institutions. Twelve hundred families, for example, can support a modern public school: if one doubles the number of families, one must double the number of schools. A still larger population is necessary for a high school, and one must draw on something beyond the immediate local area for a college or university. Similarly with other functions: fifty thousand people might support a well-equipped maternity hospital; but it would require many times this number to supply a sufficient number of cases for a cancer hospital. There is no reason whatever that, with modern transportation and communication, any one city should attempt to provide for every possible human function. Even New York does not succeed in doing that: there are certain types of operations for which one must go to Rochester, Minn., or to Johns Hopkins, if one wants the highest degree of skill, just as there are certain works of art for which one must still go to Florence or Madrid or Amsterdam.

Now, the major common functions of a community can plainly be taken care of in towns of from five thousand to a hundred thousand population quite as well—frequently much better—than they can in a vast megalopolis. But there are special institutions which require a large basis of population, and it would be futile to duplicate these in small communities and unfortunate to do without them: they must be produced on a regional scale. This suggests that the new regional pattern will be a constellation of related cities, separated by parks and permanent agricultural areas, and united for common projects by a regional authority. Each city would have all the local institutions necessary to its own effective life, local shops, schools, auditoriums, theaters, churches, clubs; and in addition each center would perhaps tend to specialize on some one institution of culture or social life, a museum of natural history in one center, a radio broadcasting station in another, a university in a third. Modern transportation and communication remove the necessity for the continuous urban agglomeration; they make this new pattern of cities possible. Each city would perhaps be a regional center for at least one function; but no city would attempt to be the regional center for everything. Without such a pattern as this, it is impossible to do away with the congestion of the central districts and our present waste of resources in providing temporary palliatives for this congestion—palliatives whose effect is speedily ruined by the further congestion that must follow in order to pay for the costs. The undoubted advantages that come with the massing of a great population in the metropolis would be even more available in a well-wrought network of regional cities. In contrast to the metropolitan planner, the regional planner seeks to establish new norms of city growth and to create a fresh pattern of regional and civic activities. To discover these various norms, to relate them to civic functions, and to embody them in communities is one of the major functions of the regional planner.

Finally, regional planning differentiates itself from metropolitan planning by its respect for new and emergent elements in our civilization. The metropolis is a large and unwieldy unit: it represents an enormous vested interest of capital, and it necessarily will take no steps that are likely to displace the real and imaginary values that have been created. As the metropolis increases in magnitude, it becomes more and more committed to the mistakes of the past, and these mistakes are more and more costly to rectify, even when they have become unbearable. This reason alone would be sufficient, if no others were important, to justify the regional planner's interest in small-scale communities: flexibility, ease of adjustment to a new situation, the speedy utilization of new mechanical and scientific advantages, all these things are more easy in a small community than a great one, provided that the intelligence is there to take command. Do we need to widen an avenue? It is easier if the buildings are four storeys high than forty. Do we need an aviation field? In New York the distance of the landing field from the center of the city nullifies the greater speed of the airplane over the railroad train on short journeys. Do we wish to take advantage of the auto or the autogiro? Once we have escaped the congestion of the metropolis it is far easier. The small industrial town may have its housing congestions, its slum area, as well as the metropolis: on a small scale, conditions may be even worse, for lack of any public conscience or remedial measures. But in the small town there are not, as in the metropolis, tremendous physical and financial obstacles to solving it.

The radio, the moving picture, the airplane, the telephone, electric power, the automobile—all these modern utilities have only increased the potential advantages of the region-as-a-whole over the congested metropolis: for with these instruments, the unique superiority of the more congested areas is removed and their benefits are equalized and distributed. Regional planning can help to realize positively all the important achievements of the new age: metropolitan planning exhausts itself in temporarily alleviating the disastrous results of its own elephantine and unregulated growth. Once the region becomes again the center of organized intelligence, as it was in the Middle Ages, as it is today in certain parts of Germany and France and Spain, the superiorities of region over the merely metropolitan area will become manifest. The region as a natural and human grouping is a fact. Regional cities and regional development are possibilities: regional planning itself is an attempt not to ignore these possibilities, in the interest of finance or abstract growth of population, but to make the fullest use of them. Regionalism is only an instrument: its aim is the best life possible.

14 The Concept of Planning

Stuart Chase

Not many days ago I was discussing the current furor as to planning
with the dean of the Yale Law School. "Why," he said, "it is getting so
that one is as loath to appear on the street without a Five Year Plan
as without his trousers!"

As a charter member of the Regional Planning Association of America,
I am strongly tempted to ascribe the whole outbreak to the cumulative
effect of the astute propaganda of that organization. But, alas, as an
inquirer after truth, I know that we are not the primary motivation. It
is a combination of Russia and a certain October 29th. The pie which
Mr. Hoover promised us was stolen—doubtless by designing Democrats
—while the economic, political, and moral systems of besotted Bol-
sheviks, which were written off the books of every Great Thinker as a
total loss not later than 1923, are going, if the expression be permitted,
like a house on fire. Even Great Thinkers, dusting the sand from whis-
ker and eyebrow, are admitting, with a singular lack of graciousness,
that the Russian Five Year Plan, whereby some thirty billions of new

Reprinted with minor changes from Stuart Chase, "The Concept of Planning,"
(11 July 1931, Address to Round Table on Regionalism, Institute of Public Affairs, University of Virginia), Avery Library, Columbia University.

industrial and agricultural capital is to be invested in half a decade, has a reasonable—if deplorable—chance of success. This combined with the morning after the big bull market—several mornings in fact—provide reasons enough for the planning pandemonium. I wish it had been our devoted little band of regionalists which inspired it, but it was not.

We have, however, unprecedented opportunity to exclaim, "I told you so!" For a decade we have maintained, individually and collectively, on all occasions, to everyone who would listen, that the choice of a machine age lay between planning and chaos. Now we awake to find, among others, Mr. Matthew Woll and the dean of the Harvard Business School in bed beside us, chanting our slogans in whole or in part. Indeed, our couch, once so cozy, seems to extend practically to infinity; even the full fashioned hosiery industry has reserved a pillow. Mr. Hoover, it is true, refuses to lie down and continues to stalk like Hamlet before Elsinore. He has split the unsplitable by announcing a plan without planning. In twenty years, he tells us, through those sublime processes—by guess and by God—the lowliest American will be embarrassed by the magnitude of his material possessions. Which is, as it may be.

But Mr. Charles A. Beard, who, it seems to me, is a better engineer than Mr. Hoover, says:

> Is the concept of national planning merely another transitory fad, an idle fantasy born of day-dreaming and destined like a thousand others to pass away to-morrow or the day after? The answer seems to be an inescapable negative. All Western civilization is founded on technology, and of inner necessity technology is rational and planful. The engineer must conform to the inexorable laws of force and materials. Technology cannot begin anything without first establishing a goal, a purpose. To proceed at all it must stake out a field of work; then in execution it must assemble materials and engines and carry on its operations according to blueprints until it reaches its predetermined ends. With irresistible might it strides across the wild welter of unreasoned actions, irrelevant sentiments, and emotional starts and fits which characterize historic politics, agriculture, and industry. As technology advances, occupying ever larger areas of productive economy, there will be a corresponding contraction of the spheres controlled by guesswork and rule-of-thumb procedures. This means, of course, a continuous expansion of the planned zone of economic activity.

In brief, if we are to elect the machine—and we have so voted—we have got to plan. To me the logic is utterly inescapable.

For the moment, we regional planners stand vindicated, not only by engineering common sense, but by hitherto inarticulate economists, professors, lawyers, senators, congressmen, editors, bankers, manufacturers, merchants, labor leaders, and heaven knows whom besides. Indeed, so unanimous is the sentiment that our duty in the premises is to keep the cardinal word *regional* from being altogether buried by more grandiose conceptions. Which brings us to a résumé of the various conceptions of planning. I shall borrow heavily from a survey I prepared very recently for the editor of the *Atlantic Monthly*.

A handicraft culture needs no systematic planning of its economic life. Each local area is self-sufficient. A mechanical culture, such as ours, cannot sustain economic stability if allowed to drift with the winds of free competition and the unlimited pursuit of private profit. A million cogwheels must mesh if food, shelter, and clothing are to be obtained. Today many of the gears are out of order. Why should they not be, since nobody makes it his business to keep them aligned and oiled? Even in times of so-called prosperity, the creaking is prodigious. Witness the plight of American farmers from 1922 to 1929, the utter disorganization of the textile industry and of bituminous coal mining.

Under these circumstances it is the contention of reasonable men that if we are to have a mechanical civilization we have got to control it. This means centralized planning; the same procedure for the economic region, the nation, perhaps the whole continent that an efficient manufacturer employs in his own office. He must organize his shop and correlate production schedules to probable demand. We must make the cogwheels mesh—or else retreat, after a frightful cataclysm, to the stability of the handicraft age.

Let us turn our attention to what might be termed the theory of master planning. What area does it cover; what types of economic activity are included; how is the planning machinery set up? The triple aspect—geographic, economic, political—is cardinal to any plan. The variations within these three dimensions are, of course, endless.

Area may range all the way from the whole planet to a small local community. The Supreme Economic Council of the Allies in World War I was the nearest we have dared to come to world control, while *town planning* has been a commonplace in America and Europe for decades. The latter has ranged from vague committees of earnest citizens with no power, no money, and no tangible objective, to complete towns, blueprinted and built from the ground up, like Letchworth and Radburn.

The world, although it grows smaller every day, is still too big to accomodate any plan not frankly utopian. In *Men Like Gods*, H. G. Wells has supplied perhaps the most stimulating of the utopian designs. The World Court and the League of Nations are the first feeble flutterings in this direction, unless one includes the gyrations of the oil, copper, and silver interests now endeavoring to restrict production. We shall probably see more and more of these international groupings.

Town planning, for all its admirable function, is altogether too small to be dignified by the term *master planning*. The latter by definition connotes an attempt to come to terms with the machine. Rome knew town planning, and Athens, and Chichen-Itza. Today we need to plan because of the specialization introduced by the industrial revolution, which, unregulated, leads to overproduction and unemployment. This specialization knows nothing of town boundaries, but operates in units of continents or more. A continental plan for North America would comprehend from 90 to 95 percent of the goods and services necessary to self-sufficiency, but here again Canada and Mexico might view co-operation with the colossus in the middle of the map with justifiable apprehension. But a plan for the United States or for Russia is not beyond the limits of reality. Both are large enough and sufficiently equipped with natural resources to approach stabilization. The point is not so clear for an island such as England.

From the psychological point of view, if not that of pure engineering, the best unit is probably the *economic region*. By that is meant an area which embraces unity of soil, climate, general topography, and racial mixture. New England is such a region, and so is the corn belt, the cotton belt, or the Northwest zone of wheat and timber. The sight of a New England village green after a long absence brings a mist to my eyes. This is where I was born, my homeland, the place I love. The Alps look cold and bleak beside the White Mountains of New Hampshire. One signboard on the Mohawk Trail hurts me more than a hundred on the Rocky Mountains; and I am content to view Los Angeles as one glittering cosmetic container. Human beings, in spite of their rushing about at fabulous speeds, are lost without a place to root. This does not mean a house as much as waving prairie, high plateau, undulating meadow land, sand and cliff and sea. Regional planning designed to make the home country fairer, happier, more to be loved is perhaps the only sort of master planning that will some day arouse the emotions of the wayfaring citizen. The competitive element supplies additional motivation. Our region shall be cleaner, more desirable than the one next door. To date, this valuable incentive has been exclusively responsible for gentlemen's buying by the acre and selling by the front foot.

So much for theories of area. Where shall the economic lines be drawn? A master plan, it seems to me, must include all economic effort that furnishes the ordinary citizen with the necessities and reasonable comforts of a civilized life. This means food, shelter, clothing, public health, education, and the rudiments of recreation—such as a great system of national and regional parks. The coordination of a specific industry—coal, copper, or railroads—however excellent and useful it may prove, is not master planning. It falls under the head of control, perhaps; but master planning must mean correlation, synthesis, meeting the challenge of specialization in the machine age. To control leather, while letting hides run wild on the one side and shoes on the other, lands us precisely nowhere—however it may affect the balance sheets of the embattled leather men. It is possible, however, and indeed necessary, to accent the essential industries and to neglect—beyond the stage of raw-material control—the superfluities and the luxuries. Thus wheat and lumber should be in the conning tower spotlight, while golf balls, cigar lighters, toys, and platinum rings should hover in the shadow. Another distinction might be drawn between the established, one-line industries where technical achievement approaches standard practice, and new, developing industries. Steel is an example of the former; airplanes of the latter. Planning should keep its hands off the new industries so far as is consistent with public health and safety, and permit them to work out their own salvation in the domain of *laissez-faire*, allowing the profits and losses to fall where they may. Only when the youngster has matured should he be admitted into the control area.

We turn last to the political area. How shall the planning mechanism be set up? We are forced to admit that history points strongly to the state. The Incas, the Pharaohs, the imperial trade of Rome, the War Industries Board, the Supreme Economic Council, the Gosplan, have all been agencies of the central government, although the War Industries Board was run largely by businessmen in cooperation with regional groups of businessmen. In the United States there is more ability and energy in the business community than in any other group. If industry itself chose to take charge of the planning machinery, and really marched on overproduction, unemployment, business cycles, and low standards of living, I, for one, would raise no objection. Even if profit ranges were excessive at times, one could not complain too bitterly if the main objectives were achieved. We do not care who controls the wild horses, as long as they are effectively controlled.

The control we are considering must pass through two stages—the drafting of the plan, and its administration after adoption. The first is passive, the second active. I see no future for master planning without mandatory powers in the second stage. In Russia, the Gosplan is theoretically an advisory body, but it is incorporated in the extremely powerful Department of Labor and Defense; its suggestions are immediately drafted into law and executive action. In America an advisory commission, drafting a plan and submitting recommendations to President, Congress, state and regional authorities, trade associations, and labor unions would undoubtedly be a move in the right direction. However, one suspects it would accomplish little beyond oratory and beautifully bound reports. . . . Somewhere there must be a set of teeth. . . . The War Industries Board, you remember, controlled fuel supply and freight cars, without which most businessmen are helpless.

Master planning, then, means a geographical area large enough to cope with economic self-sufficiency, with due regard for the psychological considerations implicit in regional planning. It means that all essential industries are comprehended, and their interrelations closely followed, failing which the problems of specialization cannot be confronted. It means first a paper program, and then executive action clothed with more than advisory power. It probably means state [control] with as much cooperation from industry as the government can secure. But there is no objection—save from embittered Marxists—to industry's taking the lead if it has the will and the intelligence.

Probably the most important feature of master planning is the orderly control of new investment. In so-called prosperous years in the United States, as much as ten billion dollars may be dispensed. This sum goes anywhere, on a glorious hit-or-miss basis—into woolen mills when there are already three times as many woolen mills as the market needs, into highly dubious foreign enterprises in which the size of the banker's commission is the primary magnet, into surplus cement plants, into new oil pools when we have a 50 percent excess of producing wells, into miniature golf courses, into skyscrapers and subways to compound the discomfort and danger of existing in Megalopolis, into land reclamation projects when bankrupt farmers are streaming from the land, into a huge advertising campaign to make us athlete's foot-conscious, into developing house lots in the swamps of Florida. (At the peak of the boom there were more house lots for sale in the palmy peninsula than there were families in the United States.) It will be a long day before a planning board can tell a man what he shall do with his surplus funds in this republic, but at least the citizen's sturdy individualism might not be outraged if there were an authority to tell him where his money had a chance of securing earning power over a term of years, and where it would be simply thrown away. The mere knowledge, now unobtainable, of where capital is genuinely needed would be a long step forward. A certain amount of capital would have to be conscripted —at a fair rate of interest—for great public improvements, like slum clearance, where the profit would mature beyond the patience of the private investor.

The whole wheel of the Russian Five-Year Plan turns on the allotment of capital to new enterprises. This is what balanced economy means. Just enough coal mines and iron mines to supply the steel industry; just enough blast furnaces to supply the rails, structural shapes, tractors, and pitchforks that the plan calls for, year by year. In five years, some thirty billions of dollars will go flooding into mills, mines, railroads, power plants, houses, schools, mechanized farms. Nearly every kopeck of it has been allotted in advance. Russia, of course, has the great advantage of starting from scratch. She had no industrial structure to scrap or remodel; hers was a handicraft economy. She can put her new mills where they functionally belong with an eye to raw material supply, transportation outlets, markets, as well as labor. In Western civilization we have always located our mills where labor could be most ruthlessly exploited, on the now-exploded theory that cheap workers mean low costs. We have to rearrange a chaos—imagine trying to unscramble New York City!—where Russia need only build fresh and clean.

We have, however, the advantage of a far higher standard of living to carry us through a transition period. We have the advantage, too, of having already started upon a program of industrial decentralization, while Russia is heading, mistakenly I believe, for the Pittsburgh ideal of huge, smoky, roaring industrial blood clots. Worshipping the machine, she likes to see her god a towering colossus. She will have to learn better, if she is really to live with the brute.

The second great task of master planning is to bring purchasing power into alignment with the growth of the technical arts, to give citizens enough income to buy back the goods which citizens make. The failure to do this hitherto has been the most bitter paradox of the whole industrial revolution. It means tinkering with the credit system, tinkering with wages, tinkering with hours of labor. The first two must expand, the third contract. Sometimes, in a fit of desperation, one is prepared to cry a halt to the technical arts, giving society an opportunity to catch up with its indefatigable engineers, the arts of consumption a chance to draw level with production—but this is begging the question, as well as desecrating all the sacred cows of progress.

The regional conception will not down. The conning tower captaining must leave no stone unturned in an endeavor to make economic regions more nearly self-sustaining, less susceptible to the ebb and flow of external economic forces than they now are. Specialization has gone too far for either human comfort or human safety. The principle, of course, is that of a wheat farmer with a garden patch. If the crop fails, or the dumpers dump, he can still eat. In the regional idea, furthermore, things of the spirit receive more consideration: the beauty and order of one's own countryside, rebirth of craftsmanship aided by cheap electric power, a local literature, a local art.

As I said at the opening of these remarks, we ride for the moment on the crest of the wave. Plans are as cardinal as trousers. But I doubt if the furor will last. I am very much afraid that Americans have clutched at it as, in the past, they have clutched at crossword puzzles and Tom Thumb golf. It is the fad of the moment, and as a fad it will pass. Indeed its curve will be in inverse ratio to that of the stock market. When the latter starts up, planning starts down. Our couch will be deserted by all the Great Thinkers who thrive on publicity. They jump with the headlines; and master planning will no longer be in the headlines.

Well, I think that we can spare them. Planning connotes rigorous and concentrated thought. As a fad it denies its own reason for being. We who are trying to think will go on, and, I venture to believe, with a considerable addition to our numbers. We shall be less lonely than we were, for many intelligent men and women—not to be confused with mercurial Great Thinkers—have in this depression been brought face to face with the paradox of a marvelous technical structure marvelously undisciplined. We shall have aid and comfort from high quarters. Our concepts will grow. We may even see the beginnings of a national plan inaugurated by the next congress. Our path is forward with renewed vitality and hope.

Perhaps our next step is to take a specific region, study it in detail, note carefully the problems involved in technique, and prepare and publish a series of blueprints. Nothing, it seems to me, would be more rewarding, both to our own knowledge and to the world outside, than a concrete intensive study.

IV Metropolitan versus Regional Planning

"Genuine regional planning, as distinguished from . . . superficial metropolitan planning . . . , is not content to accept any of the factors in city
growth as outside human foresight and control. If we cannot create
better urban conditions without changing our present methods and institutions and controls, we must be prepared to change them: to hold
that the present means are sacred and untouchable is to succumb to a
superstitious capitalistic taboo."

—Lewis Mumford

Introductory Note

Periodically members of the RPAA ventured into the stormy seas of public debate. On occasion, they uncharacteristically took a formal organizational stand in open letters addressed to political leaders. But Mumford supplied by far the most combative journey into the public arena when he reviewed the *Regional Plan of New York and Its Environs* in the pages of the *New Republic*. Although Mumford's article failed to tumble the enormous stature of the plan, it was damaging enough to shake an angry reply from the man who directed the project and wrote its final report, Thomas Adams.

The antagonism evident in both Mumford's review and Adams' testy reply would have been hard to predict prior to Adams' association with the New York project. Adams was admired by members of the RPAA for his active role in the garden city movement in Great Britain and for his unique regional planning work as an advisor on town planning to the Commission of Conservation of Canada. But his later work in New York seemed inconsistent with all that.

In 1921 the Russell Sage Foundation launched an early and certainly the most famous regional planning effort in this country—the Committee on Regional Plan of New York and Its Environs. They chose Thomas Adams to direct the effort. It took ten years, ten volumes, and some of the most distinguished professionals from many fields to complete its work. The organization continues today as the Regional Plan Association of New York. Although their name frequently confuses them with the RPAA, the two groups reflected directly opposite views, as this series of articles demonstrates.

Shortly before Mumford's article was published, the RPAA held a special meeting.

The subject of the meeting will be the Report of the Regional Plan of New York and Its Environs. The discussion will be led by Lewis Mumford who has devoted the greater part of the last month to a detailed study of the Report. Before publishing his conclusions in regard to the Report he wants very much to have the members of the Association criticise these conclusions.[1]

This illustrates the relationship of individual members of the RPAA to the group. Mumford's review expresses his own ideas, but they have been subjected to the sympathetic scrutiny of his peers.

In this article, which originally appeared in two parts, Mumford unleashed a spirited assault on the so-called regional planning that emerged in the 1920s. His characterizations apply equally well to today's regional planning. The article clarifies the distinction made frequently by members of the RPAA between metropolitan planning and what they considered true-regional planning. Mumford also explores the proper role for planners. In this respect the critique of the Russell Sage report becomes a general criticism of a style of planning that is as common and bland as a breakfast cereal.

Even in some of Mumford's detailed descriptions of the plan's nearsightedness, one can read today's headlines. For example, in a rare departure from physical and financial concerns, the report recommends the expansion of the Metropolitan Museum of Art into Central Park; Mumford quickly dismissed that idea. But unlike the recent dispute over the use of park land for the museum's new wing, Mumford focused on the concentration of art objects that such massive institutions had already obtained. Instead of monopolizing the region's cultural resources in a single shrine, Mumford suggested the establishment of sev-

1. Mumford to RPAA members, 12 March 1932.

eral small museums elsewhere in the region. In another portion Mumford discusses some of the fiscal contradictions of the growth ideal outlined by Adams. As New York slashes its budget to prevent financial default, Mumford's forty-five-year-old warning of pared school and playground appropriations to pay the interest on municipal indebtedness seems almost clairvoyant, were it not for the simple logic of the predicament.

The entire conception of planning advanced by Mumford conflicts with that of Adams and most modern-day planners as well. Mumford emphasized the need for flexibility in a plan. But more importantly, he felt it should be a basis for public education and debate. For that reason he rejected the Sage report's tendency to propose politically expedient measures. Mumford believed that a controversial report based on the Sage studies would be the basis for a compromise instead of a self-fulfilling endorsement of the existing order.

15 The Plan of New York

Lewis Mumford

*We publish below . . . two articles by Lewis Mumford criticising the
Plan of New York as produced under the auspices of the Russell Sage
Foundation. While the plan might seem at first glance to be a matter of
local interest to New York City, we believe that the principles of city
and regional planning which Mr. Mumford discusses are of universal application and importance.*

Mr. Mumford is well know to readers of The New Republic *as critic,
essayist and biographer; but perhaps not all of them know that he has
for many years closely studied the subject discussed in these articles. A
student and follower of the late Sir Patrick Geddes, who might be called
the father of modern city and regional planning, Mr. Mumford is secretary of the Regional Planning Association of America. This group, devoted solely to general study and research in the field of regional planning, regionalism and city development, is not to be confused with the
Regional Plan Association, Inc., founded six years later to "work for
the adoption of" the Russell Sage Regional Plan.*

*As a young man, Mr. Mumford made a systematic survey of the entire
New York region, for his private education. Since 1919 he has written*

Reprinted as one selection from an original two-part series in the *New Republic* 71
(15 June 1932): 121-126, (22 June 1932): 146-154.

steadily on the subject of cities and city planning and regionalism and regional planning in The Journal of the American Institute of Architects, The Sociological Review, Architecture, Die Form, *etc. He was investigator in housing history for the New York State Housing and Regional Planning Commission, and editorial secretary to the Committee on Community Planning, A.I.A., in 1924 and 1925.*—The Editors [of the *New Republic*].

The Scope of the Regional Plan

The last volume of the "Regional Plan of New York and Its Environs" appeared at the end of 1931. The Plan was conceived by Mr. Charles D. Norton, a trustee of the Russell Sage Foundation; and a committee to carry it out was formed in 1921. The full-scale investigation and survey began in 1923: a whole corps of city planners, engineers, statisticians, economists, lawyers and municipal experts have been at work on it: many preliminary pamphlets and ten sumptuous illustrated volumes embody the research and the recommendations.

This enterprise was supported by the Russell Sage Foundation; and it cost over a million and a quarter dollars. Because of the magnitude of the task, because of the money and civic good will behind it, because of the high reputation of the investigators themselves, New York's Regional Plan has been pretty generally accepted as the last word on the subject of city planning and regional development. The guiding spirit in the plan was Mr. Thomas Adams, an experienced city planner and administrator, a man of international reputation. He directed the surveys, wrote a good part of the reports and gathered the results together in a final volume. No one can confront the imposing staff of authorities and experts that assisted him without a feeling of genuine deference. If they are wrong, who can be right? If they are muddled, who can be clear?

Still, authorities must finally be judged by the same criterion that applies to everyone else: what is the quality of their thought and what is the validity of their conclusions? After a painstaking examination of this tremendous work, and after due consultation with many other authorities, I am frank to say at the outset that the "Regional Plan for New York and Its Environs" is a disappointment. It not merely fails as a specific enterprise for the benefit of New York: it fails as an example. Mr. Adams, indeed, hopes that the "plan has rendered a real service in establishing some of the principles underlying the problems of city and regional planning, and so has been of use to those struggling with similar problems elsewhere." But while in many parts of the survey, particularly in Volumes Six and Seven, many essential principles are ably set down and many current tendencies in city development are judiciously criticized, the effect of the plan itself is to upset most of the criteria that the authors, in their more detached and critical moments, have established. With respect to the general effect of the Plan—as distinguished from specific contributions within the Report—Mr. Adams' hopes are unfounded.

As a survey of the region and as a handbook on the municipal affairs of some four hundred diverse governmental units, the Regional Plan is invaluable. It presents with great skill and adroitness a good part of the merely local data that are necessary as a basis for plans and policies in the metropolitan area of New York, already a conglomeration inhabited by some eleven and a half million people. On a score of specific projects, the Regional Plan has suggested procedures or sketched out designs with which no competent person will take issue. But it is precisely in the broader aspect of regional survey and regional plan that the report is fundamentally weak: it not merely fails to demonstrate valid principles and useful methods of procedure, but by its show of authority it creates barriers against anyone else's arriving at them. Were its example and its assumptions widely followed in other cities, the results would, I think, be disastrous for them.

What is the source of this weakness? The failures of short-sighted politicians, practical administrators, to say nothing of bribe-takers, grafters and hold-up men, to give us some semblance of order in our present urban chaos present no interesting problems. But the failure of a group of technicians, men whose specialized competence and honesty and public spirit cannot be doubted, raises some very significant questions. To account for it, one should have a better understanding of the essential tasks of planning and the strategy of living in our present civilization.

The Difficulty of Criticism

In more than one way, the report on the Regional Plan is difficult to criticize. It has been written by various people, and in the course of writing it the same writer has more than once expressed contradictory opinions. Any school of planning could find considerable justification for its special point of view on some page of this report. The advocate of the garden city will find backing for the garden city, and the advocate of the skyscraper will find support for that: those who believe in industrial decentralization will find considerable ground for their interest, and those who believe that New York is destined to greater concentration will also be backed: the believer in the social control of land values and the speculator who would like no control at all: the housing expert who knows that nothing can be done for the masses without a state subsidy and the old-fashioned business man who still thinks that housing can be done by private interests: the believer in a purely mechanical theory of city growth and the believer in organic communities—all these can find exactly the words they are looking for in some corner of this report.

Sometimes, of course, the presentation of contradictory points of view is merely an honest witness to the complexity of the facts that are surveyed: but in other cases, unfortunately, it is due to a failure to think clearly and to follow a train of thought to its conclusion. The net result of this Pauline effort to be all things to all men is to neutralize the effect of any particular proposal. One must finally judge the Regional Plan not by its separate details but by its *drift*. Thus, the report talks garden cities but drifts toward further metropolitan centralization; it talks neighborhood planning and better housing, but drifts toward our present chaotic methods of supplying both; it talks of objective standards of light and air for building but drifts toward overintensive uses of even suburban areas. Hence no single quotation from the report will do it justice, either by way of criticism or defense: one must get the drift of it, and one can do this only by grappling with the Regional Plan as a whole.

With respect to the actual contents and their arrangement, the eight volumes of survey and the two on plan are likewise very difficult to characterize. Possibly because of purely accidental circumstances, the separate reports are arranged in no logical order: the surveys of geographic and historical conditions in the metropolitan area, which are preliminary to any understanding of the social and economic conditions, are mixed together in Volume Eight. They are in effect and in content perfunctory studies, which do not seem in the least to have enabled the investigators to lay down more intelligently their main problems.

On matters of critical importance for an understanding of metropolitan development, as a special phenomenon in the growth of cities, the Plan has only a slight contribution to make. In a preliminary report to the committee, Mr. Walter W. Stewart, an able economist, suggested that a regional plan for the area involved a study of the complex forces that affect the balance between farm and city populations; but neither this, nor the relation of metropolitan growth and metropolitan finance was undertaken by the surveyors—although the latter is plainly a key problem. In their anxiety to arrive at tangible recommendations for the Plan, the Russell Sage planners failed to deal systematically with more than a fraction of the forces that have created the present complex of cities and that condition any attempt to effect their improvement.

In geography, the word *region* has a fairly exact connotation; but the Russell Sage planners have used it to describe an arbitrarily chosen area of metropolitan influence. Why was an area with a forty-mile radius from the center taken as the basis of the Survey and the Plan? This question is bound up with all the population predictions and a good part of the plans for transportation and traffic; and yet the intentions and purposes which were in the planners' minds in choosing such an area are nowhere very clearly expressed or cogently accounted for. In Plan Volume One, we learn that "the boundaries were determined largely on four grounds, namely: (1) they embraced the area within which population can and does travel in reasonable time from home to place of work—that is, the commuting area; (2) they included the large outlying recreational areas within easy reach of the metropolitan center; (3) they followed the boundaries of cities and counties at the periphery of these areas, so as to relate the plans to the areas of administration; and (4) they had regard to the physical characteristics such as watersheds and waterways."

The assumptions involved in this choice are not in the least self-evi-
dent. By what criterion is two hours' commutation per day a reasonable
expenditure of time, energy, money? Why should a metropolitan area
be planned so as to increase the flow of population from a crowded
center to more and more fully urbanized but dependent outlying areas?
(Mr. Raymond Unwin, called in as consultant, posed this question, I
believe, at the very outset of the investigation.) If garden cities are to be
built up, as at one point the Regional Plan advocates, why should the
colonization of such cities be within the expensive suburban districts
of the metropolis, instead of in the cheaper agricultural areas beyond?
Why does the notion of planning for the metropolitan area carry with it in
the minds of the Russell Sage planners the notion of progressively filling
up the metropolitan area? This question of a boundary line is of critical
importance: for an area with thrice as great a radius would have altered
almost every term in the problem. The question becomes all the more
pertinent when one observes how often in the report the low *average*
density of population for the forty-mile area is cited—as if this were in
some fashion a palliation for the indecent congestion of the metropolis
itself or an earnest [illusion] of the possibility that future growth,
arising out of similar causes, would be less congested.

The boundary line suggested by the Russell Sage planners takes the
place of the walls of the bottle in which Dr. Raymond Pearl bred his
fruitflies: by a metaphorical process, he assumed that the curve of
growth which accounts for the multiplication of Drosophila in a closed
container will also account, by and large, for the future growth of population in the New York region—if that be regarded as a closed container.
The original estimates on this basis of a population by 1965 of
29,000,000 for the entire area have now been reduced by the planners
to 21,000,000; but the principle remains fallacious. Sociologically
speaking, the assumption is valueless; psychologically speaking, it must
be classed as wish fulfilment.

The New York region, then, as described by the Regional Plan, is a
purely arbitrary concept, based upon future possibilities of transportation and past facts of city growth. But the population of this area is
not simply determined by the biological ratio of births over deaths: nor
will it be determined inevitably by the social and economic forces that

have acted in the past, since these are not immutable. The actual population that will come into the area is conditioned not merely by industrial movements, changes in the form of labor organization, laws governing immigration, the rate structures established for railroads and for giant power: *it is also conditioned by the very plans and policies that are made to meet an anticipated increase or decrease of population.* To assume that growth within an arbitrary metropolitan area will continue automatically in the future, under the same conditions that prevailed in the past, is to beg the whole question: it is to place a premium upon inertia and routine and to register a vote against those possibilities of social control which a plan, by its very nature, must conjure up.

Planning for an Inevitable Growth

The Regional Plan's difficulties on the fundamental matters of area and population derive from two sources. First: they have accepted as "automatic" and "inevitable" a process of metropolitan aggrandizement which has been in good part deliberate: the outcome of consciously formulated plans and purposes. Second: the investigators do not distinguish between the actual forms of urban growth in our present civilization. In the first volume, for instance, Professor Haig, discussing the economic conditions of metropolitanism, ignores the part played by the efforts to promote congestion, such as the pyramiding of ground rents in the business districts and the establishment of differential freight rates in favor of the Port of New York, and within that Port, of Manhattan Island. Nor does he distinguish between urbanism in general and metropolitanism: hence, for him, the increase in the proportion of city dwellers to agricultural workers is a justification of the process of metropolitan expansion—as if that were the sole mode of city development!

So confidently did the Russell Sage planners accept the inevitability of metropolitan development that they blinded themselves to the significance of their own statistics, and even arranged them in such a fashion as to obscure the real trends to the casual reader. Here are the Regional Plan's own figures (Vol. I, pp. 23, 34) on the increase in the number of factory workers for the region as a whole. I have translated these figures into percentages in order to tell the story more clearly. In the case of all three zones there appear actual decreases in the period from 1912 to 1922 which are not fully accounted for. But the figures are perhaps even more important taken for the area as a whole.

1900-1922	1900-1912	1912-1917	1917-1922
24,960 per year	33,438 per year	17,082 per year	12,493 per year
83.6%	61.0%	8.1%	5.5%

Whereas the increase from 1900 to 1922 was 83.6 percent, that from 1912 to 1922 was only 13.6 percent, and whereas in the first period the factory workers increased more rapidly than the population, in the second the population increased more rapidly than the factory workers.[1]

This puts another face upon the overwhelming industrial importance of the metropolitan area, and its "inevitable" growth. More recent figures reduce the increase further: during the two-year period, 1926 and 1927, the seventy-four cities included in the New York region gained only 14,136 industrial workers, or an average of 7,068 per year (Vol. VI, p. 189).

In other words, there has been a steady decrease in the rate of industrial growth since 1912: a process which has nothing whatever to do, of course, with the present business depression. There is reason to believe that the peak of industrial centralization occurred at about 1910, and that since that time new technological factors, particularly electric power, the telephone, the motor car and the new methods of corporate direction, have been making themselves felt. Dealing with this problem almost solely in terms of local factors—the local market, the necessity for the heavy industries, like chemicals, to find cheaper land to expand on, and so forth—the Regional Plan has not concerned itself with the general conditions that are plainly diminishing the necessity and the convenience of metropolitan centralization. Even calculations as to the importance of the Port of New York as a commercial center are affect-

1. It might be well to mention here that the Regional Plan of New York, while it gives the actual figures of increase or decrease of factory workers in the three zones within the periods 1900-1912, 1912-1917, 1917-1922, is extremely misleading to any casual reader, for it prints the percentage of increase only for the whole period of 1900-1922, entirely omitting to mention the significant fact that by far the greater part of that increase occurred before 1912.

ed by proposals like those for building up Hampton Roads or opening a direct waterway from the Great Lakes to the Atlantic. In both geography and technics, the purview of this gigantic Regional Plan was essentially parochial.

With the myth of New York's greatness and the desire for metropolitan concentration to spur them, they looked for no other evidence and admitted no other necessities. Is it any wonder that from the beginning the Russell Sage planners tended to belittle the new social conditions and the new technological innovations which might, if socially applied and controlled, act as a brake upon metropolitan growth? The influence of the telephone, the radio, the automobile, the airplane, giant power, skilled industrial planning and rationalization, in flattening out the "advantages" of the metropolis, even the dubious advantage of a large labor market, part of it chronically unemployed—none of these factors has been completely canvassed and candidly assessed.

Accepting the extension and the congestion of the metropolitan area as inevitable, these planners are in the position of a community on the lower Mississippi when the river is rising: it is too late to control the flood and the only possible form of effort is to create stouter levees and to remove one's household back from the river to higher ground. All the more tangible hopes for the Regional Plan for better living conditions lie in the outlying suburban areas. "It is in the outlying fringe," writes Mr. Adams, "that the opportunities for improvement are greatest. As the regional survey has shown, it is here that the greatest potentialities exist both for creating good conditions and for the application of measures for the prevention of bad conditions."

Unfortunately, the forces which have created a mess in the center are at work, likewise, in the outer fringe. If the regional planners have no plan for controlling these forces at the center, why should they be more sanguine of their abilities on the periphery?

The Lack of an Alternative Hypothesis

Now, the capital use of a comprehensive survey is to state the problem correctly. It may be that under terms acceptable to our present financial interests no effective planning can be done within the metropolitan district, and no solution in the interest of public health and welfare and amenity and the good life generally is possible. But this is no reason for evading the problem itself or for hiding the essential facts with illusory hopes and false promises. One of the needs of a fundamental survey is to delimit those problems which can be handled immediately, those which can be dealt with by current methods once public opinion and official authority have been educated sufficiently, and those which cannot be handled at all until there is a complete reorientation in our civilization. The last are by no means the least important.

While providing a plan which was to operate over a period of at least thirty-five years, the Regional Plan has cast its solution as far as possible into terms which would admit of their immediate fulfilment. This mode of forecast and planning not merely allows precious little for changes in our economy and our institutions: it does not allow for the education and political possibilities of a well digested plan. It may be more *effective,* as well as more clear-sighted and honest, to say that no comprehensive planning for the improvement of living conditions can be done as long as property values and private enterprise are looked upon as sacred, than it is to draw pictures of parks that may never be built, playgrounds that may never be opened to children, and garden cities that will never be financed.

Judgments about the social future differ from other forms of scientific prediction. Dr. John Dewey has called them "judgments of practice" and has pointed out that the hypothesis that is provisionally assumed is also one of the factors that contribute to the results. The Russell Sage planners have assumed the necessity for the continuous growth of the population and the continuous urban expansion of the metropolitan area. Had they accepted one or another hypothesis, the area they treated would have been of different size, and the problems they set themselves would have been posed differently and answered differently.

At no point in either the survey or the plan is there the slightest indication that they seriously considered alternative hypotheses, although one of these had been broached in 1926 by the New York State Housing and Regional Planning Commission, under the chairmanship of Mr. Clarence S. Stein, in outlining a schematic regional plan for the state of New York. This weakness in the fundamentals of a planning technique and of social control ramifies through every part of the report. Mr. Benton MacKaye has pointed out that to undo a traffic snarl in Times Square the planner may have, not to build double-decked streets or belt-line railroads or multiple subways, but to reroute the movement of wheat, let us say, through the Eastern ports. No city is a self-contained entity, least of all the metropolis: it is what it is because of continental and even worldwide conditions. The solutions of most of the fundamental problems of city development in New York do not rest simply in the municipal engineer's office, and no council of local experts, however able, can deal with them adequately on local terms alone. But the Regional Plan took the underlying causes of congestion as "given," and did not inquire into them or ask how they might be alleviated or diverted.

The truth is that the Russell Sage planners did not take advantage of their theoretical freedom: they were so eager to fasten to a viable solution, a solution acceptable to their committee full of illustrious names in financial and civic affairs, to the business community generally, to the public officials of the region, that they deliberately restricted the area of their questions. In genuine research, it is a surprising matter to emerge from the investigation with the same conclusions as one provisionally had reached before entering it; and the very fact that the makers of the Regional Plan found so little need to shift their point of view or to adopt a fresh outlook during a period of eight years makes one feel that they felt, doubtless unconsciously, the pressure of limiting commitments.

But in a report of this nature, without official authority, the whole success is bound up with its intellectual and imaginative validity, with its capacity to start new lines of activity going, to suggest new methods of procedure, in short, to depart from the limited and routine thinking of the practical man, whose horizon is limited by his desk or his draughting table. There is nothing more practical than a fertile theoretical attack: there is nothing less practical than a concrete proposal which, if not immediately carried out, becomes obsolete and must be replaced. By creating a plan for immediate adoption, the Russell Sage planners have made a plan that is not worth adopting.

This superficiality accounts for no small part of the weakness of the specific recommendations made by the Russell Sage planners. Let us examine these concrete proposals in a little greater detail.

Proposals for Land Utilization

Let us take up, first, the matter of land-utilization. The scope of this planning is so broad and detailed that one can touch, of course, only some of the high points.

The chief proposals for the present built-up areas in the metropolitan districts are for new industrial zones. These areas are, very sensibly, much smaller than those which the municipal authorities have lavishly zoned as industrial. Perhaps the best of these are suggestions for improving the waterfront of Manhattan, making it more generally available for recreation at the same time that it is improved for rapid transportation and for port uses. New industrial areas are indicated for Brooklyn, and there is even the suggestion that an airport might take the place of the present Brooklyn Navy Yard, with still another airport on Governor's Island. These are all sensible proposals: the treatment of the Chrystie-Forsyth area as a wide traffic boulevard is infinitely to be preferred to the present attempts to make it a site for municipal housing—the plottage constitutes probably the very worst housing site in the city—and the elevated highway along the East River, which was omitted in a plan recently made for the East Side Chamber of Commerce, would help to open up that dead area in the heel of the island.

In contrast to the numerous industrial areas assigned, there are no major proposals for new decentralized business areas. This is all the more curious because not only are department stores, for example, a great factor in transit congestion—a four-story store, Mr. Goodrich calculates, is the equivalent in congestion of a twelve-story loft or a twenty-story office building—but because department stores themselves have begun spontaneously to decentralize and might be encouraged to go further. In Plan Volume One the opportunity is mentioned: but the only plan laid down is that for the Hackensack Meadows project. Despite the important opportunity offered by the George Washington Bridge, there is no hint in the report of a sub-business center between One Hundred and Fifty-sixth and One Hundred and Eighty-first Streets, although the short-circuiting of traffic and commerce through this area, instead of bringing it into the center of the city, would greatly relieve congestion in the Pennsylvania-Grand Central district. With the Long Island hinterland connected with Harlem by the Tri-borough Bridge, and the New Jersey hinterland connected with Washington Heights by the bridge over the Hudson, an opportunity now exists for effectively recentralizing the existing city and relieving some of the pressure on the two overcrowded centers below Fifty-ninth Street. If population continues to decrease on Manhattan this would be a real step toward lessening congestion; and should commutation increase as rapidly as the Russell Sage planners believe, it would be the only measure that would postpone the complete strangulation of business below Fifty-ninth Street. Moreover, the building up of new commercial centers in Harlem and in Washington Heights would perhaps be an effective step towards redeeming the blighted areas in the upper East and West sides on Manhattan Island. Despite Mr. Adams' frequent use of the word recentralization, he lost here a major opportunity to bring it into action.

One notes, too, that there is no suggestion of a sub-business center on Jamaica Bay, to care not only for the possible port development there, but to relieve workers and shoppers of a burdensome trip into Manhattan or into the already congested Borough Hall district. The neglect of such opportunities tends not merely to pile up traffic and transit problems: it tends also to neglect a remedy for our already overcostly transportation system—namely, a balanced load moving in opposite directions at the same time.

Within New York, the plan makes two excellent suggestions for more needed park space: one is the use of the larger part of Welfare Island, Ward's Island and Randall's Island—removing the present institutions to outlying areas. The other is the building up of a park, partly in the water, around the Williamsburgh Bridge and down to Corlears Hook. The suggestions about Central Park are not nearly as happy: one is to sacrifice strips along the Central Park West and Fifth Avenue, in order to facilitate traffic, and the other is the removal of the existing menagerie to a distant suburban park—on the quaint abstract ground that this accords better with modern park principles, and in the face of the fact that it is, on the planners' own confession, one of the most popular and humanizing attractions in the park. The only way in which the sacrifice of the park area could be atoned for would be by closing up the traffic driveways of the park proper, making this considerable amount of space open for children's play and adult recreation: but the only compensation the Plan offers is that traffic within the park be reduced to fifteen miles an hour!

In the outlying sections of the region, the Regional Plan suggests principally new park sites and new industrial sites: they also add to the areas of most of the residential villages and suburbs and zone some of the distant lake sites for residences. The admirable Westchester County Parkways system, duly described in Volume Six, has offered a convenient standard for similar projects in other parts of the region. A large park is suggested for Greenwood Lake, and a considerable extension of the Ramapo Mountains Park is added: but Lake Hopatcong, more accessible than Greenwood Lake, remains apparently in private hands.

Perhaps the most drastic transformation of land use put forward is that for redeeming the Hackensack Meadows, converting the southern part into an enormous industrial area and creating a large residential community out of the upper part, with a park area of over 3,000 acres. Such a development would wipe out a natural obstacle to transportation and would possibly diminish the number of mosquitos: but the question arises as to whether the rehabilitation of the blighted housing areas around the meadows would not be more feasible and economical. The newly made land would have the advantage of being cheaper as raw land and of being unspoiled by the subdivider; but on the other hand, the park area suggested, already reduced by almost a thousand acres by those who are pushing the plan, would be of little use to the surrounding population if 700,000 new inhabitants were likewise to use it. With the filling up of the hinterland by suburbs, with the congestion that exists in the summer in the favored recreation grounds, with the greater and greater distance in time consumed, if not in miles, between the residential areas and the recreation areas, especially bathing beaches, it is a serious question whether the filling up of the meadows during the present period would not be treason to a later generation. What the Regional Plan proposes is to swallow for housing and industry the last large potential park and open-water area. The question is not, can we afford to develop it as a park: the question is, can we afford to develop it as anything else? (In spite of all that the Regional Plan has stated so confidently about the existence of open areas in the present region, it is significant to note that almost the only area of considerable size it can point to, unspoiled by real-estate development or by topographic obstacles, is a salt marsh.)

In contrast to the very dubious Hackensack Meadows project, on which the Regional Plan sets great store, is that which Colonel William J. Wilgus put forward for a mole and breakwater across the lower bay, from Sandy Hook to Rockaway Point. This is a piece of genuine imaginative planning: it would not merely provide an area of safe anchorage before reaching Quarantine; nor would it only provide a useful roadway connection between the Jersey mainland and Long Island, making possible a rerouting of northbound traffic: it would also provide a much needed expanse of clean beach, whose bathing facilities and amusements would utlimately pay for the entire cost of the project. Mr. Adams puts this proposal on the carpet again in Plan Volume Two, but it does not appear in the Graphic Regional Plan. If it be feasible, and if it could be done without running the danger of silting up the channel, it has far more to commend it than the Hackensack Meadows project. Incidentally, this scheme was put forward independently by the Pilots' Association.

Our Stake in Congestion

Let us return to the heart of the metropolis. The Regional Plan estimates that New York City wastes roughly $500,000 a day because of congestion, and the entire region, approximately $1,000,000. (Vol. III, p. 61.) What have the planners to say on the subject of building heights and congestion?

Here Mr. Adams has taken the standpoint of the practical administrator, faced with an immediate problem and forced to compromise with all the existing interests and pressures. If the present Regional Plan were an official one, if it were to be put in force immediately, and if these proposals were the last step in drafting ordinances and proceedings to legislative action, the final results he achieves would be a regrettable—but so far understandable—attempt to make the best of a bad situation.

But, in practice, Mr. Adams' assumptions do not merely do away with a clear presentation of the problem, but with an effective solution. Despite the excellent discussion of desirable degrees of concentration and height in Volume Six, to say nothing of the monograph on "Sunlight and Daylight for Urban Areas" in Volume Seven, Mr. Adams proceeds to lay down merely "practicable" standards on the basis of the existing structure of values and the existing methods. He therefore provides no sufficient impulse to change the framework and the ideas, the structure and the standards; and the very interests he has already compromised within his report will, encouraged by his timidity, exact further compromises and concessions from any municipal officials who might actually attempt to put these ideas into practice.

In other words, by attempting to be practical and hard-boiled, Mr. Adams, so far from helping the practical administrator, has actually made his task more difficult. The time for compromise is not when one is thinking out a problem; for by hauling down one's flag to the enemy as soon as one has surveyed the field and counted his forces, one lacks the power not merely to reinforce one's friends in their attack, but to win over such of the enemy as may have sympathies in the other camp. There are business men, for example, who are not convinced that buildings over twenty stories high are desirable forms of investment, just as there are plenty of architects who do not believe that the skyscraper is the chief boast of American architecture or the only way in which to house office workers. The Regional Plan, with its genius for premature compromise, gives these people no effective aid.

The Regional Plan might have performed a useful service in examining the present forms of the skyscraper on the basis of their utility and efficiency, compared the business buildings built on the row principle—with through ventilation, a complete access to daylight and a minimum of dead interior space—with the extravagant layouts of the types that fill the entire lot area. Here again, the Regional Plan lacks the very essence of a good plan: the sense of alternative possibilities. Not alone is there no examination of other methods of planning business buildings, such as Ludwig Hilbersheimer has made in Berlin; but there is, on the contrary, the persistent suggestion that the set-back skyscraper covering the entire lot at the base is an ideal form, even in suburban areas.

The attitude of the Regional Plan on building bulks and congestion is all the more indefensible because Mr. Adams is not in the least fooled by the weird mathematics and logic by which Messrs. Hood and Corbett have undertaken to defend skyscrapers as an aid in relieving congestion. "If," says Mr. Adams quite justly, "in areas which skyscrapers are built closely it is considered essential to pull down valuable buildings for the purposes of wholesale widening of streets; to build up roads and sidewalks in two or more tiers to obtain elevated street space because of insufficiency of ground space; and to concentrate transit lines much more than elsewhere, then it is obvious that those who advocate these things are proving indirectly that the traffic and transit demands grow in proportion to building bulk. And yet it is a common thing to hear the same voice say at the same time that high buildings do not create more traffic than low buildings, and that streets in areas occupied by high buildings should be doubled in capacity."

In view of this, the compromises Mr. Adams is willing to make on behalf of business buildings are almost unbelievable. Thus he says of the quarters in which two million people spend at least eight hours a day on Manhattan Island alone, that "they may have less space about them for light and air than residential buildings because of the greater opportunities they present, as a rule, for artificially overcoming deficiencies in natural light and ventilation."

As a matter of cold fact, the office worker is far more confined than is the housewife or the school child. From the standpoint of the health and efficiency of the office worker and the loft worker, it is highly important to have plenty of sunlight and air, all the more because their resistance is lowered and the chances of infection greatly increased by daily travel in crowded subway lines. Zoning ordinances should establish a stringent regulation, not merely of height and bulk, but of building depth and exposure, for office buildings and factories.

Does the Regional Plan suggest such standards? On the contrary, even in areas of predominantly low building it does not hesitate to assign high ones: see the development of the civic and business center of Paterson, suggested on page 548, Plan Volume Two. While Mr. Adams is verbally against congestion and against unsocial modes of building, the Plan, whenever it has a concrete step to propose, automatically assumes the existence of congestion and generously provides for it: see the view of Columbia Heights, Brooklyn, see the Upper East

Side Water Front, see the Civic Center for Manhattan, with its vast tower, 1,000 feet high, see the suggestions for the midtown district of New York, see that for the Chrystie-Forsyth Streets area.

Is the Russell Sage planner's excuse that land values are already high in these areas? Not at all; for in Volume Six, page 27, he says: "Land values will adjust themselves to any density of building permitted by the city, and should not be allowed to force high building." Mr. Adams himself is not unconscious of the fact that he has faced both ways on the issue of congestion. "Viewed by themselves," he says, "some of the imaginative designs that follow may appear to picture a degree of height and density of building that is greater than our words and our standards would indicate as desirable" (p. 332, Plan Volume II). "May appear" is a curious phrase in this context: it flatly contradicts even Mr. Adams' words, even Mr. Adams' standards.

But what shall we say to the basis upon which he calculates the maximum bulk of office buildings in central areas—a twelve-story building covering the entire lot? Fortunately, the Report takes the criticism out of one's mouth; for in Volume Six one reads: "An excessive building bulk is one where buildings cover over 80 percent of the area of private land and rise above an average height of ten stories per unit area of building plot in the areas of highest densities. This is the maximum. A reasonable optimum, where it is practicable to apply it, would be 75 percent and eight stories, respectively, always assuming that at least 50 percent of the land was open public area." No one could phrase the economic objection to Mr. Adams' zoning proposals any better than he has done himself. "Probably," he says in Plan Volume Two, page 161, "if an estimate could be made of the increased income obtained by groups of men in certain districts, as a result of exercising their privilege to erect higher and bulkier buildings than the streets can serve without double-decking, and this could be set against the costs of congestion plus the cost of the remedy in double-decking, there would be a balance in favor of more stringent zoning."

But in these discussions of building heights and congestion two vital facts are fogotten. The first is that congestion in the center demands wider and wider areas for commutation: this is not merely costly in the matter of supplying new transit facilities and new terminals, but in order to make these expensive lines pay, the maximum degree of congestion must be created in the outlying areas: so that, ultimately, open spaces cannot be maintained in the suburbs so long as intensive growth is localized and encouraged in the central areas. If the sky is the limit in the metropolis, parks and gardens and parkways and playgrounds will not be the final result in the suburbs. That is an illusion. The Regional Plan does ill to foster it. Under this regime the suburb is merely a temporary transitional area, awaiting the last degree of metropolitan exploitation: those who wish the advantages of a semi-rural environment must always be on the move.

As a matter of fact, the Plan involves two contradictory sets of proposals. One is for the building of large neighborhood units and even garden cities in the suburban parts of the metropolitan region. The other is for the concentration of traffic and transportation and high buildings in the central district below Fifty-ninth Street in Manhattan, and the filling up of the open areas in the metropolitan district in such a fashion as to continue the congestion and to preserve the land values that have been founded upon this congestion. The first of these proposals is, within the region, a platonic hope: the actual ground is so badly chopped up into private parcels and the financial interest in long-term and low-paying investments like garden cities is so meager that, without a complete reversal of our present financial institutions, the prospects of building them in the local area are infinitesimally small. Nor would it do the slightest good toward lessening congestion unless new industries were planted in the garden cities: this means large state subsidies for workers' housing; for without an industrial base the garden city is only a fancy name for a suburb. If anything were needed to make the Regional Plan's allusions to the garden city more futile, the plans for further congestion at the center would be sufficient.

The second fact about building heights is equally important to the planner, who must look forward to the continued adaptation of the city to human uses and functions. This is the fact that radical changes can be easily made only in districts of low building density. Congestion, in other words, lack adaptability. It fixes inordinately high values on land which do not permit its change in function except at the cost of incorporating the capitalizable value of congestion rents, plus the costs of demolition, in the new value of the land: a fact which automatically prohibits low buildings in an original skyscraper area even should a change in urban use demand them.

An obsolete small building can easily be demolished; a street of low buildings can be widened to meet new traffic demands; a section of such buildings can be torn down to meet a new civic need. Skyscrapers, on the other hand, tend to ossify capital and to restrict the necessary adaptation to new uses. So heavily does the skyscraper have to capitalize its unusable equipment and its unrealizable advantages that it is unable to make terms with a new situation. In other words, the costs of congestion are never amortized and written off the books: on the contrary, they form a standing charge which can be written off only by a revolution or a final declaration of bankruptcy.

If the past hundred years have taught us anything, they should have taught us the advantage of traveling light. It is because we have sunk such vast fortunes into what is now obsolete equipment that our cities present a massive resistance to change and improvement. Only by simplifying our equipment can we meet new situations and take advantage of new opportunities. Today the motor car has an efficiency value in the country town that far outweighs its value in the traffic jam of Fifth Avenue: this generalization applies to the small city itself, as opposed to the metropolis. The small city can spend on real improvement what the metropolis must spend on the mere amelioration of a condition fundamentally bad.

Neighborhood Communities and Housing

We come now to a highly important phase of any constructive policy of regional planning: the building of houses. The section on housing really consists of two parts. One deals with the conception of the neighborhood community and the other with the problem of housing in relation to general city development.

Mr. Clarence Perry, who conducted the first survey, has seized upon three important facts in connection with modern housing. The first is that arterial traffic roads, being dangerous and tedious to cross, tend to act as delimiting boundaries of neighborhood communities. The second is that such neighborhood communities, in order to ensure children's safety in going to and from schools and playgrounds, should not be through-traffic areas, but rather should be insulated: this is a corollary.

Finally, Mr. Perry holds that it is possible to define such neighborhood communities as to the area and the number of families in terms of the type of housing and the elementary school that can economically serve them. With such definite requirements of population established at the beginning, the amount of space devoted to shops, community institutions, parks and playgrounds can be calculated and worked into the ground plan.

In establishing a desirable standard size—160 acres—Mr. Perry has worked with criteria that have not been criticized with sufficient care: even though he shrinks from accepting the gigantic, understaffed, over-equipped prison school developed to meet the high costs and curtailed budget of megalopolitan New York, he probably places the maximum number too high. This holds likewise of his calculations for shopping centers, where the figures are loose and inaccurate. I mention these deficiencies, not in a spirit of carping, but to warn against their being accepted as the last word in accurate scientific study, and as such, a basis for all future planning. But Mr. Perry's principle is, nevertheless, a valid one. Orderly city growth does not consist in following the standard practice of platting new areas in endless rectangles on the map, permitting them to be broken up into innumerable building lots and sold for speculation, providing areas so opened up with new transit lines and utilities, long before the settlement is compact enough to pay the taxes and assessments on the services, and then, finally, when the area has been completely mangled, paying a great advance in price for the necessary school sites and playground areas, in most cases so late that adequate space for either cannot be obtained.

Not merely does our present method automatically wipe out the possibility of a sound community development; but in the very platting of the streets it creates a large unnecessary expense. Mr. Robert Whitten, for example, shows in a comparison of the cost of utilities in a standard New York street, as compared with a neighborhood plan, that the total cost for a regulation lot is $856.31 for the present type, while it is only $485.09 for the neighborhood plan.

Our present scheme of city development, with its premium upon early subdivision and speculation, makes the economies of large-scale operations impossible except in a completely unsettled area. In order to gather together a neighborhood sufficiently large to be planned and developed as a whole, a new financial charge, the charge for assemblage, has to be added; and without the power of public condemnation, the builder is at the mercy of the first person who gets wind of the fact that the tract as a whole is in demand.

In introducing the insulated neighborhood community as a unit of city development, Mr. Perry has made a valuable clarification which was worked out in practice, at about the same time, in Radburn, New Jersey. There is no doubt as to either the economy or the social necessity of this type of development. But the concept is unrealizable by any scheme of two-dimensional planning: it needs planning in four dimensions, that is, the timely municipal purchase of the land, the building of houses as part of the neighborhood unit, as well as streets and parks, and the setting up of an administrative authority which will carry the whole project through *in time*. This involves the coordination of city-planning and housing authorities, as has been done, for example, at Amsterdam and at Frankfurt-am-Main. To conceive of neighborhood communities and to rely upon the fitful and unreliable efforts of a limited-dividend company to achieve them, is to accept our present chaos and disorder and waste as inevitable.

Unfortunately, in housing the Russell Sage planners are prevented by their prejudices and their principles from looking the problem full in the face. "The housing problem in New York," says Mr. Adams blandly, "differs in character and in some of its divisions and origins from that of other great cities. This is particularly so in its economic aspects. For example, the problem is less associated with real poverty than it is in great European cities. It might almost be said that the greatest problem in New York up to the present has been to provide more healthful accommodation for those having sufficient income to pay an economic rent, whereas the great problem in European countries has been to make provisions for those who cannot pay an economic rent."

When one remembers that there are still 66,000 insanitary old-law tenements in New York, when one remembers that the New York State Housing and Regional Planning Commission, more closely and authoritatively in touch with the problem than Mr. Adams, stated that two-thirds of the population could not afford housing that met modern standards of sanitation and decency, one wonders whether the rest of Mr. Adams' generalizations are as subjective and unreal as those he makes on housing.

At another point, however, Mr. Adams dismisses the basic housing problem in this area by simply placing it in the category of a general social problem whose solution lies outside the province of the planner. The reason for Mr. Adams' diffidence here is plain: he believes that "all housing should be economic, in the respect that it should yield a fair return on the investment in building and land." Since two-thirds of the needed housing in New York cannot come under this head, the report suggests no method for dealing with it. "The state and city should, however," he believes, "give financial aid in the poorest quarters of the city toward the acquisition of parks and playgrounds, the improvement of sanitary conditions, the widening of streets and the opening of lanes through congested blocks. It should also encourage the investment of money at a low rate of interest for low-cost housing." These would have been brave and heartening words if Mr. Adams had written them for the Tenement House Report of 1884. They are a little inadequate now.

But the fear of giving state and municipal aid for the building of houses would be a little more convincing if the Regional Plan were not so lavish in investing public moneys on every device that will increase congestion and permit the constant growth of the metropolitan area. The city has been subsidizing subway travel, since 1918, to the extent of something more than one cent a ride. Mr. Daniel Turner, an authority on transit, shows in Volume Four that future transportation needs will cost the city, after 1940, some $350 per capita for every million people added to the population of the metropolitan area—which would be something more than an investment of $1,400 per family merely to provide transportation from dingy and unsalubrious areas of residence to an overbuilt skyscraper center. This amount would be a tidy aid to housing; and if the housing were properly correlated with the recentralization of big business and commerce and the decentralization of industry, it would go a long way toward making the transportation bill lower, if not wholly unnecessary, since on the Regional Plan's own showing, there is room for another three million people within the present city of New York, without rebuilding and repopulating its blighted areas.

Megalopolitan centralization tends to sink into the business of mechanical movement the resources that a regional scheme of distributing the population in balanced communities would expend on equipment that directly subserves the life and welfare and health and education of the community. *The colossal highway and rapid-transit schemes outlined by the Regional Plan are really an alternative to a community building program;* certainly not a means to it. The fact that financiers and bankers will sink money into obsolete forms of business enterprise which once were profitable, and have nothing but indifference for the more modest possibilities for profit that conservative forms of investment like housing and city development present, does not give the Regional Plan's scheme any greater validity. The bankers miscalculated our capacity to absorb skycrapers; they may easily make a similar mistake about our capacity to absorb tunnels, bridges and transit systems.

Metropolitan growth has its own inherent limitations. In "The Sociology of City Life," Professor Niles Carpenter points out that there is some evidence that "a process of the increase of costs, because of the lengthening of the lines of transportation, has already begun to be operative. . . . Further than this, it appears probable that, barring important technological improvements, most extensions of transportation facilities will before long involve increasing costs, and hence eventuate in a situation where continued extensions, and the urban growth predicated upon them, cease to be economically feasible."

What is true for food and transit lines is true for water, sewage disposal, garbage disposal, as the Regional Plan itself points out. It may be difficult to define the limits of metropolitan concentration: but one cannot doubt that they exist. Blighted areas, unbalanced budgets, bankruptcy, are the symptoms of decay: the first warnings of a much greater collapse. The Russell Sage planners have succumbed to the illusion from which the average American of Middletown suffered during the boom period: he spent his money riotously on a new-model car every year, while his house was leaky and obsolete and his neighborhood was a civic disgrace. The mere fact that we produce motor cars and transit systems more easily than we produce balanced conceptions of personal

domestic life and of civic existence is certainly no proof that we are
not riding swiftly towards disaster.

An Obsolete Pattern

Now, the fact is that the basic pattern of Megalopolis, as the Russell
Sage planners have accepted it, is anachronistic: it does not conform to
our modern social and economic needs. Its streets and blocks were designed for easy speculation: they "work" only in so far as lots are as
negotiable and fluid as Wall Street paper. The skyscrapers of Megalopolis
were designed to obtain a maximum income out of land made exorbi-
tantly expensive by speculation on future congestion: they "work"
only in so far as they can uphold these paper values, and no heights-of-
building regulations which would upset this false scale of values would
be tolerated by our bankers and our realty interests. The subways and
other modes of transportation were designed to facilitate congestion
and to increase the outlying tributary areas: they, too, "work" only in
so far as they are overcrowded.

Our present municipal governments reflect in the political sphere the
anachronisms and basic inefficiencies of our physical equipment. These
governments operate on the premise that a majority of the population
is indifferent, poverty-stricken, slum-dwelling, demoralized. Municipal
politics "work" only so long as the mass of citizens remain in this state.
The vested interests of the metropolis, therefore, are in impermanence,
speculative facilities, low degree of living amenities, congestion, indifference, poverty, corruption and demoralization: this is the basic metropolitan complex, well described by Spengler in "The Decline of the
West," and incisively formulated by the late Sir Patrick Geddes in his
diagram of the rise and fall of cities: Polis: Metropolis: Megalopolis:
Parasitopolis: Patholopolis: Necropolis.

Any effort to relieve or reconstitute the metropolis must go *against*
the basic pattern; for to carry it further is only to broaden its capacities
for mischief. The ever rising cost of running Megalopolis, a cost which
increases directly with the size of cities, depends upon a proportionate
rise in property values and a proportionate increase in the total income.
The present economic scheme of the big city, in other words, depends

The economic reason for repairing the blighted areas should be plain. With curtailed budgets and resources, we must temporarily plant our new building where the costs of site development and utilities have already been met: namely, in those areas already adequately served by sewers, water mains, transportation services. This is not merely true of New York: it is equally true of Chicago, Philadelphia, St. Louis, Detroit —in fact, of every city that has been on the make and overexpanding during the past twenty years. None of these municipalities can continue to afford the luxury of blighted areas. The exodus of population from these miserable run-down neighborhoods must be prevented: but the only way in which it can be prevented is by razing them and rebuilding them as desirable neighborhood communities, with healthy, efficient houses and better sunlight, air, garden space and playgrounds than most of the suburbs can boast for the higher income classes which they chiefly serve. In the case of the large areas of two and three-story buildings throughout the metropolitan area, the population can, as Mr. Henry Wright has suggested in *The Architectural Record,* be more intensively housed, with an increase of usable open space. Whether Mr. Wright's particular solution be desirable and feasible or not, he has at least defined an important field of investigation within which a solution must be found.

Writing as late as 1931 with the confidence of the boom period still buoying him up, Mr. Adams rejects this possibility. "Mr. Henry Lee Block, vice-president of the Long Island Title Guarantee Company," says Mr. Adams, "has pointed out that one of the greatest needs in the city of New York is to rebuild large areas that have become deteriorated and that only by large-scale developments can this be successfully accomplished. Whole neighborhoods are involved in these improvements, for, as Mr. Block points out, builders cannot obtain profit from erecting one new building in a blighted neighborhood." Mr. Adams goes on to say: "In considering what can be done in the central as compared with suburban areas, this question again recurs, namely, why, if it be true that a certain openness is desirable for health in the suburbs, should not the same degree of openness be attempted in the central areas, in spite of the enormous cost. The answer is mainly that the citizens have convinced themselves that the idea is unattainable in the center."

The answer is rather that Mr. Adams and his investigators apparently at no point in their survey took any serious account of the problem or asked themselves how it could be met. On the contrary, they have prepared elaborate plans, to be carried out only at a staggering cost, to lead the population farther and farther out into the suburbs, without bothering to ask what will become of the wasted districts that remain. At present, the tenements in the Lower East Side do not, according to the Regional Plan, earn a return proportionate to the assessed value of the property: if this goes on without a change in use, this property will presently be recapturable for state-aided housing at more modest rates—all the more because a change in use grows less likely, with the over-building of office buildings and lofts in other parts of the city. As for the "enormous cost," Mr. Adams was doubtless thinking only of the old super-congested East Side, where the land is still too expensive for economic housing: but he was forgetting the cheaper areas where, without the intensive congestion, the blight is just as deep and disreputable.

Many of the blighted areas in the metropolitan district are at least fifty or sixty years old; but a good part of the cheap building in Queens during the last ten years already constitutes a blighted area and must be rebuilt presently, if it is not to be a constant economic burden to the city. In spite of tax exemption, in spite of differential assessments, favoring the small houseowner, the amount owed to the city in uncollected taxes in 1930 was $113,492,006, and in assessments, $53,375,219. Of the latter, no less than $22,294,201 represented the amount due in Queens, with its extensive speculative developments of new subdivisions.

To further the extension of the metropolitan district while these conditions prevail in the developed sections is a suicidal policy. It is only because the Regional Plan is committed, by reason of its faith in the magic of population graphs and in skyscrapers, to the policy of expansion that it did not even bother to make a serious study of the comparative costs of reversing the past order of expansion and rebuilding the metropolitan area from within. If there is room for three million people on the unbuilt land, at a density of ten houses per acre, there would be room, at a rough guess, for another five million on the areas that are now hopelessly blighted in the region at large: a good part of this has low land values and small houses. So even if the population predictions for the region proved true, a more sound social and economic policy would consist of making the maximum use of the existing built-up area —instead of obliterating more of the countryside and spilling out in the sort of growth which, by the very terms accepted by the Regional Plan, could not be appreciably more orderly or more effective than that already achieved.

Meanwhile, if the new factors that have entered into the situation must be given more weight than the Russell Sage planners are willing to allow, there is further reason for metropolitan reconstruction from within. In the long run even our banks and insurance companies, wild and reckless though their conduct has been in promoting congestion, may be forced to write off the spurious land values that are on their books and accept a reasonable compensation in order to promote sound replacements. In all probability, the city itself will have to go through a period of bankruptcy, canceling its fictitious values, its false hopes, its spurious ambitions. Then, and not till then, will rebuilding on a large scale be possible in the congested areas, although Mr. Henry Wright gives us reason to think that with skillful planning and large-scale operations it might be done on areas where the land costs are still low. This sort of internal reconstruction is an example whereby cities that are already wastefully overexpanded, like Cleveland, Detroit and Chicago, could vastly profit.

The construction of completely planned neighborhood units within the existing centers is worth undertaking for itself, it goes without saying: but it is also a key to eventual municipal solvency, and to obtaining the advantages of open areas and public recreation grounds of convenient access outside the metropolitan district. If once we master the political and economic means of creating such communities within the existing city, we will have a means of creating them outside as well; and when industry is ready for completer rationalization and socialization, we may build up new regional cities outside the sphere of metropolitan influence. Transitory suburban dormitories which we wistfully call garden cities are no substitute for either form of constructive city development.

The Failure of Regional Plan "A"

What is the upshot of these criticisms of the "Survey and the Plan of New York and Its Environs"? With respect to basic method and plan the work is, I think, a monumental failure. The Regional Plan, by committing itself to a single hypothesis, and to an arbitrary area, failed to examine and to present alternative possibilities.

But the strategy of real planning, as Mr. Benton MacKaye has pointed out, is the strategy of warfare: one must provide plans A, B and C, in order that one may be ready, when an actual situation arrives, to throw them all in the scrapheap and improvise plan D. One such emergency is here: an economic depression; there will be other new factors in the future, many of which were plainly emergent in 1925.[2] Plan A, gigantic, comprehensive, closely articulated, is all that the Regional Plan possesses for meeting the situation.

If they discard it, they will lose seven years of effort. If they keep it, they will fail to deal with realities. Like the real-estate operators who went on building skyscrapers after 1929, their Plan assumes that in the essential bases of city development nothing will change during the next forty years. No assumption could be more fantastic than this. The very Plan that the Russell Sage planners have so confidently offered and so widely publicized makes it plain that decisive changes in the methods and the ends of city growth *must* take place—if we are to avoid complete ruin. If we follow the path to ruin, we cannot say in excuse that we were not warned. The very steps that the Regional Plan Association now urges us to take for the "improvement" of the city are fair enough warning indeed. The fact that the Russell Sage planners have treated their warnings as hopes and promises should not deceive us for a moment. We must thank them for presenting most of the facts: we are at liberty to draw our own conclusions.

The Sociological Failure of the Plan

The Russell Sage plan is not the first comprehensive plan for providing for the future growth of the city. Like Washington, New York is a plan-

2. See "Regional Planning" in the *Survey-Graphic* of May, 1925. [Reprinted as Part One in this volume.—Ed]

ned city; but, unlike Washington, New York did not have the direct influence of the city-building tradition of the Renaissance, imported by Major L'Enfant: the plan of 1811 was conceived from the narrower standpoint of merchants and land-speculators, and its aim was to create the maximum number of building lots and street frontages.

The Regional Plan, while not as official as that of 1811, is nevertheless not so different as it might, by reason of its technical elaboration and its more humane professions, appear. It, too, was conceived first of all in terms which would meet the interests and prejudices of the existing financial rulers: indeed, the very project was conceived by and sponsored originally by enlightened members of this caste, and its aim, from the beginning, was as much human welfare and amenity as could be obtained without altering any of the political or business institutions which have made the city precisely what it is.

Both the planners of 1811 and those of 1931 believed in the Manifest Destiny of New York. One saw Manhattan Island, the other the metropolitan region, as a limited area, waiting to be filled up. As it happened, the plan of 1811 became technologically obsolete within less than a generation, when the growth of railroad transportation reduced the need for numerous cross-streets from waterfront to waterfront: but the early planners succeeded by their large-scale methods and their flat disregard for existing communities, such as that in Harlem, in putting their city in a strait-jacket from which it has not escaped, from which perhaps it can never altogether escape. The transit and highway system proposed by the Regional Plan for the metropolitan district as a whole may prove such another strait-jacket. In this place one may well remember Mr. Herbert Croly's excellent words in *The Architectural Record* for July, 1904: "If a city needs new streets and buildings, let them be built, of course; but contemporary work should be restricted to contemporary needs, and no attempt should be made to build very much for a future that may be much better capable of building for itself."

In both cases, the planners were thinking either of the physical city alone, or of those even greater abstractions, the plots and values and investments and trends of population. Meanwhile, *they completely neglected the sociological fact of the city*—a collection of groups, within a limited area, housed in appropriate permanent structures, serving the common life in related institutions. *The city in its complete sense,* a physical organization, an institutional process, an esthetic reality, an incorporation of groups, *cannot be increased indefinitely in size;* for to be effective, the nuclear institutions must, beyond a certain point in growth, split up again into units conceived on the human scale and responsive to human needs and human requirements.

Without the whole corps of essential civic institutions, in active operation and in continual process of renewal, every new area added to the city is by definition a blighted or suburban area—an area devoid of citizens because destitute of the very organs of citizenship. The political corruption of the city, its gangsterdom, its thieving officialdom, its demoralized police, its lax and apathetic public, is not an accidental result but an inevitable product of inorganic forms of urban growth.

That the growth of the city is something other than a process of extending transit lines and laying down blank subdivisions is obliquely presented in just one part of the Report—that on the neighborhood unit. But what applies to this unit applies to the city as a whole; for the nucleus is not alone the school, but all the other social groups and institutions which make the difference between an integrated corporate life and a private, isolated life. Through the concentration of rich individuals, the present financial metropolis claims a disproportionate share of the institutions of art and culture in the country; but by the very act of expanding its urban areas, it removes or lessens the opportunity to enjoy these advantages on the part of any considerable share of its population.

When one speaks of "decentralization"—Mr. Adams remains willfully obtuse on this point and at various times seeks valiantly to confuse the issue—when one speaks of decentralization one naturally means something more than the decentralization of the overburdened physical plant and equipment of the metropolis: one means equally the spread and reintegration of the organs of the common life; and no form of city growth is tolerable which does not supply this opportunity. To conceive of an expanding physical plant and a contracted area of sub-urban cultural and civic opportunity, such as now takes place in our present form of expansion, is to conceive of the death of the city as a social organization—although, like any dead and putrefying organism, such a metropolis may show unwelcome signs of intense local activity.

As an instance of the failure of the Russell Sage planners to consider any other aspect than the physical and financial one, one may take its failure to mention the possibility of coordinating a recentralization of its facilities with the needs of our universities, our museums and our library system for greater diffusion and wider influence. The planners mention the necessity of permitting the extension of the already preposterously overgrown Metropolitan Museum of Art in Central Park: but that this extension might profitably take place, as suggested in the example of Barnard's "Cloisters," by the building of well covered specialized museums in other parts of the region, is not even hinted at or examined as a possibility.

The same is true of universities. The three leading institutions of higher learning in New York have already taken partial steps, as a necessity of administration, towards founding centers in other boroughs and towns: in terms of regional development, rather than of metropolitan aggrandizement, the Regional Plan might have contributed impetus and intelligent direction to this movement. The planners' blindness here gives their polite gestures in favor of "garden cities" and "recentralization," words that recur frequently throughout the report, an entirely Pickwickian flavor.

The weakness of the Russell Sage planners in this department is not unique: it reflects the lack of adequate sociological study and preparation of American planners generally, a lack not without parallels in Europe. But how can any body of men plan cities and the relationship of cities to each other and to their regional background, if it lacks even an elementary conception of what the city, as such, is? If buildings, streets, transportation system, constituted a city, the Russell Sage plan might be inadequate, but it would be at least founded on a present-day reality. But since the physical plant is only one aspect of a city's being, the Russell Sage plan is inadequate in its basis as well as in its superstructure.

Almost a generation ago Patrick Geddes read a paper before the Sociological Society in London on "Civics as Concrete and Applied Sociology." The conception of the city which he set forth there in elementary form—the city as "Town," "School," "Cloister" and "University"—has not yet percolated through to the planners and the municipal engineers: they still think it is possible to plan merely the physical organization of the "Town." But this means that such planners are dealing only with a vicious abstraction—a physical equipment unrelated to the life-needs and the spiritual impulses that bring men together in groups.

"Men come together," said Aristotle, "in order to live: they remain together in order to live the good life." Until the planner has a guiding notion as to what the good life in his generation is, how it is expressed in communities, what organs must be created for it, his elaborate surveys and his vast engineering projects will remain disoriented—disoriented and wasteful. The lack of a sociological concept of the city is at one with the planners' lack of an organic geographical concept of the region: it means a failure to approach the problem scientifically and to make use of such tentative results as already have been achieved. Maps, charts, tabulations, surveys, statistical analyses, are useful accessories of thought: they do not take the place of it.

Lacking an adequate technical and scientific method, a good part of the Russell Sage investigation was futile, not because accurate answers were not found, but because the correct questions were not asked.

In what way, then, does the Survey and Report serve as a model? Like the city with which it so largely deals, it is a warning rather than a good example. Every proposal that the Russell Sage planners bring forward could be carried into effect immediately, and yet the existing metropolis would remain remarkably the same, and it would lack a good part of the desirable and attainable attributes of a great city. It would still contain large areas of slums and blighted districts. The central areas and a good part of the suburbs would still be inadequately served with parks and playgrounds; except for Manhattan, there would also be a dearth of civic and cultural institutions. The amount of private capital available for housing and city building would still be infinitesimal in relation to need. The amount of energy wasted in the tedious transportation of human bodies would still run into millions of man-hours per day; and if the plan proposals were carried out, this would be greatly increased. The crowding, the congestion, the wear and tear, the enervation, so much more impressive in human terms than even in estimated expenditures and wastes of money, would still be up to our present standards of misery. (Mr. Adams' belief that overcrowding on transportation lines can be remedied contradicts both common experience and expert opinion.)

In short, the Regional Plan, since it carefully refrains from proposing measures which would lead to the effective public control of land, property values, buildings and human institutions, leaves the metropolitan district without hope of any substantial changes, or more than minor and accessory improvements. In the future, even more than in the past, school budgets and playground appropriations would be lessened in order that the interest on municipal indebtedness for transportation could be paid.

The older school of city planners who initiated the movement for the City Beautiful in the nineties were later condemned as superficial because they did little more than map out boulevards and create civic centers. The condemnation on the whole was just; but at least both the civic centers and the parkways were new elements in the American city's life: so far the work of these planners was positive and fruitful. The planners of New York and its environs would disdain the label of the City Beautiful: but their conception of the city is even more shallow. The city projected by the older school of planners at least *looked* a little more spacious and elegant. That was something.

In sum: the "Plan for New York and Its Environs" is a badly conceived pudding into which a great many ingredients, some sound, many dubious, have been poured and mixed: the cooks tried to satisfy every appetite and taste, and the guiding thought in selecting the pudding-dish was that it should "sell" one pudding to the diners, especially to those who paid the cooks. The mixture as a whole is indigestible and tasteless: but here and there is a raisin or a large piece of citron that can be extracted and eaten with relish. In the long run, let us hope, this is how the pudding will be remembered.

16 A Communication: In Defense of the Regional Plan

Thomas Adams

Sir: In one of his books Mr. Lewis Mumford designates the Place de l'Etoile in Paris as a square. As I see it, in plan and on the ground, it is a circle. Mr. Mumford could no doubt demonstrate that his description was correct in theory. I could prove my conception correct in fact and geometrical form. But probably each would remain unconvinced.

Here we have an illustration, first, of the relativity of truth, and second, of the wide gap between Mr. Mumford and me. He conceives regional planning as a square closed in by one fixed idea. I conceive it as a circle having a focal point, or definite major objective, in social improvement, but including numerous radial avenues affording access to different ideas as well as exits for ideas that every sincere person must abandon, after proper test.

In other words, Mr. Mumford has a theory of what regional planning should be which experience has taught me to distrust profoundly as affording a desirable social objective. That it is visionary is not in question even by its author. I, on the other hand, have no definite theory but am merely an experimenter and student who has been endeavoring to discover where the largest measure of truth is to be found.

Reprinted from the *New Republic* 71 (6 July 1932): 207-210.

Chief Justice Hughes might have been referring to the differences between our conceptions when, referring to political philosophies, he said recently:

There is no lack of schemes for the regeneration of society, schemes not infrequently of a sort which would not be needed by a society capable of freely adopting them. The construction of a theoretical paradise is the easiest of human efforts. The familiar method is to establish the perfect or almost perfect state, and then to fashion human beings to fit it. This is a far lighter undertaking than the necessary and unspectacular task, taking human nature as it is and is likely to remain, of contriving improvements that are workable. . . .

Mr. Mumford prefers the lighter and I the heavier undertaking. With such a fundamental difference between us there is little to be gained by arguing on the pros and cons of the Regional Plan of New York—but there are certain features in his "critical inquiry" published recently in *The New Republic* that call for an answer. I must be excused, however, from attempting to reply to such points as our failure to consider Mr. Benton MacKaye's scheme to untie the traffic snarl in Times Square by rerouting the movement of wheat!

Mr. Mumford declares that we *evaded* the problem and hid essential facts with illusory hopes and *false* promises. As a staff, he says, we *tried* to find a solution "acceptable to the committee," consisting of a caste of bankers, and *deliberately* restricted the area of our questions. These charges are not worthy either of Mr. Mumford or of any reply except to say that our studies have been from the beginning a simple search for the truth, and our conclusions uninfluenced by any other consideration.

Unfortunately, too, Mr. Mumford supports his contentions by a show of authority which, to say the least, is open to question. He claims for example, to be a follower of Sir Patrick Geddes. I knew Geddes, probably before Mr. Mumford was born, and have never ceased to derive guidance and inspiration from his writings. Although he was not a city planner himself, he had a gift that amounted to genius in analyzing the growth and evolution of cities. He had the gift of seeing a social organization, as was said on the occasion of his death by Sir J. Arthur Thompson, "not merely as something that had evolved but *as something that had evolved in a particular way and was still evolving.*" This insight, which he could not transmit to his disciples, qualified his idealism, for it enabled him to see things as they were in their practical nakedness. Those who plan a city like New York must be prepared to give consideration to the way it is evolving and not merely to the way in which they want it to evolve.

Sir Patrick admired the efforts in city planning being made in the United States. Mr. Mumford has invariably criticized these efforts as superficial; among other things he has said in effect that the Washington plan sacrificed social values to "classical order." Geddes said that the scale of Washington in some ways surpassed the greatest European capitals. As to what he meant by scale he said: "The evolution of American cities is plainly upon the very greatest scale, no longer merely in output of wealth, in increase of population, *but also in quality of civilization.*"

Mr. Mumford considered the Chicago Plan to belong to the "Imperial Order" and correspondingly lacking in true quality. Geddes called it a "comprehensive vision" and spoke of many modern plans of American cities as "ample and convincing evidence that before long the European citizen and town planner, of whatever nationality, may have to draw his best examples and incentives to civic reorganization and evolution— and these not only in material accomplishments, *but in moral uplifts which lie back of them*—from the great cities and towns and even the villages of the United States." My view is that Geddes would have given enthusiastic approval to the proposals in the New York Plan as fitting in with that process of civic evolution which no planner could ignore.

Mr. Mumford does not write as a man who has faced the facts and difficulties of making a thorough survey of urban conditions and tendencies, or of planning a city or region in a democratic country; rather as an esthete-sociologist, who has a religion that is based on high ideals, but is unworkable. His main quarrel with the Regional Plan is its *drift.* Precisely. It drifts away from his ideal conception of what a plan should be, and he is intolerant toward any other conception.

Thirty years ago I had ideas similar to those expressed by Mr. Mumford. In words quoted from him they were "pathetically immature." I was like Walter Pater's friend, to whom he referred as a steam engine stuck in the mud, but withal "so enthusiastic"! I have found that *movement* is essential to progress in reform and that one must keep to the

road, and as nearly the middle of it as possible, if any improvement is
to be made. This is the main point on which Mr. Mumford and I, as
well as Mr. Mumford and Geddes, differ—that is, whether we stand still
and talk ideals or move forward and get as much realization of our ideals
as possible in a necessarily imperfect society, capable only of imperfect
solutions of its problems.

Mr. Mumford reveals himself as an apostle of economic changes that
would require the combined power of the President, Congress and state
legislatures to bring about. The Regional Plan goes far in proposing
restriction on rights of property, but no further than it is reasonable
to expect public opnion to go, or government to authorize in the
future. It would have been folly to have attempted to make it a
charter for rebuilding the social state in tri-state regions, as Mr. Mumford implies it should have been. Moreover, if planning were done
in the way he conceives it should be done, it would require a despotic
government to carry it out. I would rather have the evils that go with
freedom than have a perfect physical order achieved at the price of
freedom.

While I shall presently show that Mr. Mumford's picture of the New
York Plan is not a true picture, yet, even if it were, there is no reason
why the Plan cannot in future be expanded and modified to suit any
possible change in economic or sociological ideas. It is a flexible plan
and no proposal it contains will bar progress that may be shown to be
desirable.

It would be presumptuous for me to claim that our conception of
tendencies and possibilities is an entirely accurate one, and the plan
volumes contain our disclaimer that the Plan is or could be perfect.

Of course, in certain physical respects the Plan cannot be changed.
The boundaries of the region is one of these. I am not impressed with
the claim of Mr. Mumford that his knowledge of what the boundary
should be is superior to that of the five leading experts who collaborated
with me in confirming its selection, after careful study. The region was
not arbitrarily chosen, as he suggests, nor is it forty miles in radius, except in New Jersey. In one direction it extends to one hundred and
thirty miles. It includes open territory sufficient to house the whole
population of the United States in densities similar to those in garden

cities. In this connection Mr. Mumford suggests that the area should have been large enough to provide for garden cities. It happens that I took a prominent part in selecting the site for the first garden city in England in 1903. Many sites were available, but the necessity of being in proximity to a large city, for economic reasons, dictated the choice of Letchworth, thirty-four miles from London. When Sir Ebenezer Howard chose the second site at Welwyn, after twelve years of experience of Letchworth, it was not chosen farther away from, but seventeen miles nearer to, London.

Mr. Mumford's specific criticisms are so much interwoven with his opinions that it is difficult to select them for specific reply. Throughout the whole of his article he returns again and again to the assertion that the Regional Plan supports further concentration. As a matter of fact, what we say against additional or excessive concentration would fill a volume, and I can give here only one or two illustrations of the inaccuracy of the article on this subject.

Our zoning proposals are based on an initial assumption that not more than 40 percent of the gross area of land should be built upon in any part of the city, thus leaving 60 percent open as a condition precedent to building. At present these figures are often reversed and only 40 percent is left free of building. In neighborhoods where land coverage is already greater, we cannot hope that public opinion will force its reduction. In regard to bulk of building, we advocate as a definite limitation that no building in central or downtown Manhattan shall exceed 144 cubic feet per square foot of lot. This compares with 385 cubic feet per square foot of lot in the Empire State Building, which has much less cubage than the existing zoning law permits. Thus the standards of the Regional Plan, which are declared to encourage further concentration, would restrict building bulk, within the city, to a little over a third of that resulting under the present zoning law.

In outer areas we propose that all business buildings shall have a 45-degree angle of light at front and rear, a more stringent regulation of bulk than obtains in most communities at present. We propose that apartment houses should have the same area of open space per family unit as the minimum permitted for single-family residences, which Mr. Mumford knows is a revolutionary proposal in favor of lesser concentration.

In general, we propose a distribution of industry and population which would result in obtaining a ratio of about twice as much open space to building area as now exists. In order to obtain this, we put forward a plan of highways and transit lines which was essential for proper distribution but which Mr. Mumford considers as likely to prevent distribution. On that point we must agree to differ. It happens to be one on which facts are too convincing to permit me to have an open mind.

Mr. Mumford says that the speculator "who would like no control at all" will find backing in the Report. This is untrue. There is no question on which we are more definite than in regard to the necessity for proper control and indeed for absolute prevention of injurious forms of speculation.

As to the ultimate population to be provided for, the staff of the Regional Plan did not assume that growth would continue automatically but that the rate of growth would be much reduced in the future. However, the Plan was made so that it would provide either for little growth or for the maximum predicted by persons of authority.

Mr. Mumford is wholly wrong when he says that we have omitted proposals for business sub-centers. He has overlooked specific suggestions for decentralized business areas in Harlem, the Bronx, Long Island City and elsewhere, and the general fact that new sub-centers would be created at intersections of circumferential and radial routes throughout the region.

He commends the scheme of Colonel Wilgus for a causeway from Sandy Hook to Rockaway Point, but attempts to cheapen it by saying that it was first advanced by the Pilot Commissioners. There was no similarity between the two schemes—the second one merely calling for an isolated anchorage off Staten Island.

Mr. Mumford criticizes the statistics of industrial workers given in summary in Survey Volume I, and their interpretation. If he had consulted the several economic monographs, published as Survey Volumes IA and IB, and the analysis of future needs for industrial areas in Survey Volume IV, he would have discovered that the significance of these figures was fully understood and taken into full account in formulating the Plan, particularly in the assignment of areas for future industrial development.

Mr. Mumford is wrong in the assumption that there is any inconsistency between skyscrapers and garden cities.

He disputes the conclusions of Clarence Perry and Robert Whitten as to the proportion of shopping area to residential areas, but presents no evidence to support his own conclusions. On this point there is no place for arbitrary opinion and it is misleading to give the impression that there is.

That the highway and rapid-transit programs are alternative to housing, as he asserts, is absurd. They are essentially complementary.

It is incorrect to say that we do not bother to ask what will become of wasted districts. We show both in general terms and by specific illustration how they should be dealt with. To talk about solving this problem by "skillful planning and large-scale operations" is merely to play with words. We include, as definite parts of the Plan, proposals for rebuilding the deteriorated areas in the Lower East Side and elsewhere.

We propose neighborhood units for city as well as suburban areas but, contrary to Mr. Mumford's idea of promoting more concentration in residential centers, we put the emphasis on the promotion of development in the open environs. We are well aware of the economic difficulties involved.

The confusion which characterizes much of Mr. Mumford's discussion of the Plan is illustrated by his reference to the Jamaica Bay area. He laments the failure to propose a sub-business center there. Such a center is an essential element of a self-contained community such as the Regional Plan proposes for that area.

In spite of our proposals to increase greatly the open spaces in upper Manhattan, we are condemned for yielding to the necessity for proposing the taking of small strips from the avenues adjoining Central Park, and moving the menagerie to Ward's Island (which is not a "distant suburban park"). Our proposed removal of through traffic from Central Park would have the same effect as Mr. Mumford would obtain by stopping *all* traffic through it, which is neither practicable nor desirable. The criticism that a park area of 3,000 acres in the Hackensack Meadows is insufficient for that section of the Region deserves no comment.

It should be unnecessary to go on showing that Mr. Mumford is not referring to the Regional Plan in his criticisms. It is obvious that his thesis and conclusions are based on a misreading of the facts, as well as a different conception of what a Regional Plan should be. He attempts to saddle the Regional Plan with the double responsibility of providing a plan on a scale large enough to embrace a state on the one hand and detailed enough to correspond to a city plan on the other hand. When he does introduce practical suggestions, we are in accord with him, and the Plan already provides for them: for instance, in submitting proposals for lessening congestion by recentralizing the congested building areas, advocating new cities and neighborhood units in outlying areas and rebuilding blighted areas. Only we go further in that we do not propose to rebuild the blighted areas so compactly as they now are, which would be the effect of Mr. Mumford's suggestion. People need room to breathe and for recreation in the central as well as in the suburban areas.

Mr. Mumford indicts the nation's Constitution and not the Regional Plan when he says that "property values and private enterprise are looked upon as sacred." But why should they not be if they are values and enterprises based on healthful and proper uses of property and on sound social principles? The Regional Plan could not have been more insistent than it is in condemning property values that are based on wrong use, and private enterprise that is injurious to public well being.

Mr. Mumford shows ignorance of what it is possible to include in a regional survey and plan when he suggests that ours should have dealt with "the complex forces that affect the balance between farm and city populations," as a problem in economics; or with all the complicated factors of metropolitan finance. Incidentally these problems were dealt with to the extent that they were relevant. Because we confined ourselves to essential matters in our investigations we failed, the critic says, to deal with "more than a fraction of the forces that have created the present complex of cities." Apparently he does not agree that the forces that enter into the life of cities are inexhaustible and that the human mind cannot grasp them all.

Finally, he comes to the conclusion that the Plan, as conceived by him, is a "monumental failure." But as the "failure" is based on a wrong diagnosis, the conclusion may be dismissed.

Index